Personality and
Peer Influence
in
Juvenile Corrections

Recent Titles in
Contributions in Criminology and Penology

Personality and Peer Influence in Juvenile Corrections

MARTIN GOLD
AND
D. WAYNE OSGOOD

Contributions in Criminology and Penology, Number 38
MARVIN WOLFGANG, Series Adviser

GREENWOOD PRESS
Westport, Connecticut • London

HV9105
.M5
G65
1992

Library of Congress Cataloging-in-Publication Data

Gold, Martin.
    Personality and peer influence in juvenile corrections / Martin
Gold and D. Wayne Osgood.
        p.   cm. — (Contributions in criminology and penology, ISSN
0732–4464 ; no. 38)
    Includes bibliographical references (p.   ) and index.
    ISBN 0–313–27970–5 (alk. paper)
    1. Juvenile delinquents—Michigan—Psychology—Case studies.
2. Juvenile corrections—Michigan—Psychological aspects—Case
studies. 3. Peer pressure in adolescence—Michigan—Case studies.
I. Osgood, D. Wayne. II. Title. III. Series.
HV9105.M5G65. 1992
364.3'6'019—dc20   92–9328

British Library Cataloguing in Publication Data is available.

Library of Congress Catalog Card Number: 92–9328
ISBN: 0–313–27970–5
ISSN: 0732–4464

First published in 1992

Greenwood Press, 88 Post Road West, Westport, CT 06881
An imprint of Greenwood Publishing Group, Inc.

Printed in the United States of America

The paper used in this book complies with the
Permanent Paper Standard issued by the National
Information Standards Organization (Z39.48–1984).

10 9 8 7 6 5 4 3 2 1

Dedicated to the memory of

Ted Newcomb
(1903–1984)

mentor, colleague, friend

CONTENTS

FIGURES AND TABLES

FIGURES

TABLES

PREFACE

This book was written for a wide audience, including administrators, policy makers, and social scientists. It is a report of the findings of continuing research on over 300 youth who were remanded to medium security institutions because of their delinquent behavior. We observed the boys from the time they arrived at the institution until six months after their release, as well as the staff who were responsible for them and the other boys in their residential groups. We took advantage of a rare opportunity to conduct a field experiment in which individuals were randomly assigned to unfamiliar social environments that varied in important ways. This enabled us to assess systematically the effects of the encounter of individual personalities with different natural social environments on the behavior, values, and feelings of the youth involved.

Our research has both practical and theoretical purposes. Our practical purpose is to contribute systematic and objective knowledge to the formulation of corrective programs for delinquent youth. We have tried to discover what variations in intervention in combination with variations in individual personalities help youth to lead more prosocial and personally satisfying lives. Our findings will be useful to those responsible for the broad spectrum of delinquency prevention and treatment programs because they are derived from observations of the most delinquency-prone youth, both while they were institutionalized and after they were freed. The findings offer guidance for community-based and residential treatment programs on matters including staff management of youth, peer influence, and education. They also reveal an important dimension of personality by which delinquent youth can be identified for differential treatment.

Our theoretical purpose is to test hypotheses in several social scientific disciplines under natural conditions in the context of a longitudinal field experiment. We drew our hypotheses from the fields of corrections, criminology, group dynamics, and social and personality psychology. We have tested these hypotheses with the advantages of controlled laboratory studies more common in group dynamics and social psychology. At the same time, we made our observations under conditions more common in corrections and criminology, in which the personalities of the participants are powerfully engaged. Thus, our findings might on the one hand be more generalizable to prevailing social conditions, and on the other be more clearly interpretable as to cause and effect. They reveal how people generally are both affected by and arrange their social environments.

While the conditions under which we observed the delinquent youth in this report were "natural," they were not in some potentially critical ways "normal," nor were the boys themselves. Our respondents were all heavily delinquent, sufficiently so to warrant their incarceration. For two-thirds of the time covered by this report, the boys were incarcerated; that is, subject to unusually coercive influence. This has provided the study of group dynamics and social psychology with tests of hypotheses about certain individuals under social conditions rarely available for observation in these fields. The importance of our respondents' deviance and the coercion in their lives should not be exaggerated, however, and it should not limit generalization of the findings too narrowly. The degree of constraint varied among the forty-five residential groups of boys we observed, and we have thus been able to take into account the effect of coercion, both real and as felt by the boys. And, as extreme as they surely were on the dimension of delinquency, the boys nevertheless were subject to and could reveal the workings of social and psychological principles as any others might.

We often referred to the research among ourselves as a study of "Bennington Behind Bars." We allude here to the famous groundbreaking study of the experiences of Bennington College students by the late Theodore M. Newcomb (Newcomb, 1943; Newcomb, Koenig, Flacks, & Warwick, 1967). Ted was one of the original principal investigators. This research got its initial impetus from his eagerness to move methodologically beyond his earlier studies of the interaction of personality and social conditions that he conducted at Bennington and in juvenile corrections (Vinter, Newcomb, & Kish, 1976). He was enthusiastic about the opportunities afforded here for close observation under more controlled conditions. Unfortunately, Ted died just as our research was beginning to yield findings, and was able to participate in the writing of only one article (Osgood, Gruber, Archer, & Newcomb, 1985). It is fitting that we dedicate this book to his memory.

Many people contributed to this study, assisting us in its design and implementation. Over the years we have surely lost track of some of their names; if so, our apologies. We invite them to get back in touch with us so we will not neglect them in future reports. Special thanks to: Mark A. Archer, Lisa Baum, Bruce Belzowski, Paula Boffa-Taylor, Catherine Buck,

Ann Cobau, Diane Cranston, Mary Cullen, Michael DiConti, Muffy Ep-
pler, Sara Freeland, Elizabeth Gearin, Enid Gruber, Zoanne Snyder Joy,
Lee Jussim, Myung Un Kim, Kathleen Malley, Frank Martim, Jay Mattlin,
Carolyn Miller, Sun Yong Ming, David Pais, Monica Robinson, Cheryl
Slay, Ronald Taylor, Phyllis White, Peter Williams, and Martin Young.

Throughout this research, we have been advised by an administrative
committee of representatives of the four institutions that participated in this
research. They devoted many hours to reviewing our procedures, measures,
and reports, and were indispensable in communications between ourselves
and the institutions and agencies that made this study possible. Serving on
the committee from time to time have been: Alec Allen, Chris Ameen,
Carletta Anderson, Nancy Coleman, Carl Lagore, Eleanor Langley, Gregg
Peters, Dale Shears (Chair), and Dennis Swiggum.

The cooperation of the Michigan Departments of Corrections, Social
Services, and the Secretary of State are much appreciated; as well as that of
the staffs and boys at the Adrian Training School, Boysville, Maxey Boys
Training School, and Starr Commonwealth.

This research was supported by a grant from the National Institute of
Mental Health Center for Studies of Antisocial and Violent Behavior, a
grant from the State of Michigan Office of Criminal Justice Programs, and
a grant from the Edna McConnell Clark Foundation.

Personality and
Peer Influence
in
Juvenile Corrections

1

THE PROBLEM

At this writing about 1,000 delinquent children are institutionalized in Michigan, about 33,000 nationwide (Lerman, 1989). Most have been removed from their homes because authorities judged that they inflicted serious harm on others or on themselves. One purpose for their institutionalization is to treat them while they are held so that they will not continue to harm others or themselves after their release. One of our purposes here was to discover ways to achieve this rehabilitative aim.

Locking delinquent children up together is fraught with so many problems that it may be counterproductive. Indeed, history tells us that even institutions founded on the highest ideals easily can become the scene of great inhumanity toward children (Empey, 1982; Platt, 1977; Prescott, 1981). Knowing no other way to prevent them from doing harm, our society will undoubtedly continue securing delinquents in institutions. Incarcerated children will be with us for the foreseeable future, even if their incarceration does not achieve their rehabilitation, but actually increases their depredations upon release, and not withstanding how miserable it may make them to be locked up. Therefore, it is extremely important, for their sake and the sake of the rest of us, that the problems of institutionalization be overcome so that the humane and rehabilitative aims of the practice can be more fully realized. For this reason, our research is as concerned with the lives of children during their incarceration as it is with their behavior after their release.

Among the problems to be overcome are these: First, when heavily delinquent children are locked up together for extended periods of time, it is likely that they influence one another. In this way, institutions may become "schools for crime." Residents may teach each other delinquent skills and encourage their practice during institutionalization and afterward. A counterculture may develop that supports opposition to the staff and the program, thereby circumventing rehabilitation. Second, the "pains of imprisonment" (Sykes, 1958) may embitter the children, further fueling their antisocial behavior. Third, the stigma of incarceration may impose a criminal label on the children, isolating them from prosocial influence and leading them to adopt a criminal identity. These are well-recognized problems of juvenile and adult corrections. Various treatment programs have been devised to overcome them, such as strict military discipline, vocational training, camping and conservation work, behavior modification, psychotherapy, group therapy, and social group work.

The four institutions participating in this study all use some form of Positive Peer Culture (Vorrath & Brendtro, 1985), Inasmuch as these institutions held over 90 percent of Michigan's incarcerated delinquent boys, Positive Peer Culture (PPC) was and remains the dominant form of treatment for institutionalized delinquents in the state. PPC attempts a kind of social judo to deal with the problems of institutionalization: It recognizes that institutionalized delinquents may exert a great deal of negative influence on one another, so it attempts to turn that force against itself, to convert it to prosocial ends. The program is heavily group-centered, and the staff works to enlist group influence to rehabilitate group members. By fostering group norms in support of prosocial behavior, mutual respect, and caring, the program is intended to lessen the "pains of imprisonment" and prevent the adoption of a delinquent identity.

Because of PPC's reliance on group norms and a prosocial culture to realize its rehabilitative goal, a great deal of social psychological theory and research is relevant to the program. Our contribution as social scientists has been to make the theoretical and empirical connections explicit. We have drawn hypotheses about the conditions that might affect the impact of the program from theory and research about reference groups, group dynamics, interpersonal relations, and personality. Certain characteristics of groups and individuals have been identified as potential determinants of the strength and direction of peer influence. We have also drawn from the methodology of social science to design this study and to measure group properties, boys' personalities, and changes in boys' attitudes, values, and behavior. We hoped that bringing together relevant theory, method, and practice would further all of them.

This study's contribution to practice is that it has identified some of the conditions of the encounter between individuals and groups that promote positive adjustment to institutions and to communities after release. Some of these conditions are characteristics of the individuals involved, some are properties of the peer groups in which they lived, and some are joint or interactive functions of both. Because we found these conditions by systematically observing practice in its natural environment rather than in a special experimental situation, the findings should be directly applicable to institutional programs with similar rehabilitative goals and group-oriented means. We did not intervene in the program. Instead, we measured variations that occurred naturally among the residential groups and among the individual members. We then tested our hypotheses about which combinations of group and individual would generate positive outcomes.

Our study is not an evaluation of PPC treatment. All of the individuals in this study participated in a variation of PPC; there was no comparison group of delinquents in a different program. Nor is the applicability of our findings limited to PPC programs: to the degree that institutionalized delinquents are organized in groups—and this is true of most residential programs—our findings are relevant to their treatment.

Our research may also further our theoretical understanding of the way groups influence their members. This field study of forty-five groups living in moderately secure institutions presented an opportunity to test social psychological principles under conditions different from previous research.

The preponderance of research on group influence has been done in groups created briefly for the purpose of experimentation. The usual settings have been academic laboratories, and the groups' purposes have had little if any real import for their members. Most participated in the groups merely in order to satisfy requirements of introductory courses in psychology or sociology.

In contrast, the 336 closely observed boys in this study joined their groups under duress. They remained members for an average of a year, none less than four months, and their membership required intensive interaction for almost every waking hour of every day. The quality of their participation was extremely important to them, for it determined the quality of their present lives, the length of their residency, and where they were sent when they were released. These conditions meant that we were able to extend our understanding of group influence to higher levels of coercion, duration, density of interaction, and gravity of consequences.

Furthermore, the participants were different from the usual population of college undergraduates that have served as subjects for experiments on group influence. Virtually all of them had a history of serious deviance from social norms, indicative of strong resistance to powerful sources of social influence. We found that the principles established in academic research held up fairly well under these new conditions, but that they required some modification.

In Chapter 2 we review the theoretical and empirical literature from which we drew ideas about what to observe and how. In Chapter 3 we describe the settings, design, and methods of the study and the research design that we constructed in order to distinguish the individual from the group determinants of outcomes. The findings about determinants of boys' adjustment while they were institutionalized are presented in Chapter 4. There we also describe the specific measures we used. In Chapter 5, we present the findings about boys' adjustment in the first six months after their release, most of them to the open community. Chapter 6 considers how a two-fold typology of delinquent boys furthers our understanding of the determinants of adjustment to an institution and to the open community. Chapter 7 is a discussion of our findings in terms of theory and practice, including a description of our continuing follow-up of the boys—now young men— whom we met initially in the first few days of their institutionalization. The discussion of the implications of this study for practice includes comments by Dale Shears, administrative assistant to the director of the Residential Care Division, Michigan Department of Social Services, who chaired the administrative committee of this project since its inception.

2

THEORETICAL BACKGROUND

We bring together some major contributions of theory and research in corrections, crime and delinquency, and social psychology to derive both specific hypotheses and a general strategy for studying incarcerated adolescents. Our goal is to explain variation in their adjustment during and after incarceration. Our approach encompasses prior individual differences in personality, the nature of the institutional experience, the norms of the institutional peer group, and later experiences in the community.

General theories of crime and delinquency have often been brought to bear on the study of juvenile corrections. However, theoretical social psychology has of late tended to neglect practical problems in real-life settings. Just as Newton's theories of dynamics did not account for observed phenomena beyond the earth, so principles of group behavior based on experiments using college students as subjects cannot be assumed to be generalizable to quite different settings. In particular, findings obtained with volunteers may not generalize to institutional settings in which participation is definitely forced. Our study of four institutions for juvenile offenders was an opportunity to apply some social psychological principles to the practical problems of juvenile corrections and to discover whether these principles hold up under some of the special conditions of institutional life.

The application of social psychology seems all the more appropriate in the context of programs that use Positive Peer Culture (Vorrath & Brendtro, 1985), which is intended to bring about prosocial change by marshalling

Portions of this chapter are adapted from Gold et al. (1989), Jussim and Osgood (1989), Martin and Osgood (1987), and Osgood et al. (1985).

peer influence in the service of treatment goals. Social psychological theory and research should have much to offer as a basis for rehabilitative programs that give a prominent role to social influence. Unfortunately, there has been little input in this regard from social psychologists. We hope that our work will help to bridge that gap.

THE INSTITUTIONAL COUNTERCULTURE

The concept of an institutional counterculture is one of the cornerstones of the study of corrections. It has long been regarded as fact that residents of correctional institutions tend to develop a counterculture characterized by opposition to institutional rules and goals, norms against informing authorities about rule violations, and the use of physical coercion to influence residents (Clemmer, 1958; Sykes, 1958). In several studies of institution-alized delinquent girls, Buehler, Patterson, and Furniss (1966) found that the girls agreed with and encouraged one another's antisocial remarks and they denigrated prosocial talk. Though the major societal goal of incarcer-ation is the long-term reduction of illegal behavior, there seems to be little chance of reaching that goal as long as residents are enmeshed in a coun-terculture. Thus, a correctional program must convince residents to support institutional goals. Some institutions may accomplish this—in contrast to the observations of Buehler et al., Sanson-Fisher, Seymour, and Baer (1976) found that delinquent girls in a New Zealand institution supported the prosocial talk of their peers.

The counterculture concept provides a point of departure for our pre-sentation of the varied theoretical background for our study. The notion of an oppositional culture implies that group norms and peer influence are important in correctional institutions, and assessing their nature and im-portance is a major theme of our study. Furthermore, we can organize many of our research questions in terms of the primary theories of the formation of the institutional counterculture.

A major theoretical issue has been whether the counterculture is due to the character of the incarcerated youths, or whether it is generated out of the conditions of institutionalization. The classic statements of these posi-tions were set forth by Clemmer (1958), who asserted that the counter-culture is imported by the residents; and by Sykes (1958; Sykes & Messinger, 1960), who concluded that the counterculture is a functional response to the setting. Clemmer questioned whether the appearance of a counterculture actually indicated an effective social organization of residents. He observed no such organization empirically and found none of the conditions that theory and research posit are necessary for one. He attributed the appearance of shared resistance to reform to the same personal intransigence that leads individuals to be selected for incarceration. Sykes, on the other hand, noted that incarceration constitutes a pattern of extreme personal deprivation or "pains" that residents have in common. According to Sykes, the presence of recognized common problems and opportunities for communication and interaction are the conditions sufficient for the generation of culture, and the natural cultural adaptation to the shared deprivations is countercultural.

Empirical tests of the relative validity of the importation and functional theories have produced mixed results. Some studies have shown that background factors account for more of the variance in the presence of an institutional counterculture and individuals' commitment to that counterculture (e.g., Jensen & Jones, 1976; Mathiesen, 1968; Propper, 1976; Selo, 1979). Others have found that institutional conditions account for as much if not more of the variance (e.g., Akers, Hayner, & Gruninger, 1974; Berk, 1966; Street, Vinter, & Perrow, 1966; Thomas, 1977; Vinter, Newcomb, & Kish, 1976). The reason for the seemingly contradictory findings is clear enough: each position has merit. The strength of the counterculture, and individuals' commitment to it, depends both on characteristics of the residents and on institutional conditions. The relative weights of these two sets of factors undoubtedly depend on the specific measures chosen and on more complex interdependent effects.

Some research suggests that the strength of the counterculture is especially variable for younger offenders. Most of the research on institutional countercultures has been done in institutions for adult criminals rather than for juvenile delinquents (with some notable exceptions, e.g., Empey & Lubeck, 1968; Empey & Rabow, 1961; Street et al., 1966; Vinter et al., 1976). It is plausible that juveniles are more responsive to peers because of such forces as adolescents' heightened concern for autonomy, the greater age differences between staff and peers in juvenile institutions, and the greater fluidity of adolescents' personalities. Both Akers et al. (1974) and Jensen and Jones (1976) found that younger residents were more committed to the rules of the institutional counterculture—the "inmate code"—and Akers et al. found that the characteristics of the institutions made more difference for this commitment among the younger residents.

These theories provide two of the major themes of our research. From Clemmer's importation theory we take the general hypothesis that residents' prior characteristics influence their involvement in the counterculture, as well as their overall adjustment to the institution. From Sykes's functional theory we take the general hypothesis that adjustment is influenced by the conditions of institutional life. After discussing these two themes in greater detail, we will turn to peer influence, which is at the heart of the idea of a counterculture.

The Importation Theme: Prior Characteristics and Institutional Adjustment

Commitment to the delinquent subculture. We begin our consideration of prior individual differences with commitment to the delinquent subculture.

Clemmer (1958) asserted that the existence of a counterculture is a simple consequence of residents' prior involvement in a comparable subculture in the community. Accordingly, some students of corrections have noted institutional differences in the degree to which their populations were previously committed to a deviant subculture (e.g., Mathiesen, 1968) and others have noted individual differences (e.g., Hewitt & Jenkins, 1946; Propper, 1976; Selo, 1979). Also, Empey and Lubeck (1968) have observed a delinquent subculture in the open community that is quite similar to the "inmate code," both stressing noncooperation with legitimate authority, in-group solidarity that is exemplified by refusal to inform on one's companions, and elevation of the value of certain deviant acts. Wellford (1967), Lerman (1968), Miller (1958), and Thomas (1970) have all suggested that this subculture is more indigenous to the lower class in America, from which most incarcerated offenders are drawn.

A number of studies have addressed the relationship between prior commitment to a delinquent or criminal subculture and adaptation to incarceration. Some researchers have defined this commitment in terms of values at incarceration (Tittle, 1969) and others in terms of previous delinquent career (e.g., Akers et al., 1974; Jensen & Jones, 1976; Propper, 1976; Selo, 1979). Neither Tittle nor Akers et al. found that the preinstitutional variables were significant predictors of commitment or of behavior in the institutions observed, while Jensen and Jones, Propper, and Selo found them to be significantly related. There were wide variations among the studies in the nature of the institutions, and of the independent and dependent variables, so it is to be expected that these findings would not be uniform. It is clear, however, that there is not a uniform strong relationship between commitment to deviant subcultures outside an institution and commitment to one inside an institution.

In our study, we did not limit our attention to delinquent subcultures, but included delinquent involvement more broadly. The subculture concept is appealing because it more directly corresponds to the notion that opposition to institutional authority takes the form of a counterculture. We would prefer, however, to avoid the assumption that deviance in either context is essentially a subcultural phenomenon. We will, instead, address that issue more directly in our analysis of peer influence. Therefore, we assessed prior delinquent orientation in terms of attitudes, behavior, and offense history present upon arrival at the institutions. We did not attempt to identify the group or subcultural context of prior delinquent involvement, although this could have caused some of the boys' orientations. In fact, despite theoretical language concerning subcultures, this has been the common practice in prior research, which generally used measures of individuals' delinquent behavior or values as indirect indicators of involvement in subcultures.

Other prior individual differences. Though prior delinquent involvement seems particularly pertinent to involvement in an institutional counterculture, other individual differences might also be relevant. The personalities and life histories that incarcerated adolescents "import" include much more than prior delinquency.

Prior functioning at school is important in several ways. School is a major part of institutional life, just as it is for adolescents in the open community. Students who have been more successful at school and have maintained a positive attitude toward school are likely to feel more comfortable and be more successful in this aspect of institutional life, and this should reduce the chance of a countercultural adaptation. There is also ample evidence that school failure is a factor contributing to delinquency (Gold & Mann, 1984; Hirschi & Hindelang, 1977), so it seems likely that it contributes directly to opposition to institutional authority as well.

If opposition to institutional authority takes the form of a counterculture, then involvement in this counterculture may also be a function of residents' more general orientations to social relations. If some youths are loners who shy away from others, they would be less susceptible to joining with others in opposing institutional authorities. Youths who are adept at relating to their peers would seem most likely not only to become involved in the counterculture, but to become its leaders. On the other hand, we would expect a very different pattern if resistance is not socially organized, especially in institutions using the Positive Peer Culture program. In this case stronger social skills and more interest in relationships with peers could easily be positively correlated with support for institutional goals. In a similar vein, incarcerated adolescents who have had positive relationships with their parents and other caregivers might be more likely to have positive relationships with the adults who are responsible for them at the institutions. To our knowledge, these are not subjects that have been directly addressed by prior research.

Research has shown that low self-esteem is associated with delinquent behavior (Coates, Miller, & Ohlin, 1978; Gold & Mann, 1972; Shore & Massimo, 1966; Kaplan, 1980). An interpretation of this relationship is that adopting a delinquent identity enhances youths' self-esteem, at least at the conscious level, because it is supported by at least some peers. Thus, we wished to determine whether self-esteem, conscious and unconscious, is related to incarcerated adolescents' orientations to an institutional counterculture. This theme of delinquency as a psychological defense is also the basis for a typology of adolescent offenders that is a central part of our study.

A typology of adolescent offenders. Our typology is grounded in a general theory of delinquent behavior whereby delinquency is a defense that many adolescents employ successfully to ward off conscious feelings of self-derogation (Gold & Mann, 1972). Some heavily delinquent youth continue to display low self-esteem, however. This persistent self-derogation indi-

cates that delinquency is an inadequate defense for these youth, and as a
consequence, they should experience high levels of anxiety and depression.
These youth constitute a discriminable type of delinquent from those for
whom delinquency is an effective defense. We submit that these youth are
the type of delinquents that Hewitt and Jenkins (1946) labeled "unsocialized
aggressive" and distinguished from "socialized" delinquents in their classic
typological study. In Chapter 6, we address whether distinguishing institutionalized delinquent boys on the basis of their anxiety and depression
constitutes a useful typology.

Hewitt and Jenkins' typology is based on an assessment of enduring
personal characteristics. In this respect, it is more similar to the personality-
based typological approaches of researchers such as Quay (1964), Eysenck
(1970), and Megargee (1979), than to those whose classifications are based
on the kinds of offenses the delinquents committed (e.g., McCord,
McCord, & Zola, 1959; Hindelang & Weis, 1972) or on the social milieu
in which offenders live (e.g., Cloward & Ohlin, 1960). Hewitt and Jenkins
claimed to have found three "fundamental patterns of maladjustment," of
which only two were delinquent. It should be noted here that, of these two
types, Hewitt and Jenkins found the unsocialized aggressive to be more
"neurotic" and "nervous," but not more "depressed" (1946, p. 95). Hewitt
and Jenkins' typology has held up well in previous research (see Gold and
Petronio, 1980, and Quay, 1987, for reviews of studies).

The theoretical and empirical differences between the two types led us
to hypothesize that they would differ in their life-histories and other personal
characteristics. Hewitt and Jenkins believed that the two types had been
treated differently by their parents. They observed that parents rejected the
unsocialized aggressives from infancy, while parents' loss of control during
adolescence was typical of the socialized aggressives. In an English repli-
cation of Hewitt and Jenkins' study, however, Field (1967) found no relationship of the three types to any particular type of upbringing.

Hewitt and Jenkins (1946) labeled their two delinquent types "unsocialized" and "socialized" because of the differences in their relations with peers.
They found the former to be more quarrelsome, unable to get along with
other children, and lacking close friends. The corresponding "undersocialized aggressives" in Quay's (1987) scheme are also characterized by poor
interpersonal relations and are "likely to be at odds with everyone in the
environment" (p. 121).

Our version of the typology originates in Gold and Mann's (1984) study
of the effectiveness of alternative school programs. They distinguished only
two types of delinquents, using a measure of anxiety and depression to
classify the boys and girls they observed. Gold and Mann recognized the
similarity of their typology to Hewitt and Jenkins's and to Quay's. They
labeled their types "beset" and "buoyant" in order to call attention to the
emotional condition by which the youths were classified, rather than to

assume any particular differences in their peer relations. The beset are like Hewitt and Jenkins' unsocialized type and probably includes both Quay's undersocialized and anxious-withdrawn-dysphoric types. In comparison to the buoyant youth, the beset were not only more anxious and depressed, but Gold and Mann also found that they got along worse with their peers and tended to commit more solitary delinquent acts, thus conforming to the "unsocialized" description of Hewitt and Jenkins.

Types based on Hewitt and Jenkins's system have also been found to differ in their responsiveness to treatment. Quay has concluded, "It is abundantly clear that the Undersocialized Aggressive group is the most troublesome in the institutional setting" and that "failure while on probation [is] more common among this group" (1987, p. 128). Gold and Mann (1984) reported that an alternative school program had a positive effect on buoyant youth, but not on beset youth.

We investigated two hypotheses concerning this typology. One concerns the life-histories of the delinquent respondents; the other, their adjustment to the group-oriented institutional treatment programs to which they were committed. According to our theory, the beset delinquents suffer from low self-esteem due to personal difficulties that are too deep-seated to be resolved by engaging in delinquent behavior. Therefore, they would be more likely to have experienced events that could interfere with normal socioemotional development. Parental divorce and early separation from one's primary caregiver are examples of such events. Thus, we reasoned that buoyant delinquents would commit more of their delinquent acts in the company of others. This is based on our assumption that their self-esteem is maintained by an audience of peers who applaud their delinquent behavior.

As to their responses to treatment, we expected that the buoyant residents in this study would adapt in whatever fashion is most consistent with positive relations with peers. If there was a strong counterculture, they would participate in it. On the other hand, in these group-oriented programs, the more social orientation of the buoyant residents could well be a resource for success in reaching program goals.

Furthermore, we expected that the two types would respond differently to certain variations in programs. We supposed that the buoyant boys would feel more autonomous because they would generally feel less put upon and more in control of themselves than the beset boys would. Later in this chapter we discuss our rationale for expecting that a sense of autonomy would coincide with more favorable adjustment and less support for an institutional counterculture. We also thought that autonomy would have a greater impact on the adjustment of the buoyant than of the beset.

The second dimension of program variation we investigated was the closeness boys felt to their staff, which is widely considered a prerequisite for successful treatment. Supposing that the beset boys would have experienced a less stable home environment prior to their institutionalization, we reasoned that they would be more in need of supportive relationships with adults. Therefore, whether they felt close ties with adult staff members would have greater effect on their adjustment.

The Functional Theme: The Institutional Experience and Adjustment to Incarceration

Sykes's (1958; Sykes & Messinger, 1960) theory posits that incarcerated offenders form a counterculture of opposition to defend against the deprivations of institutional life. This perspective leads us to the general theme that adjustment to incarceration can be understood in terms of the nature of the institutional experience. Accordingly, variations in the nature of that experience should produce differences in adjustment.

Custodial versus treatment-oriented institutions. Most studies that have addressed whether institutional conditions affect the presence of a counterculture have compared custodial institutions with treatment-oriented institutions (e.g., Akers et al., 1974; Berk, 1976; Street et al., 1966; Vinter et al., 1976). Their main hypothesis has been that treatment orientation enlists the residents' social organization on the side of reform by reducing the deprivations of institutional life that encourage an institutional counterculture. Furthermore, treatment effectively reduces the motivations that prompt individuals to become committed to a delinquent/criminal subculture prior to incarceration and to remain committed during incarceration. The empirical evidence from these studies supports this hypothesis.

We wish to go beyond this research in three ways. First, if Sykes's theory is correct, that the counterculture arises from the "pains of imprisonment," then other factors affecting the quality of the institutional experience should also be important. We discuss several such factors below.

Second, we believe that these studies have focused on the wrong level of analysis in comparing entire institutions whose residents usually number in the hundreds. They have assumed that institutional programs are uniform over their entire respective populations and therefore will have internally undifferentiated effects on residents' social organization and on individuals. This assumption is probably more valid for custodially oriented institutions. But treatment-oriented institutions, especially those that Selo (1979) calls "participatory," organize residents into smaller residential groups located in cottages, wings, and the like. Juvenile institutions are more apt to do this than adult prisons. When residents are organized into smaller groups, then it is likely that the institutional program is not delivered uniformly to all groups and that the composition of groups differs in ways significant for the informal social organization and for effects on individuals.

Research by Jones (1964) provides data to support this idea of intrainstitutional differences. He studied two large juvenile institutions, one that stressed control and obedience, the other, psychological change. Residents in both places were housed in cottages of from sixteen to thirty-two boys each. Because there were clear differences between the two institutions in the boys they enrolled, the researcher tried to control for this by pairing cottages in his study, including the cottage with the most troublesome boys, the cottage with the least troublesome, and an average cottage in each institution. Interviews with the boys revealed more marked intrainstitutional than interinstitutional differences in the strength of the counterculture. In order to gain a clearer view of the nature of the institutional experience, we avoid institution-level comparisons. Instead, we seek a more specific characterization of institutional conditions experienced by each individual. We obtain this in terms of both individuals' perceptions of their situations and more objective characterizations of conditions for their small living units.

Third, we have attempted to overcome a pervasive methodological weakness of studies comparing custodial and treatment programs. Rarely do these studies control for differences in the selection of residents to custodial and treatment programs. That being the case, it is reasonable to advance an alternative explanation for the differences found in the strength of the institutional counterculture—that custodial institutions most often serve "hardened" offenders who are more strongly prone to antisocial behavior and to organize a counterculture. For example, Eynon and Simpson (1965) found that at intake boys who were assigned to an open camp setting had greater scholastic achievement and had a briefer history of delinquent involvement than boys assigned by the same judicial system to a more custodial training school. Similar differences in assignment to the different kinds of institutional programs have been documented by Coates et al. (1978), Vinter et al. (1976), Jones (1964), and elsewhere. The general tendency is for less serious offenders (who could be expected to be more cooperative during incarceration) to be assigned the less restrictive and oppressive conditions. Research designs that disentangle institutional conditions and offender characteristics are a prerequisite to advancing our knowledge about the effects of institutional conditions.

Closeness of interpersonal relationships. We focused on the closeness of residents' relationships with institutional staff and with their fellow residents as two important features of the nature of the institutional experience. Relationships with the staff are of interest, in part, because it is widely assumed that positive feelings toward treatment staff are a prerequisite for the success of a treatment program. People must accept the treatment provider in order to accept the treatment. Also, in light of Sykes's deprivation theory, positive feelings toward the staff indicate that the institutional experience is less oppressive. This seems particularly apt in the case of adolescents. Institutional staff are the only adults present for these youths who are still at an age when adults are expected to play a nurturing and authoritative role in their lives. Thus, Coates et al. found that "youths who at the end of their program experiences looked favorably upon their primary group [which included institutional staff] are less likely to report further delinquency than youths who seem more alienated from their primary group" (1978, p. 159).

Relationships with peers also should be an important aspect of the quality of life for incarcerated adolescents. According to Sykes, close peer relationships are the basis of the counterculture. On the other hand, PPC attempts to build close relationships among peers as the basis for its treatment program. Thus, we can make no clear prediction about the relationship between close peer ties and adjustment to the institution. As with individual difference factors such as sociability, this will depend on whether opposition to institutional authority takes the form of a socially organized counterculture.

Autonomy and participation in decision making. Sykes identified the lack of personal autonomy as one of the principal deprivations of incarceration. Inasmuch as incarceration means being forced to live away from one's home, family, and friends, a tremendous loss of control over one's life is necessarily part of the experience. Even so, there is a great deal of room for variation in just how much autonomy, independence, and participation in decision making incarcerated adolescents are granted. Three well-established lines of research in social psychology lead us to expect that lack of autonomy and participation in decision making are deprivations that will be associated with opposition to the institutional program.

The first area of relevant research is the impact of leadership style on group functioning. In their classic study, Lewin, Lippitt, and White (1939; Lippitt & White, 1943) experimentally varied the behavior of adult leaders and examined its impact on the groups of children they supervised. The most favorable results occurred with a democratic style of leadership in which group members helped determine policy and group activities. Compared to an autocratic style, in which the leader made all decisions, the democratic style resulted in greater internalization of the group's goals, greater satisfaction with the group, and less hostility and aggression among members. Thus, to the degree that staff members maintain control over all decisions and activities, it can be expected that the residents will fail to accept institutional goals as their own and that aggression will be common.

French and Raven's (1959) concept of coercive power, one of six bases for social control that they distinguished, is also pertinent. Because coercive power is based on punishment, its use is one important way in which incarcerated adolescents may be denied autonomy and participation in decision making. Similar to research on autocratic leadership, studies of coercive power have found that its use tends to decrease the attractiveness of those in power and of the goals they support (French & Raven, 1959; French, Morrison, & Levinger, 1960; Raven & French, 1958). Compliance obtained through coercive power depends on surveillance, so it has little chance of generating genuine acceptance of a treatment program and consequent pro-social change.

The concepts of "cognitive dissonance" (Festinger, 1957) and "reactance" (Brehm, 1966) provide a third social psychological perspective on autonomy and participation in decision making for incarcerated adolescents. Both theories predict that attitudes will become consistent with behavior if the behavior is perceived as being freely chosen. If, instead, the behavior is clearly coerced by external factors, reactance theory predicts that attitudes in opposition to the behavior may become even stronger. Thus, these theories imply a limiting condition on the prosocial impact of autonomy. For prosocial change to occur, a sense of autonomy must be accompanied by a meaningful level of involvement in prosocial activities. We hypothesized, therefore, that residents who experienced relatively high levels of autonomy and participation in decision making would adopt prosocial behavior and attitudes. PPC prescribes peer group autonomy and peer participation, so the treatment modality encourages prosocial effects for these reasons. We expected substantial variations in autonomy and participation from one group to another, however, and among individual members of each group.

Peer Influence

Several theoretical approaches of social psychology, such as reference group theory (Newcomb, 1950; Sherif, 1948), balance theory (Heider, 1958; Newcomb, 1953), and symbolic interactionism (Mead, 1934) contend that interpersonal relationships are a major basis of social influence. Indeed, friends are generally similar to one another in many respects (Rubin, 1973). Accordingly, interpersonal influence has a prominent role in social explanations of many topics, such as political preferences (Berelson, Lazarsfeld, & McPhee, 1954), academic and occupational attainment (Sewell, Haller, & Portes, 1969), illicit drug use (Kandel, 1978), and illegal behavior (Sutherland & Cressey, 1955). Indeed, many theories of deviance in general, and delinquency in particular, have placed considerable emphasis on peer influence (e.g., Akers, 1977; Cloward & Ohlin, 1960; Cohen, 1955; Elliott et al., 1985; Sutherland & Cressey, 1955).

It is generally assumed that peer influence among incarcerated offenders is likely to interfere with attempts to bring about their reform. Given the intensive contact that occurs among people who are incarcerated together, there is ample opportunity for influence. Furthermore, because these offenders have a history of violating conventional standards of behavior, peer influence in correctional settings will likely oppose the aims of the authorities. This idea is captured in the lay notion of correctional institutions as "schools for crime," and it is central to sociological conceptions of an institutional counterculture (Clemmer, 1958; Sykes, 1958). In this vein, Elliott et al. (1985) argued that peer influence is such an important source of delinquency that peer-group-oriented correctional programs, such as those in the institutions we studied, are doomed to failure.

One of the major goals of our research has been to assess the nature and extent of peer influence in this setting. Despite widespread assumptions, there has been little well-designed research on this topic. Furthermore, not all authors agree that peer influence is prominent in correctional institutions.

Peer influence is implicit in Sykes's conception that a counterculture derives from solidarity in opposition to the deprivations of the institutional experience. This is not true of Clemmer's assertion that opposition to institutional authority is a function of previous involvement in a delinquent subculture. From that point of view, influence is not an especially important part of the institutional experience itself.

Furthermore, social control theory (Hirschi, 1969), one of the most prominent theories of crime and delinquency, denies that peer influence leads to deviance in any setting. This theory provides an alternative image of interpersonal attachments as social bonds that reduce the chance of deviance, regardless of the norms of the groups to which one is attached. Any similarity of individuals' deviance to that of their friends is seen as reflecting their preference in friends rather than their friends' influence.

The most common view of the role of peers in deviant behavior, however, is that the individual is socialized to conform with peer group norms. This image is central to differential association theory (Sutherland & Cressey, 1955), strain theories (Cloward & Ohlin, 1960; Cohen, 1955), and social learning theories (Akers, 1977; Elliott et al., 1985; and Jessor & Jessor, 1977). This perspective also is consistent with the major social psychological theories mentioned above. These theories led us to expect that group norms would be an important determinant of whether incarcerated adolescents opposed the institutional authorities and violated program rules, or accepted the goals of the treatment program and cooperated with the staff.

In examining peer influence, we focused not only on group norms but also on the individual's attachment or attraction to the group. The simplest model of peer influence is that individuals are influenced by the groups with which they associate. Reference group theory and balance theory indicate, however, that the amount of influence is dependent on the strength of the individual's attachment to the group. According to this view, no matter how much time a person spends with a group, that group will have little impact on the individual's attitudes and values if he or she dislikes or rejects the group. Theories of deviance tend to be more consistent with this point of view as well. For instance, differential association theory posits that some associations have more impact than others (Sutherland & Cressey, 1955), and Cloward and Ohlin's (1960) strain theory stresses the close interpersonal bonds in delinquent gangs. Nevertheless, Hirschi's social control theory presents a radically different prediction that group norms will have little impact on individuals, that close bonds to peers will reduce deviance (even if the peers are deviant).

Peer influence is a particularly important component of our research. This is partly because the assumption that peer influence is a major problem for correctional institutions needs to be tested; indeed, this assumption is critical for the treatment modality of Positive Peer Culture. In addition, our results also bear on important questions for theories of crime and deviance. Further still, they extend the social psychological study of influence to important conditions that cannot be created in typical laboratory settings, namely that group membership is not voluntary, and the group and the issues of influence are extremely salient. As we will describe in later chapters, we were able to implement an unusually strong research design for the study of group influence.

Adjustment to the Open Community

Up to this point we have considered factors likely to affect adjustment during incarceration. Of course, juvenile correctional institutions eventually release their residents, and they are charged with releasing them in a state less prone to deviant behavior than when they entered. Accordingly, we wished to understand the sources of more and less prosocial adjustment to the open community as well. Unfortunately, few follow-up studies of incarceration have been done except to document that there frequently is too much recidivism. Follow-up studies comparing institutional conditions are rare (see, for example, Coates et al., 1978), and controlled studies even more rare.

The first question that arises is whether changes that are observed during incarceration will carry over to post-release adjustment. Results from evaluations of treatment are ambiguous. Persons (1967) found that therapy reduced deviant behavior after as well as during incarceration. Empey and Lubeck (1968) found that Guided Group Interaction made a difference only during incarceration. Murray and Cox (1979) reported that institutionalization deters post-release delinquency. We will address this issue more broadly by examining both the continuity in individual adjustment from incarceration to the open community and the relationship between program characteristics and later adjustment.

We also consider whether residents' prior characteristics will carry over beyond the institutional stay to later adjustment. In the extreme, adjustment to the open community could be consistent across pre- and post-incarceration, with residents' responses to the institution irrelevant beyond that setting. Of course it is also possible, and undoubtedly more likely, that both prior characteristics and institutional adjustment will be useful for explaining later adaptation.

As our respondents returned to the open community, we also considered potential influences there. It is likely that important influences are operating in the community because substantial change in the amount of delinquent and criminal behavior is quite common among even the most seriously delinquent youths, quite apart from the influence of any treatment program (e.g., Empey & Erickson, 1972; Murray & Cox, 1979). Nevertheless, remarkably little is known about the naturally occurring processes that would account for the reform of some youths but not others.

The concepts of reference group theory, which are at the heart of our approach to group influence in the institution, are useful here as well. An excellent example of the relevance of this approach to the study of long-term change is Newcomb's follow-up of the students of Bennington College (Newcomb et al., 1967). Newcomb and his colleagues reported changes in attitudes toward public issues over a twenty-five-year period on the part of more than 100 women whose attitude changes during college years were known. During their four years in college, most of them had become distinctly more liberal. Two major findings were that during the twenty-five-year interval the majority of those who were distinctly liberal on graduating had remained distinctly liberal, and that those for whom this was true had developed personal friendships with persons in their post-college communities who also tended to be liberal or had maintained close acquaintance with their classmates who were also liberal. Similarly, Coates et al. (1978) have reported that prior characteristics of youths in delinquency treatment programs and their situation in the open community after release were stronger determinants of post-release adjustment than their institutional experiences were. Among the factors in the community, Coates et al. found that "following the program the youths . . . most likely to report delinquency look up to, trust, and relate well with people who themselves break the law" (p. 159). These findings are consistent with the central proposition of reference group theory: People tend to maintain previous attitudes if their close associates have attitudes that are similar to their own. Thus, our primary approach to studying community influences is in terms of social relationships with people who are tolerant versus intolerant of deviant behavior. We considered social relationships in the contexts of peers, family, school, and work.

In summary, in order to understand incarcerated adolescents' adjustment during and after their institutional stays, we draw on a variety of theories and empirical findings from corrections, crime and delinquency, and social psychology. We found them invaluable for guiding our study. We hope that our findings will in turn both further our understanding of processes in institutions for juvenile offenders, and that they will also contribute to knowledge in those fields of study.

3

RESEARCH DESIGN

This chapter describes how we designed our study in order to determine, with as much certainty as possible, how institutionalization affected our designated 336 focal students. The research design was intended to assess the effects of natural variations among the staff teams and among the boys' groups on their adjustment to the institution and to the open community after release. The design has enabled us to investigate the effects of these variations independent of characteristics of the boys themselves, which also affected their adjustment. Furthermore, the design has allowed us to test whether the encounter between boys with certain characteristics and certain kinds of peer groups had special joint effects.

We did not design our study to evaluate Positive Peer Culture as a treatment modality. To do that, we would have had to include a comparison group of focal students in one or more other treatment programs. But we were primarily interested in testing hypotheses about how groups affect their members' attitudes, values, and behavior, particularly under the condition of involuntary membership. Observing people in measurably different kinds of groups was sufficient for that purpose, and all of the boys in our study experienced some variation of Positive Peer Culture. We assumed—correctly as it turned out—that in the natural course of treatment, boys' groups would differ in theoretically and practically important ways, permitting us to study their differential effects.

However, our study might shed light on the effectiveness of Positive Peer Culture as a specific treatment. One might evaluate the degree to which each of the forty-five boys' groups fit the "ideal" of PPC. Then boys' adjustment could be correlated with the closeness of the groups' program to the ideal. If more ideal groups had more positive effects, that would indicate that the treatment modality was effective. Some of our findings could be interpreted in this way. That is, some kinds of staff management and group functioning follow more closely than others do the way PPC is supposed to operate. In general, however, we have no set notions about what constitutes the ideal PPC treatment. Therefore, we will refrain from interpreting our findings in terms of the effectiveness of PPC. We will instead comment on their relevance for guiding group treatment programs in general. Others may wish to consider whether our findings have implications for the effectiveness of PPC specifically.

RESEARCH SITES: THE INSTITUTIONS

Four residential institutions for delinquent boys participated in this research. The W. J. Maxey Boys Training School and the Adrian Training School were administered by the Michigan Department of Social Services. The two private, nonprofit institutions were the Starr Commonwealth Schools and Boysville, a service of the Catholic Holy Cross Brothers. They were all located in rural areas in southern Michigan. All four were moderately secure institutions where boys were locked into their residences, school buildings, dining halls, and so on. Each practiced its own version of Positive Peer Culture, relying heavily on the boys' groups to rehabilitate their members. Together, these four institutions held more than 90 percent of the incarcerated boys in Michigan, almost all of whom were referred by Michigan juvenile courts.

W. J. Maxey Boys Training School

The Maxey School was by far the largest of the participating institutions. It housed about 420 boys when all of its wings were open and all of its beds filled. Maxey's total size can be misleading however, because its program was highly decentralized. Maxey was divided into three centers, Olympic, Sequoyah, and Summit, separated by rolling lawns. Each center was divided into six L-shaped wings, with a group of ten to twelve boys in each leg of the L. Each boy had his own room. Central facilities in each wing provided a dayroom with some kitchen facilities to prepare snacks, and table tennis or other recreational space and equipment, a TV room, a meeting room, and staff offices. In addition, each center contained a gymnasium, an isolation room, maintenance facilities, and administrative offices.

Other buildings on the Maxey campus included a school that matched in all respects a well-equipped comprehensive American secondary school, with classrooms, media center, workshops, large gymnasium, indoor pool, and a playing field. There was also a medical services building and an administration and reception building.

In keeping with the PPC modality, the small group was the operational program unit at Maxey. Each wing had its own staff team of six youth specialists and a teacher, and each team was headed by a group leader. Although the two groups of boys on a wing shared a staff and central space, a group was quite self-contained. The group ate at its own table in the dayroom of the wing. Boys in a group attended the same classes mostly taught by their wing's teacher, studied together after school, played together during recreation periods, and took trips off campus together. They also held formal group meetings, which are a central feature of the PPC program, for an hour and a half, five days a week. A student had little contact with boys in any group but his own, and he was almost never away from his group. Shower schedules, work details, and such were arranged so that the two groups on a wing were kept largely separated. When one boy went somewhere, like to a dentist or to be interviewed in the central administration building by one of our research staff, he was usually escorted by two or more members of his own group—his "deuce."

Group leaders held a least a bachelor's degree in some field related to human services, such as psychology, sociology, or social work. Youth specialists had at least two years of higher education or a few years of experience in a similar position. Group leaders and youth specialists also had to pass civil service examinations. Teachers were certified by the State Department of Education.

In addition, the program staff of each center included a career education teacher, a physical education teacher, a lead group leader, a program manager who supervised the staff teams, and a center director.

Youth specialists and group leaders were primarily trained by a center's lead group leader. New staff would begin by rotating among shifts and groups for about two weeks before taking on their regular position. During that time, newcomers would of course observe other staff members at work and received instruction from them.

Adrian Training School

The Adrian Training School's organizational structure was similar to Maxey's because both followed the program of the Michigan Department of Social Services. Adrian was in effect a fourth center to Maxey's three. It was an older institution, established originally as a training school for female delinquents. At the time of our research, forty beds were allocated to girls and eighty to boys.

Seven red brick cottages, from twenty to over fifty years old, housed two groups of boys or girls in two wings of two- and three-person bedrooms. The wings were joined by a central dayroom for recreation. Cottages also included staff offices and lavatories. Because two groups shared a cottage, most inter-group contact occurred in the central dayrooms.

Some of the specialized service buildings were built before the oldest remaining cottage. The gymnasium was a remodeled chapel, with a heated swimming pool in its basement. Several buildings housed the educational program, including classrooms, vocational education shops, and a green-house. One newer building was devoted to reception and administration, and another was the central dining facility where everyone ate, each group at its own table.

New staff members at the Adrian school received two weeks of orien-tation that included on-the-job experience and one-on-one sessions with supervisors. Several times a year, new staff members would gather for training in such skills as first aid, situational leadership, and suicide pre-vention. Especially important among these training sessions was one on Positive Peer Culture, centering around discussions of the Vorrath and Brendtro text.

Starr Commonwealth Schools

Starr Commonwealth is a privately endowed agency that maintains two campuses for delinquent youth, one in Michigan and one in Ohio. Only the Michigan campus participated in this study.

The Michigan campus contained three "villages" of four or five cottages each. Each cottage housed a group of eleven or twelve boys, who shared two-, three-, or four-person bedrooms. The boys dined at their cottages and participated with staff in preparing their meals in the cottage kitchen. Each cottage also had a central meeting and recreation room, laundry fa-cilities, and the usual lavatories. Some staff members—a "house mom" or in one case, a resident couple—also had living quarters in the cottage.

Cedar Village had its own school, which included a well-equipped shop. The Lakeview and Maple Villages shared a school building. Elsewhere were a gymnasium and an administration/reception building. There were several playing fields and ponds as well.

The Michigan campus of the Starr Commonwealth Schools is among the most attractive of institutions for delinquent boys in the United States—perhaps the world. The newer boys' cottages look like nothing less than large suburban ranch homes, with immaculate lawns and tasteful landscap-ing. The roads and pathways are tree-lined. The buildings are well-furnished. Everything is neatly kept. George Orwell (1953) once observed that when upper-class English boys were sent away to their famous "public" schools, their standard of living dropped precipitously to a level below the average of the English population. Something of the reverse was true of boys sent to Starr: They were almost all from disadvantaged families, in the kind of surroundings enjoyed by few youngsters anywhere.

A group of boys had little contact with other groups. While all the groups attended chapel together on Sundays and one group might invite another over for games occasionally, students at Starr spent almost all their time with their own group. They attended school together, did their homework together, dined at their cottage, and traveled off-campus as a group.

For the most part, each group had its own staff. The staff team consisted of a senior educateur who was the group leader, an educateur I who acted as a kind of associate group leader, three educateurs II, a house mom or couple, teachers, and family service workers. When this study began, one or two teachers were part of each team, but midway along, Starr departmentalized its scholastic program so that students were taught by several teachers each day as in most American secondary schools. Each team was served by all of the agency's family service workers, for these staff were assigned to geographic areas around the state; but the workers met with staff teams on a rotating basis so that they could remain generally familiar with student life at the school.

Senior educateurs and educateurs I held bachelor's degrees and were encouraged to earn master's degrees as well in counseling, educational leadership, or another relevant discipline. Educateurs II also held bachelor's degrees or had extensive experience in a similar position. House moms did not typically have a college education, some not even a high school diploma; they were older women with a special talent for relating to troubled adolescents.

Each team trained its own new staff, with the senior educateur having specific responsibility for this. Newer staff members also met from time to time with higher-level supervisors to discuss their progress. The agency also supported staff attendance at professional conferences as part of its inservice training program.

Boysville

Students at Boysville lived in three dormitories, with four groups in two dorms and two groups in the third. Unlike the other institutions, Boysville did not lock its residence doors. There was also a central dining hall, where groups assisted in preparing meals; the Thomas More High School; a large gymnasium; an outdoor pool (during the winters, Boysville students would sometimes swim in nearby Adrian's indoor pool); a medical building that also contained two isolation rooms and rooms for visiting families; and an administration and reception building.

Each group of twelve boys occupied one wing of its dormitory. Boys slept in an open dorm room, a small cabinet between each bed. Each wing had a common room with TV and stereo sets. Each dormitory had a central living room and recreation room shared by its groups.

A staff team at Boysville consisted of a treatment director, three treatment specialists, a teacher, and a family service worker. The treatment director and the treatment specialists had to have earned bachelor's degrees. The teacher was certified in special education, and the family service director was expected to have a master's degree in social work.

New treatment specialists spent an initial week getting oriented to the agency as a whole, two days of those on the campus and three with the central administration and out in the community with family service workers. They would rotate around the ten groups on campus during the second week, under the general supervision of the treatment department head. Then they would substitute for other treatment specialists for three to six months until they got a regular assignment.

Family service workers and teachers, after the initial orientation week, received on-the-job training from the family department head and the school principal respectively.

PROGRAM: POSITIVE PEER CULTURE[1]

The Positive Peer Culture (PPC) program is based on the premise that *"the peer group has the strongest influence over the values, attitudes, and behavior of most youth"* (Vorrath and Brendtro, 1985, p. 2. Emphasis in the original.) The primary rehabilitative instrument of PPC, therefore, is the peer group. PPC's aim is to create a group of peers for students that will contribute positively to their rehabilitation.[2] PPC staff try to impress upon students that they are responsible not only for their own behavior but also for the behavior of all the other members of their group. Students are encouraged to be helpers as well as recipients of help, and progress in the program is evaluated in substantial part by the degree to which one functions more as the former than needing the latter. This implies that students' readiness for release from the institution is reflected in part in the behavior of their group's members and depends on their contributions to everyone's positive behavior.

Following from this emphasis is the normative value placed on "caring." Vorrath and Brendtro write that "a positive peer culture can exist only in a climate of mutual concern" (1985, p. 21). Thus, each student's behavior is weighed against the standard of whether it displays as much concern about the welfare and improvement of the other group members as about one's own—"Is this [behavior] helping or hurting?" (1985, p. 21). In the PPC program, staff is supposed to devote great effort to inculcating this value as a group norm.

A few examples will demonstrate how PPC puts its principles into practice. Fights sometimes erupt among institutionalized delinquent boys. The staff and the institution accept the ultimate responsibility for the safety of their wards. Nevertheless, whenever possible the group is expected to protect its members from hurting one another; staff will not rush in to break up a fight unless the group is unable to handle it. So when a fight is threatened or breaks out, or when one boy attacks another, the other group members are expected to separate the antagonists with the least necessary force. In the observation of the research staff, this usually meant that each antagonist was surrounded by members of the group and kept thus contained until the threat passed. Sometimes two or three boys would actually sit on a bellowing group member in order to neutralize him.

Although the participating institutions were considered at least moderately secure, boys had to walk across the grounds to attend many activities. None of the campuses were heavily fenced; a boy could easily abscond. The institutions took a lot of flak from a lot of critics—their rural neighbors, the local sheriff, the referring juvenile judge, and so on—anytime a resident "got away." Still, staff seldom accompanied their group from place to place on the grounds. The students were expected to monitor each other's behavior, making sure that everyone got where they were supposed to go. When only one group member had to go somewhere on the campus, he would be accompanied by at least two other boys in his group. Misbehavior could lead to being placed on "total," meaning that a boy's movements had to be monitored by his entire group; he could move about only at the convenience of all of them. If a student revealed his intention to abscond, his fellows were supposed to try to dissuade him or report his intention to the staff. Residents were expected to intervene in actual absconding, short of doing physical harm. Thus, a member's running away became the group's as well as the individual's problem.

Because the program was designed so that group members were together during virtually all their waking hours—and except at the Maxey school, while asleep as well—peer interaction was continuous. It was most concentrated and intense, however, at the daily meeting. Each group met formally for an hour and a half five days a week, usually in the late afternoon or early evening, to focus on one member, usually to help him overcome his problems, sometimes to assess his readiness for release. In the process, the group's general capacity to contribute to positive rehabilitation was supposed to be enhanced.

The format and even the physical layout of the group meeting is carefully detailed by Vorrath and Brendtro (1985, chap. 8). We observed that their instructions were followed fairly closely. Boys sat on chairs in a circle that included a desk, behind which sat the group leader. Meetings started promptly with a census of each member's problems, as described by himself or by the other members, each in his turn around the circle, with or without the urging of the group leader.

In the second phase of the meeting, the members awarded the session to one boy, by consensus. While the decision to "give the meeting" to a particular boy was supposed to emerge from the preceding census of problems, we observed that the decision had often been made before the meeting had even convened. Perhaps a group member had attracted the group's special attention because of some recent particularly problematic behavior or because it was time to consider his release. In any case, it was often agreed beforehand which boy would "have" the meeting.

The third and longest phase of the meeting consisted of the problem-solving discussion. The focus was on the behavior and attitudes of the meeting's "owner." Group members would describe his misbehavior and challenge him to explain or justify it. Peer influence was exerted to get the boy to acknowledge his errors and vow to do better. If a boy's readiness for release was under consideration, then he was challenged to demonstrate, through a review of his recent behavior and testimony as to his good intentions, that he could handle his freedom constructively.

While the behavior of the group leader during the session is carefully prescribed in Positive Peer Culture, we observed a great deal of variation. Some group leaders played a much more active role in the discussion than others did; some limited their contributions to leading questions, while others intervened with substantive comments more in keeping with the role of group member. On one occasion, we observed a group leader act as a kind of choral conductor, prompting the group to chant in unison certain phrases like, "That's not the way we see it!" in response to the "owner's" account of his behavior.

The last five to ten minutes of a session was allocated to the group leader's summary. Again, there was much variation in leaders' styles at this point. In general, leaders followed the PPC prescription that they summarize the group process in terms of whether the group was helping its members and how the group might help better next time. Sometimes, however, a group leader would deliver an interpretation of the "owner's" behavior and advise him how to change, thus taking over a function that the PPC modality assigns to the group.

Variations in the way the treatment modality was delivered to each group and each student arose from at least four sources. These were the institution; the staff team; individual staff members, especially the group leader; and the students.

Differences among the institutions arose partly because the institutions deliberately chose to modify PPC in some way. Boysville staff, for example, introduced two innovations. First, it did not employ the language of PPC's "problems," such as "inconsiderate to others" and "fronting." Instead, boys were prompted to describe problematic behavior in its particulars without trying to classify it according to the PPC list. Boysville abandoned the list because they felt that its use had developed into a jargon. Second, each boy met about once a month with a staff member and two of his groupmates to discuss personal matters—such things as his clothing needs, his medi-cations if any, and perhaps feelings that he was not yet ready to discuss at a group meeting. The staff member would attend to those details that could appropriately be handled without group involvement, and all three of the boy's "advocates" would advise him about how to use the group to meet his needs.

Starr Commonwealth adhered fairly closely to the Vorrath and Brendtro model of PPC, with one elaboration. (It is notable that when this study began, Brendtro was the director of the agency.) Starr energetically reached out to its students' families. This was the function of its family service workers. These workers met with families in their homes and arranged for them to come to the campus, providing transportation when necessary. On the campus, families met not only with their boy and his staff but also with their boy's group. About 75 percent of the students' families were involved in this program.

The public institutions also followed Vorrath and Brendtro's PPC model quite closely. Nevertheless, there were differences between the two public campuses, partly attributable we believe to differences in the population from which staff were drawn. Adrian and Maxey were both located in rural areas, but Maxey was located on the fringe of suburban Detroit and not far from the university city of Ann Arbor. Because of the population from which it was drawn, Maxey's staff was decidedly more urban in its values and styles than the staff at Adrian, which was sixty miles from any urban center. There also existed at Adrian a staff culture that pre-dated the introduction of Positive Peer Culture; for employment on Adrian's staff not only went back many years in some staff members' lifetimes, employment also went back two or three generations in some staff members' families. Moreover, while the proportion of black students at Adrian was as large as at Maxey, the proportion of black staff at Adrian was much smaller. These rural–urban, ethnic, and historical differences seemed in our observations to be reflected in relatively less tolerance for diverse behavior and, as one supervisor at Adrian put it, less "empowerment" granted to groups.

There were also differences in treatment from group to group within each of the four participating institutions. Staff teams differed in their level of cohesiveness, the effectiveness of their informal organization, and their enthusiasm for PPC; and these differences affected how they delivered the program to their students. Staff members differed from one another, of course, in the way they did their jobs. And there was constant turnover among the boys, because one or two were admitted to each group most months while one or two others were released. According to the staffs, these changes sometimes prompted alterations in treatment.

We did not attempt to determine systematically the reasons for inter-group differences in treatment. As we will see in the next chapter, we found evidence that variations were due largely to differences among the institutions and the staff teams, rather than due to turnover among students and consequent changes in peer group composition and dynamics. Without trying to trace the sources of differences in treatment, we measured the differences that they generated among the groups. These measurable differences in hypothetically important group characteristics were essential to our research design.

SIMILARITY IN THE COMPOSITION OF GROUPS

Because we did not create inter-group variations, our research design is properly termed a "field experiment." It differs from a pure experiment in that the researchers did not have control over the inter-group differences that we hypothesized would cause differences in boys' adjustment. The inter-group differences were generated mainly by the different staffs, and we captured the naturally occurring variations with our measures. Then we related these measured differences among groups to measured differences in boys' adjustment.

It was important to the integrity of this field experiment that, while groups differed in certain important ways, the composition of group *members* was very similar from group to group. This would not be the case if boys had been assigned to their groups selectively upon their admission so that some groups were composed, for example, of much more seriously delinquent or much more anxious boys than other groups. Such selective assignment would have made it impossible to determine how group characteristics affected boys' adjustment independent of how much adjustment was affected by the condition of boys when they were admitted. A crucial facet of our research design was therefore that boys were randomly assigned to their groups upon admission.

In this research, random assignment could not be a technical matter of consulting a table of random numbers to determine each boy's group assignment. Random assignment occurred only to the degree that the institutions' policies were such that group placement was unrelated to any of the boys' characteristics that might be associated with the outcomes that we wished to study. Fortunately, such policies were the norm for these four institutions.

Well before actual data collection began, we made a thorough investigation of the processes by which boys were assigned to groups. The official policy of all four institutions was that boys would be admitted in the order in which they had been referred by juvenile courts or other agencies. Typically, the institutions had waiting lists of a week to a month and a half. To the degree that this policy was strictly followed, it would generate random-like assignment. That is, which group a boy entered would have nothing to do with his personal characteristics, properties of the group, or characteristics of the staff. Instead, assignment would be entirely a function of the date of the boy's referral and the time when a place opened in a group.

It was of course possible that administrators would not adhere strictly to this policy. Therefore, we discussed group assignment practices at great length with all administrators responsible for group placements. Indeed, almost all of them acknowledged that exceptions sometimes occurred. Our concern was with the nature of these exceptions. Administrators of three of the four centers at the public institutions (Adrian, Olympic, and Sequoyah), and at Starr Commonwealth all reported similar practices that were quite compatible with the desired research design. These administrators considered all of their groups essentially equivalent, with none more appropriate for one type of boy than another. Consequently, they followed the basic policy of random-like assignment in almost every case. They felt it necessary to make exceptions only when the normal policy would lead to creating divergent groups. For instance, they would avoid making placements that would lead to groups having an almost entirely black or entirely white membership, they would avoid a concentration of boys with a history of drug abuse, and they would not place several boys together who had known each other previously. While these exceptions diluted the strict randomness of group assignment, they tended to further the research goal that strictly random assignment was meant to achieve—creating groups with equivalent memberships. Thus, we felt satisfied that the groups at these four centers suited our field experimental research design.

The assignment practices at Boysville and at the Summit center at the Maxey Boys Training School were quite different. In both of these centers, administrators tried to compose groups that would be homogeneous in a way conducive to management and rehabilitation. At Boysville, the boys were assigned to groups according to their size, and consequently, Boysville groups tended to be different in the ages of their members as well. While students were admitted to Boysville in the order of their referral, they were assigned initially to an intake group where they were oriented to the program and awaited a vacancy in a group appropriate to their size. Because Boysville conceived of its ten groups as falling into four size categories, it was still possible that assignment would be random within pairs of groups whose members were about the same size.

Assignment practices at the Summit center were more complex. As at Boysville, boys first entered an intake group where they waited for an opening in a group considered appropriate for them. Summit's administrators had rather elaborate conceptions of the types of boys appropriate to each group. For example, one group might be composed of older boys with especially poor verbal skills, while another was designed particularly for boys with drug problems and emotional difficulties. Our discussions with Summit's administrators revealed that they did not consider any of their groups to be comparable to any of the others. We therefore did not include Summit's groups in our study.

During the preliminary phase of the study, we sought empirical verification of the impressions we had gained about assignment practices. We extracted information from institutional records about age, physical size, offense history, prior placements, grade level, and standardized test scores. The data confirmed that groups at Boysville differed in physical size and age in the expected pattern, and that there were numerous differences among the groups at Summit. On the other hand, differences among the groups within each of the other centers were no larger than could be expected by chance, even while there were significant differences between the centers in several respects.

These findings gave us confidence that the four participating institutions provided an opportunity to design a study of the effects of the groups on their members, independent of the characteristics of the individuals. We proceeded to select our focal sample from boys entering the ten groups at Sequoyah center and the ten at the Olympic center of the Maxey school, the eight boys' groups at the Adrian school, the fourteen groups at Starr Commonwealth, and the three groups at Boysville that proved comparable to one another, forty-five groups in all.

What we have just described as natural randomization of boys to groups needs to be qualified, however. To begin with, while the population of boys referred to the public and private institutions in our study overlapped considerably, delinquents were not assigned at random across the public– private line. Although juvenile court judges and their staffs often placed boys on the waiting lists of both the public and private agencies and sent a boy to fill whatever opening occurred first, they were sometimes selective in their referrals. Furthermore, boys who absconded from a private insti- tution might be sent to a public one, but not vice versa. Consequently, the focal students whom we found at the public institutions were as a group different in some important respects from the boys at the private ones.

Table 3.1 displays twelve characteristics of the 356 focal students who participated in our research at their admission. Figures are presented for the total group and for each of the public and private residential centers. Note that the three centers administered by the Michigan Department of Social Services admitted boys who, during our intake interview, reported signif- icantly higher levels of delinquent behavior in the preceding three months than their counterparts at the private institutions. They had also been ar- rested significantly more often. The distribution of the instant offenses for which the delinquents were institutionalized also differed: The public in- stitutions admitted a larger proportion of boys who were charged with disorderly conduct—predominantly fighting—than the private institutions did.

Boys at the private institutions were significantly more likely to have been classified as either Emotionally Impaired (EI) or Learning Disabled (LD) than the boys at the public institutions were. This difference may not reflect an actual difference among the boys, however, as much as a difference in the agencies' policies. Any institutionalized delinquent could be classified

Table 3.1
Selected Characteristics of Focal Students at Admission by Center

	Total (n=356)	Department of Social Services		
		Adrian (70)	Olympic (77)	Sequoyah (70)
age	15.90 (12.00-17.90)	16.20	16.30	16.30
% white	52	54	40	56
social status	32.10 (6.00-92.30)	28.70	33.60	31.00
% living with two parents	34	51	35	20
N prior out-of-home placements	.71 (0-4)	.80	.69	.73
N prior arrests[f]	5.50 (0-20)	7.40[g]	5.50	6.20
self-report delinquent behavior[a]	65.20 (27-12.60)	67.50	70.50	64.20
Instant offence[b]				
% assault robbery	29	30	29	30
% property	49	33	47	44
% disorderly	15	24	19	25
% other	7	13	4	1
% emotionally impaired[c]	25	8	2.40	23
% learning disabled[d]	7	3	1	3
besetment[e]	40.20 (15-72)	41.30	39.20	41.50
% in school	67	61	61	70

Table 3.1 (*continued*)

| | Starr Commonwealth | | Boysville |
	Lakeview-Cedar (86)	Maple (31)	(22)
age	16.00	13.80	15.30
% white	56	52	64
social status	34.30	30.50	32.30
% living with two parents	28	39	41
N prior out-of-home placements	.58	.84	.68
N prior arrests[f]	4.60	3.00[h]	4.10
self-report delinquent behavior[a]	64.40	59.60	53.70
Instant offence[b]			
% assault robbery	24	43	17
% property	68	43	44
% disorderly	2	-	6
% other	6	13	33
% emotionally impaired[c]	15	77	46
% learning disabled[d]	8	3	46
besetment[e]	38.40	43.60	39.10
% in school	67	87	68

[a] public/private difference p = .01: public mean = 67.5, private mean = 61.6, t = 2.50 (df=353)
[b] public/private difference p < .001: chi square = 33.2, df = 3
[c] public/private difference p < .001 by Fisher Exact Test
[d] public/private difference p < .001 by Fisher Exact Test
[e] Maple/other difference p < .03, F = 4.79 (df=2, 352)
[f] public/private difference p < .001, public mean = 6.3, private mean = 4.2, t = 5.65 (df=350)
[g] Adrian more than Olympic p = .01; more than Sequoyah p = .06
[h] Maple less than Lakeview-Cedar, p = .01

as EI or LD simply by virtue of having been institutionalized. The private agencies classified many of their students as EI or LD in order to facilitate their access to special education programs after their release. Boys who emerged from an institution as EI or LD were assured of at least consideration for special education. The public institutions were more reluctant to classify their students as EI or LD because they feared that these labels would be stigmatizing. The classifications had little or no effect on the students' educational programs at the institutions; their effect was post-release.

The figures in Table 3.1 reveal a great deal of similarity among the boys we found at the public and private institutions. The data also demonstrate some important differences, notably in the frequency and nature of their prior delinquency. Because of these differences, it is not appropriate to compare the public with the private institutions in terms of their treatment processes or effectiveness. That was, in any case, not an aim of our research. These differences alerted us to the need for certain statistical controls as we analyzed our data. These controls enabled us to attribute causality with more certainty either to the personal characteristics of the boys, to the groups to which they were assigned, or to some combination of these.

Anticipating that we would be comparing groups, we also needed to check on differences in their membership within the public institutions and within the private ones. We knew that there were some systematic differences in who was assigned where. The public centers did not draw their residents from the same populations. The Adrian Training School and the Olympic and Sequoyah centers at the Maxey Boys Training School admitted delinquents from different geographical areas of the state. Each was allocated a portion of Wayne County, including the City of Detroit, in addition to a slice of the state outside of Wayne County that extended from the northern peninsula to Michigan's southern border with Ohio. The populations of these sections were roughly equal. The purpose of these divisions was to assign each center about the same proportion of delinquents from urban areas and to avoid racial segregation.

We compared the composition of the groups on those variables listed in Table 3.1. According to our data, this apportionment did not generate any important differences among the boys admitted to the three public centers or from group to group within these centers. The only marked differences that we found were in the number of prior arrests and the proportion of boys who had been living with both a father and mother prior to their admission. The delinquents sent to Adrian while we were gathering our sample had been arrested more often; and the range in the number of boys who had been living with both parents extended from seven out of nine of the focal students in one of the groups at Adrian to none of the twelve focal students in one of Sequoyah's groups. These were undoubtedly chance differences and did not reflect any systematic selectivity in assignment.

There was one systematic difference in assignment among the villages at Starr Commonwealth: Maple Village was assigned the younger boys. Note in Table 3.1 that the boys at Maple Village averaged about thirteen years, ten months old compared to the predominantly fifteen- and sixteen-year-olds at all the other public and private centers. Lakeview and Cedar Villages at Starr accepted the same kinds of boys depending on available bedspace and could be considered essentially as one center, as we have done in Table 3.1. The Lakeview and Cedar boys were not significantly different in age or in comparison to the boys at the other private institution, Boysville, or from the boys in the public institutions.

Apparently associated with their relative immaturity, the focal students at Maple Village had been arrested less often and were also more anxious and depressed—"beset"—upon their admission than the rest of the focal students were. As we expected, prior levels of delinquency and besetment proved to be significant psychological characteristics of boys, so it was important to control for these differences in order not to confuse them with differences in treatment that the boys at Maple Village may have received. The groups of focal students outside of Maple Village did not differ significantly in either of these respects.

Finally, one other difference was found among the centers at the private institutions only: The groups varied widely in the average socioeconomic status of the delinquents' families. The average status in the private institutions did not differ markedly from the average in the public institutions, but the variation among the former groups was greater. This also was a chance difference, and it required no statistical control.

In the first stages of the statistical analyses of our data, we explored what control variables were sufficient to account for the systematic and chance differences that we had found among the residential groups and centers. We considered the factors of age, race, and the public/private distinction because we had determined that centers differed in these respects. We found that controlling for these factors effectively eliminated any substantial differences among forty-four of the forty-five groups during the period in which the focal students were admitted. One group at Starr's Maple Village appeared to receive systematically more delinquent youth than the other groups did, so that group was eliminated from all analyses of the effects of groups on individuals. Thus, with relatively simple statistical controls, we were able to disentangle differences in the referred populations from the factors we wished to study, particularly differences in the personal characteristics of the focal students and in the properties of their groups.

We should point out that we had expected to find some of these systematic differences in assignment which we would have to control systematically. That Maple Village housed younger boys was, of course, obvious. That the public institutions admitted somewhat more delinquent boys was also expected, if for no other reason than that boys who absconded from the private institutions could then be sent to the public ones.

Despite excluding some groups because of selective assignment practices, the focal students in our study well represent the population of delinquent boys institutionalized in Michigan at the time we collected our data. The participating institutions accounted for over 90 percent of all the institutionalized delinquent boys in the state, and the focal students we included were a fair sample of their residents. From the total column of Table 3.1:

• Most were fifteen or sixteen years old
• Virtually all had been arrested at least once, some as many as twenty times
• A little over half of them were white
• About a third lived with a father and mother prior to their admission
• Their average family social status was in the bottom third of the U.S. population
• Forty-four percent had at some time been placed to live elsewhere than with a parent
• A third of them had not attended any school just before their admission

DATA COLLECTION

We spent almost a year collecting preliminary data on the four campuses. During this time, we continued our informal observation of the programs, selected and trained our first set of interviewers, worked out schedules and procedures, pretested our measures, and validated our decision about which groups should be included in the study by virtue of their similarity or known differences.

Selecting and Training Interviewers

Three field interviewers were hired initially, two to interview at Starr Commonwealth and one at the Adrian Training School and Boysville. These interviewers were recruited through classified ads placed in the Sunday edition of the local newspapers that served Adrian and Albion. Prospective candidates were selected primarily on the basis of personal interviews. All three of these interviewers were female. The two Starr interviewers had college degrees; the Adrian interviewer did not. All three were bright, responsible individuals who remained with the study the entire time we were interviewing at the institutions.

Interviews at Maxey Boys Training School were conducted initially by members of the central research staff (research assistants and graduate student research assistants). Later on additional interviewers were hired to handle the increased load at Maxey and to free up some of the central project staff. These interviewers were recruited through job postings at the Institute for Social Research (ISR) and the University's central job board. All but one of the interviewers were college students, most of whom were looking for research experience. They generally stayed with the project for one or two semesters. There was one male interviewer in this group.

Training ordinarily required three days. It included an introduction to the study and its goals, a training film, a manual on interviewing procedures, and a review of the interview itself. Then trainees observed a practice interview conducted by one of the project staff with a student at one of the institutions. This interview was followed by a discussion of the process.

Next, each trainee conducted her own interview with a resident. (These students were not included in the study. They were boys who agreed to be interviewed to help us with the training process.) These practice interviews were conducted under the observation of a member of the research staff who reviewed the interview with the trainee afterward.

Finally, each interviewer's first interview with an actual participant in the study was observed by her supervisor. If the interviewer or supervisor felt there was a need, additional interviews were also observed until both were confident that the interviewer was ready to proceed on her own. Additional training sessions were held in Ann Arbor before the beginning of each new wave of interviews.

Regular contact was maintained with the interviewers throughout the study through informal meetings, memos and, in the case of the interviewers at Albion and Adrian, weekly phone calls. Each interview was reviewed and edited by the supervisor as soon as it came in. Any problems or questions were handled as soon as they arose. When necessary, the interviewer recontacted the respondent to ask missed or mishandled questions.

Selecting Focal Students and Obtaining Informed Consent

"Focal students" were those institutionalized delinquent boys who were the primary objects of our observations. They were selected by the criterion that they joined one of the forty-five groups that we had already determined would participate in our study and were among the first eight boys to be admitted to that group (and to agree to participate) after the starting date. Focal students are to be distinguished from the other boys in their group, that is, boys who were already present when the focal students were admitted to their group or who joined the group after we stopped enlisting newcomers to that group. Only the focal students were interviewed periodically during their institutionalization and after their release. Only their records were abstracted from institutional and justice system files. They and the other boys in their group all responded to group-administered anonymous questionnaires. The first focal student was recruited and interviewed at Starr Commonwealth on September 16, 1982; the 364th and last, at the Adrian Training School on October 7, 1983.

Enlisting a boy as a focal student required first obtaining informed consent for his participation from the boy himself and from his parent or guardian. At Starr and Boysville, packets for obtaining consent were left with the intake workers who interviewed families before boys were admitted to the institution. Each packet consisted of a letter to the parent introducing the study, a parent consent form, a letter to the student, and a student consent form. During the preadmission interview at Starr or Boysville, the intake person would explain the nature of the study and ask the parent and the student to give consent by signing the appropriate consent forms. It was made clear that admission did not depend on the boy's participation in the research. If the parents were unsure about the boy's participation and had further questions, this was noted on the consent form along with a phone number and a time when we could contact them. We in turn called, answered questions, and if possible obtained consent over the telephone, following up by mail to get a signed form. It should be noted that this happened infrequently. We obtained parental and student consent at intake for almost all the boys admitted to Starr and Boysville.

Obtaining consent for the students sent to the Maxey and Adrian Training Schools was not so easy. These boys were ordinarily not accompanied to the institution by a parent or guardian, so another method of reaching the parent/guardian was employed.

As soon as the decision was made to admit a boy to one of the participating public institutions, a letter of notification was sent to the parent/guardian by the Department of Social Services. The letter explained that the University of Michigan was conducting research and that a member of the research staff would contact the parent, and it urged him or her to allow the boy to participate. If there was no phone number for the family on file, a version of this letter urged the parent to call the research staff collect.

A boy might arrive at the training school anytime from a day to several weeks after the decision to admit him was made. In any case, the intake staff person explained the study to the boy as part of the initial orientation and asked him for signed consent. If the boy agreed to participate, then the research staff was informed as soon as possible by phone. If we had not already contacted the parent, we attempted to do so then, by phone if we could or by mail, requesting again that the parent call us collect.

We explained the study and the boy's part in it to the parent over the phone and requested consent. If consent was given, we then mailed a letter again explaining the study and confirming that consent was given. The parent was also informed in this letter that consent could be rescinded at any time by a collect phone call. Of the parents or guardians that we contacted, 98 percent consented to their boys' participation.

We found it impossible to contact forty-one of the boys' parents or

Table 3.2
Numbers and Proportion of the Initial Sample Interviewed at Each Wave

Interview

	N Attempted	N Complete	% Completed
Initial	400	364	91
Interim	336	326	97
Release	336	306	91
Post-release I	306	253	83

guardians despite many phone calls and letters, and in four cases we were instructed by the referring court that we were not to contact them because parental rights had been severed. These and all the other boys at the public institutions were legally wards of the Department of Social Services (DSS), which was empowered to grant consent. We had been working with the Residential Services office of DSS all along, however, and that staff was thoroughly familiar with our research, had observed our pre-tests, and had helped us to design our procedures and methods. DSS was fully supportive of the research effort and was willing to consent to a boy's participation on condition that the boy had agreed. While DSS administrators preferred that parents gave consent, they were willing to take this responsibility for those boys whose parents could not or should not be contacted. After obtaining agreement from DSS for this 15 percent of our sample, we informed the parent by mail where this was possible and allowed, with notification that they could revoke permission if they wished.

In this way, we obtained informed consent from each boy and from some adult who presumably had the boy's best interests in mind. Consent forms were placed in a locked file. Only after the boy and a concerned adult had consented to his participation did we attempt to interview him.

Interviewing Focal Students

For that part of our continuing research that we report here, we tried to interview each focal student four times—upon his admission, four months after his admission, just prior to his release, and six months after his release. We were successful in most cases. Table 3.2 presents the number and proportion of interviews that we completed.

We asked 400 boys to participate in our research, and 364 consented and were interviewed shortly after their admission. Thirty boys or their parents/

guardians declined to participate, and the remaining six boys simply slipped through our intake notification procedure so we did not know that they had been admitted until it was too late to conduct an intake interview.

Of these 364 boys, 336 were eligible for an interim interview four months later. We wanted to interview these 336 focal students because they were members of their group for at least four months. Their data files include the minimum information that we required to satisfy the aims of our research; that is, data on what the boys were like when they first arrived at an institution and data on a group with which they subsequently had at least four months' experience. Twenty-eight boys either absconded within four months of their arrival and were not returned; were transferred to another group or perhaps to another institution; or absconded, were apprehended, and then were transferred to another institution. As Table 3.2 shows, we obtained 326 interim interviews; ten boys declined to participate at that time.

We attempted to obtain release interviews from all 336 boys, whether we had obtained an interim interview or not. Of those ten who had declined to grant us an interview four months after their arrival, four were willing to be interviewed on the threshold of their release. We interviewed 302 of the focal students whom we had interviewed at the interim, for the total of 306 release interviews. Thirty boys declined to be interviewed upon their release or slipped through the notification procedure unnoticed, were gone before we could interview them, and could not be contacted in the open community for an interview within a reasonable time afterward.

We attempted to follow up with six-month post-release interviews only for those 306 boys who had granted us release interviews. While we searched the post-release records of all the 336 focal students whom we consider participants in our study, the purpose of our post-release investigation focused on those boys for whom we had data as to their condition when they left the institution. We found and interviewed 253 of these.

Table 3.3 demonstrates the wave-by-wave effects of attrition of the sample from the 336 interviewed at intake and still in their group at the interim to the 253 from whom we obtained post-release interviews. This comparison includes the same set of characteristics listed in Table 3.1. Note that the figures are highly similar from one wave to the next. Because we lost relatively few boys over time, attrition did not disturb the representativeness of the sample. It is not apparent in Table 3.3 that attrition was nevertheless in some respects selective: more heavily delinquent boys, even among the generally heavily delinquent boys in the sample, were more likely to drop out of the study, while boys who were more emotionally disturbed tended to remain in the sample throughout. The effect of this on our analyses of data was to reduce the number of initially heavily delinquent respondents available for comparisons in later waves of data. Nevertheless, enough of these remained so that there continued to be wide variation in respondents'

Table 3.3
Selected Characteristics of Focal Students at Intake by Wave of Interview

Characteristics at Intake	Intake (n = 336)	Interim (n = 326)	Release (n = 306)	Post-Release I (n = 253)
age	15.9	15.9	15.9	15.9
% white	52	52	51	52
social status	32.1	32.2	32.0	31.4
% living with two parents	34	32	32	32
N prior out-of-home placements	.71	.69	.67	.66
N prior arrests	5.5	5.4	5.5	5.3
Self-reported delinquency	65.2	65.5	65.7	65.1
Instant offense				
% assault or robbery	29	29	30	30
% property	49	47	45	46
% disorderly	15	16	18	15
% other	7	8	8	9
% emotionally impaired	25	26	25	27
% learning disabled	7	9	6	6
Besetment	40.2	40.5	40.5	40.6
% in school	67	67	67	71

delinquency, sufficient to explore what effect this had on the focal students' adjustment.

The important point, to repeat, is that at all waves of our interviews, the respondents well represented all the institutionalized boys. It is likely that our findings can be generalized to all of them.

Intake interview. We interviewed 355 boys within ten days of their arrival, nine more within two weeks. The intake interview was designed to assess boys' personal characteristics before they might be affected by their institutional experience and to collect life historical information.[3] While interviewers were trained to adopt a conversational style, they followed a structured set of questions very closely. They deviated from the interview schedule only to accommodate to unusual conditions. The interview consisted of both "open" questions to which the respondent answered freely in his own words, and "closed" questions to which the boy responded by selecting an alternative from a list such as "almost always," "often," "sometimes," "almost never." The intake interview lasted about an hour.

During the intake interview the respondent described his delinquent behavior during the most recent four months that he was free, where and with whom he had lived during the past two years, when he had last attended school, whether he had been employed in recent months, and other life experiences. Some of the attitudes and values that we measured were the respondent's admiration for certain prosocial and antisocial behaviors, how he got along with his parents or guardians, his feelings about school, his self-concept and self-esteem, his eagerness to have friends, and the degree of his anxiety and depression ("besetment"/"buoyancy").

Interim interview. Four months after his admission, we interviewed each focal student to find out, first, what he thought of his group, his staff team, the institution as a whole, and the Positive Peer Culture program. We also questioned him about his adjustment to the institution up to that time, in terms of his behavior and attitudes. In addition, we asked about his contacts with family and friends back home. This interview took about forty-five minutes.

Examples of the subjects covered in the interim interview include the boy's assessment of the strength of his group's counterculture, that is, the degree to which the group was united in breaking institutional rules. Other questions asked about the degree to which the respondent himself subscribed to a group counterculture. We also asked boys whether they liked their group, whether they had made any good friends, and if they had, what their friend was like in terms of his values and adjustment. Another line of inquiry concerned the degree of autonomy that the boy felt he had from his staff and his group.

Release interview. We interviewed as many of the focal students as we could between the time that they "got their date" for release and the time they actually left. This interview was the longest of the four because it combined elements of the first two and also asked boys about what they expected in the near future. It was understandably a happy interview for most of the 306 boys because they were anticipating their freedom. Twenty-four of them expressed some anxiety however, because they were going to a place they had never been before, into the care of people they did not know, and they were not confident that it would work out for them. Twenty others were unhappy because their "release" was not really a release but rather a placement in a more secure institution. Because many of the latter were moved quickly and often without prior knowledge, their interviews were delayed a week or so, after they had settled into the other institution. We did not feel that we should ask these boys the questions about anticipating life in the open community.

In order to measure change in personal characteristics over the course of institutionalization, we repeated several of the questions we had asked boys at their admission, questions measuring their delinquent values, anxiety and depression, self-esteem, and interest in school, among others. We also asked boys for their exit assessments of their institutional experience—the boys in their group, the staff, and the program—in order to relate these to their adjustment at release. And we asked them to look ahead. One of the major purposes of the release interview was to measure the psychological condition of the boys at release in ways that might help to understand their subsequent adjustment.

Six-month follow-up interview. Upon a boy's release, the institution gave us the address and phone number where he was going. Anticipating that finding some boys after they had been released would be a problem, we also asked each boy at his release interview for the address and phone of someone else who would probably know his whereabouts. Three months after each boy's release we began to call these numbers to arrange the first post-release interview. We also checked the rosters of the state's jails, prisons, and juvenile detention facilities. A newly-trained staff of interviewers phoned persistently day and night to make contact and in each case kept at this for up to three months after the target date if necessary. We conducted most of these post-release interviews over the telephone because the boys were scattered all over the state of Michigan, and some beyond. A few interviews were conducted face-to-face because most of the eighteen boys whom we found in jail, prison, or mental hospital could not come to a phone. We paid boys ten dollars for granting this interview. The interview lasted about an hour.

The follow-up interview was designed mainly to assess respondents' post-release adjustment. (At this point we started to refer to our respondents as "young men" rather than "boys.") We asked the young men, for example, whether they were going to school or working, with whom they were living, how they were getting along with the people they were living with, what contact if any they had with the justice system, and how much delinquent/criminal behavior they had committed since their release, caught or not. We inquired also about their psychological condition—their self-esteem, besetment, and the subjective quality of their lives. We asked them to think back to their institutional experience and evaluate it from their present standpoint. At this point, we instituted a new line of inquiry in order to test hypotheses about critical determinants of the young men's adjustment to the open community by asking them about their reference groups; that is, we questioned them about the kinds of people they were associating with, about influence and advice they valued, and about who they felt really cared about them, if anyone.

Group questionnaires. Every six months, beginning the month after the admission of the first focal student, we administered questionnaires to all the students in the forty-five groups we had selected for observation. This was the source of data on group properties such as group norms and cohesiveness. Questionnaires were administered in October 1982, April 1983, and October 1983.

Group questionnaires were typically administered in the group's classroom during school hours. The institutions were very cooperative in this respect, recognizing that many boys would consider responding to our questionnaires pleasurable in comparison to schoolwork. This took less than an hour each time, so boys were not taken "off task" from school for long.

We only required that the boys give their consent for this level of participation, because the anonymous and benign nature of the group questionnaire did not require the consent of parents or guardians. The response rates were quite high, from 92 percent of group members in the first wave to 90 percent in the third.

Because many of our respondents had poor reading skills, the questionnaires were read aloud to the group by one of the research staff while another circulated about the classroom giving help and monitoring. No member of the institutional staff was present at these sessions.

The questionnaires provided the data on groups as a whole. To assess group norms, we asked boys not only about their own support for antisocial behavior and values, and attitudes toward the staff, but also how they thought "most of the other boys" in their group would respond. The average of the beliefs about the others' responses constituted our measure of group norms. We took a similar approach to the cohesiveness or attractiveness of the group. The questionnaire included questions about how much autonomy from staff directive the group enjoyed. We also asked about the basis of peer leadership in the group: Were certain boys leaders because they were feared? Because they were popular? Smart? Caring and helpful?

The questionnaires also gave us another view of the focal students, from the perspective of their group mates. We asked boys to nominate up to three group members who fit certain descriptions such as "a leader," "really tries to deal with his problems," and "doesn't want to go straight." These data enabled us to validate focal students' own reports of their personal characteristics. For example, group members named beset boys as fitting different descriptions than buoyant boys.

Staff questionnaires. At about the same time that we administered questionnaires to groups, we distributed questionnaires to the staffs of those groups to obtain another, independent assessment of group properties (e.g., the autonomy of the group), measuring differences in the way staffs treated the group (e.g., relative emphasis on boys' emotional problems or antisocial behavior), and measuring certain characteristics of the staff teams themselves (e.g., morale).

Collecting these data from the staffs proved to be the second most difficult of all of our data collection procedures (after contacting the young men six months after their release). Staff members were very busy, and they had higher priorities for their time than helping us with our research. Some doubted its usefulness, and some suspected that our study was actually designed to evaluate their performance. We had to keep after many staff members to complete their questionnaires and return them, and we never got some. Consequently, response rates were relatively low: 77 percent in wave 1, 67 percent in wave 2, and 66 percent in wave 3. We set a criterion that we needed at least three members' questionnaires out of the six to nine members of a team in order to compute a staff team variable. With this criterion, forty-three of the forty-five groups' teams responded on the first wave and thirty-seven on waves 2 and 3.

Records. Several sets of records proved informative, especially about boys' life histories. With the permission of their parents or guardians, we abstracted data from boys' records at referring juvenile courts, participating institutions, county prosecuting attorneys, and the Michigan State Police. From these we learned about boys' official delinquency, including number of arrests and adjudications; the number of times each boy had been placed outside of his own home; classification, if any, as emotionally impaired or learning disabled for the purposes of special education; scholastic test scores; and other variables. The records of prosecuting attorneys and the state police were particularly helpful for finding respondents after they had been released. In cases where we could not contact the young men for post-release interviews, we were at least able to obtain official post-release crime data.

Special care had to be taken, when approaching agencies for access to their records, not to reveal that a boy had been incarcerated for delinquency. This presented no problem when our research staff searched the files, as was the case in the larger jurisdictions; we simply kept the list of names to ourselves. When an agency's personnel performed the search and completed the forms for us, we supplied them with a list of names to search that explicitly included dummy names. In this way, agency personnel did not know which individuals on the list were actually in our study. (We were sent no records for dummy names.)

Census data. We wanted to find out how the community to which they had been released affected young men's adjustment. There are a great many findings that link characteristics of communities to the official records of delinquency and crime of the people who live there. Many people trying to rehabilitate juvenile delinquents and adult criminals feel that poor neighborhoods exert almost irresistible negative influence. We tested hypotheses about these social ecological factors with data from the U.S. Census.

We were able to compile information on neighborhood characteristics for 231 of the participants. These are the young men who we knew had resided at a known address after their release for at least two of the six months, and that address was not a closed institution. We determined the census tract in which each address was located and obtained data on the characteristics of each tract from the 1980 Census. If a young man happened to reside in two places for about three months each, the average of the characteristics of both neighborhoods was used. We selected neighborhood characteristics that have demonstrated relationships with crime and delinquency in previous research: the average annual income of households, transiency of heads of households in terms of the recency of their arrival in the tract, racial composition of the tract; and crowdedness of living quarters in terms of per capita occupation of rooms.

DATA ANALYSIS

The findings that we report here were all generated through the computing facilities of the University of Michigan. In almost all cases, the statistical programs were part of the MIDAS software package created and maintained by the university's Statistical Research Laboratory. Special applications were found in widely available software (e.g., BMD, SPSS, LISREL). The Institute for Social Research Coding and Keypunch sections assisted in entering the data into computer data files as numbers. ISR and the Statistical Research Laboratory also provided valuable consultation on computing and data analysis.

Almost all the variables that we considered were constructed from responses to several related questions on interviews or questionnaires. That is, variables are typically scores on indices rather than on single items. We gauged the internal consistency of respondents' answers to the several items in each index with Cronbach's alpha (Cronbach, 1951) and assured ourselves of a satisfactory degree of internal consistency before entering the index score into the dataset. Following Nunnally (1967, p. 226), we built indices whose alphas were at least .50. Most of the alphas exceeded this aspiration. We will describe each variable's content when it is first introduced in presenting findings in later chapters.[4]

As will be seen in the next chapter on findings about institutional adjustment, we tested hypotheses and explored the data with statistical tools ranging from simple comparisons of means to complex multivariate techniques employing structural equations. The bulk of the analyses utilized partial correlation and multiple regression. Partial correlations indicate the degree of relationship between a pair of variables after controlling for their relationships with one or more other variables. Our main use of multiple regression is to assess the power of a set of scores, taken together, to predict to the value of an outcome, or dependent variable. The set of "predictors" may consist of variables of interest as well as control variables. For example, one analysis addressed whether boys' perceptions about their groups explained the relationship between group norms and individual adjustment. To do so we used measures of institutional adjustment as dependent variables (e.g., delinquent behavior and support for a counterculture) and measures of group norms as independent variables. Intake measures that had proven relevant to each independent variable in earlier analyses served as control variables. We then examined the partial correlations between independent and dependent variables, comparing their magnitude and statistical significance depending on whether perceptions about the group were added to the list of control variables. If perceptions did explain the relationship, then partial correlations would drop considerably after controlling for perceptions. In a similar fashion, the increase in variance explained (R^2) by adding the independent variables (norms) to a regression equation for a measure of institutional adjustment would be less if we had already controlled for perceptions than if we had not.

Multiple regression and other statistical tools enabled us to test hypotheses that related variables at one point in time or hypotheses about change over time, depending on the times at which variables were measured. For example, we determined what differences in life histories and current attitudes there were at intake between boys who were buoyant and beset at that time; and we also tested hypotheses about differences in the way buoyant and beset types would respond to the institutional experience by attempting to predict later adjustment of boys classified as buoyant or beset at admission.

SUMMARY

We have covered a lot of ground in this chapter in the course of explaining the methods of our study. It is worth a quick review. We first explained that the purpose of our study was to determine the effects on the boys of variations in their institutional experiences. Because of the organization of life at these four institutions, it is most reasonable to treat the group or living-unit as the principle source of variation in these experiences. We briefly described each of the four institutions as well as the treatment program they all use: Positive Peer Culture. We then focused on the process of assignment of youths to groups at the various institutions, which is at the heart of our research design. Empirical analysis supported the impression that this process was essentially random for most of the groups. We further found that the forty-five groups included in our analyses were fully comparable after differences between the institutional centers were eliminated by controlling for age, race, and state versus private institutional affiliation. This chapter also describes the collection of data for the study, including the selection and training of interviewers, the selection of focal students (the main participants in the research), and the content and administration of the interviews. We also presented information about our success in maintaining their participation through successive interviews, and we compared the original sample to that which remained after attrition. There were several other sources of data in addition to these interviews, such as group and staff questionnaires and institutional records. We concluded the chapter with some information about how we analyzed the data.

NOTES

1. The most complete and authoritative account of the principles and practices of Positive Peer Culture is contained in *Positive Peer Culture* by Harry H. Vorrath and Larry K. Brendtro. 2nd edition (New York: Aldine de Gruyter). Copyright © 1985 by Harry H. Vorrath and Larry K. Brendtro. This section is based largely on that book, as well as on conversations with the staffs and students at the participating institutions and on direct observations of the program in action there. All materials from the book have been reprinted with permission.

2. Throughout this report we refer to "students," "focal students," "delinquents," "residents," "participants," "group members," and "boys." "Students" is the term preferred by the institutional staffs; "group members" is the most frequent reference in *Positive Peer Culture*. We use these terms interchangeably here and try to be clear about when we are referring to those boys upon whom we focused particularly—the "focal students," who were interviewed and tracked after their release, and whose records we collected—and when we are referring to all the boys in their groups. We always use masculine pronouns when we refer to the students in our study because all the participating youths were male. We employ gender-neutral terms when we refer to youth or delinquents in general.

3. Copies of all of the interview schedules and other measures may be obtained from Martin Gold, Institute for Social Research, Box 1248, Ann Arbor, MI 48106.

4. Alphas and descriptive statistics for the major measures are available from Martin Gold, Institute for Social Research, Box 1248, Ann Arbor, MI 48106.

4

INSTITUTIONAL ADJUSTMENT

In the next three chapters, we present the major findings of our research so far. This chapter contains the findings about boys' adjustment to the institution in terms of their attitudes, values, and behavior. The next deals with boys' adjustment to the open community six months after their release. For both settings, we trace both the influences of their personal characteristics and background when they first entered the institutions and their experiences there on the boys' adjustment.

Our interest in the boys' adjustment while placed at a residential institution is two-fold. Of course, we wanted to identify the personal and institutional variables that accounted for the boys' successful return to the open community. That is, we are interested in the conditions conducive to rehabilitation. In addition to that, we are interested in boys' positive adjustment to the institution as a desirable outcome in its own right. Regardless of its contribution to his rehabilitation and regardless of what he did to deserve incarceration, the quality of a teenager's life while he is a ward of the state warrants earnest attention.

By "positive institutional adjustment" we mean that an adolescent will conform reasonably well to the rules of the institution; his tolerance, even admiration for delinquent behavior will decline; he will adopt a cooperative rather than an adversarial relationship to the institutional staff; his interest in school will grow; his sense of well-being will grow; and, even though he would much prefer to be free, he will not be unhappy during his stay. Adjustment in these terms is not an all-or-none matter. For instance, a boy might behave quite well and remain uninterested in school, or he might abandon delinquent values while he becomes very unhappy. We therefore report separately on the determinants of each facet of adjustment.

Our strategy for discovering the conditions for positive institutional adjustment began with the characteristics of the boys when they were admitted to the institutions. There were three reasons for this. First, it established baselines for change in characteristics such as delinquent values and delinquent behavior. Second, in order to investigate differential responses to the program by different delinquent types, boys were classified on the basis of characteristics at intake. Third, characterizing the boys at intake provided opportunities to compare the impact on institutional adjustment of the personal characteristics that the individual carried with him with the impact of the conditions of his residency.

In addition, we measured properties of the group to which the focal student was assigned and of the staff team responsible for that group. This was done primarily by administering questionnaires to all the group and staff members. In most cases we obtained this information before the focal student joined the group, and in the remaining cases no more than two months elapsed between a focal student's arrival and the assessment of group and staff characteristics.

Thus, in trying to discover the determinants of boys' adjustment to institutions, we have taken into account both what each boy was like and what his immediate institutional environment was like. Because the boys were assigned to groups at random, the measures of individuals at intake and the measures of groups were unrelated. This simplified our analyses and interpretations of findings considerably. As we demonstrated in Chapter 3, the demographic characteristics of groups within an institution were indeed quite comparable as a consequence of assignment to available bed space, although groups were not comparable across institutions. Therefore, we did not attempt to trace the conditions affecting institutional adjustment to differences among the institutions. These differences were confounded with differences among the students they admitted. We have examined differences in adjustment in relation to differences in *groups within the institutions*—the immediate environment at the institutions.

In addition to assessing the joint effects of prior individual characteristics and current group characteristics on institutional adjustment, we looked at mediating factors. We reasoned, for example, that the effects of a strong group counterculture on a boy would be conditioned by the degree to which the boy recognized its presence. It is conceivable that the personal characteristics that a boy brought to the group would affect his perception of the group's culture, and that distorted perception would affect the boy's adjustment. Thus, while the group might on the average have warm relationships with its staff, an individual member might feel quite antagonistic, or vice versa. So we investigated whether individual and group characteristics determined institutional adjustment because they shaped members' perceptions of the group and their feelings about the group and its staff. Boys' perceptions and other mediating factors were measured mostly with the interim interview, conducted four months after a boy's admission.

Finally, we tried to identify the factors that shaped the norms of the groups. For this purpose, we looked at some characteristics of the staff team responsible for each group as well as at the interpersonal climate of the group. As we shall show later, there is reason to believe that the way the staff delivered the program to their students affected the boys and the group more than the boys themselves affected their staff team's practices. An important implication of these findings is that a delinquency treatment program can affect the institutional adjustment of its wards through the selection, training, and supervision of its staff. This has of course long been an assumption of institutional management. There have been little or no data to support this assumption, however, nor have the essential properties of the staff been specified. We conclude this chapter with our findings about the effects of particular staff variables.

Figure 4.1 depicts the general model that we followed in our analyses and interpretations of the data. The arrows indicate hypothetical cause–effect sequences. Influences originate at the far left with the set of staff variables and with prior individual characteristics. Next is the set of group variables, which is influenced by the staff variables. Our research design provides that individual characteristics are not related to the group variables (once we control for differences between institutional centers). Between these and the primary goal of boys' institutional adjustment is the set of mediating factors, perceptions of group norms and of the group climate. We expect that the effects of individual, group, and staff characteristics are mediated by the perceptions, and in turn, the attitudes, values, and resources they engender in individual boys. (We assume that there are other effects on adjustment by variables that we did not measure.) The arrows signify, but do not differentiate between, two kinds of joint effects: additive effects, that is, those to which variables make independent, cumulative contributions; and interactive effects, in which the contribution of one variable changes the nature of the contributions of others.

MEASURING INSTITUTIONAL ADJUSTMENT

As we defined it, institutional adjustment has four components: the degree to which a boy's attitudes and behavior during his stay are prosocial; a boy's satisfaction with the institution and its program; his interest in school; and his feeling of well-being. These were measured in personal interviews conducted four months after the boy arrived and just prior to his release.

Measuring Delinquent Attitudes and Behavior

Delinquent behavior. To assess boys' delinquent behavior during their residence, we asked them, in strictest confidence, which of a series of laws or institutional rules they had broken in recent months.[1] We asked these questions after a four months' stay and just prior to a boy's release. We report

Figure 4.1
Model of Process by Which Boys' Institutional Adjustment Is Shaped

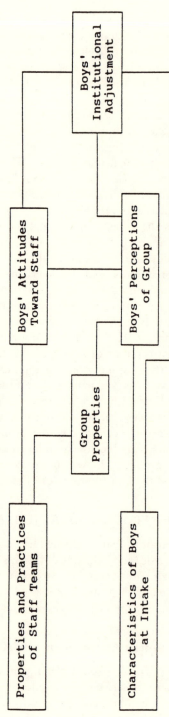

first on boys' adjustment after four months' stay—interim adjustment. We will take up adjustment at release later.

One might wonder whether boys would confess to their delinquent behavior so that the measure is valid. Studies have been done on boys' responses to such questions, and the consensus is that self-reported delinquent behavior is an accurate indicator (Elliott & Ageton, 1980; Gold, 1966; Hindelang, Hirschi, & Weis, 1981). In our study, boys often told our interviewers about infractions for which they had not been caught, infractions that could have resulted in delay of release, transfer to a more secure institution, or prosecution on new charges. We also have data on independent observations of boys' behavior: we asked the other boys in the focal students' groups to nominate those who, among other things, "lie to the staff" and "do not want to go straight." Boys who reported themselves to be more delinquent received more of these two nominations. The correlations during a boy's stay were .17 and .18 (p<.01) and at release, .15 and .25 (p < .01). These correlations are not high, although they are highly significant statistically. They indicate that there was at least some validity to boys' reports of their delinquent behavior at the institution.

Delinquent values. We measured boys' delinquent values by asking them eight questions about how much they admired people who engaged in various acts, some of which were clearly delinquent, like out-racing police cars, and others that were clearly socially approved, like almost always obeying one's parents. The more admiration they showed for the former and the less for the latter kinds of behavior, the more we considered boys committed to delinquent values. Individuals' values are not usually as public as their behavior, so a validating criterion like other people's observations is not available for boys' reports of their delinquent values. It appears, nevertheless, that boys' reports in this regard were not merely responses to an interview but reflected something about them observable to others, for boys' reports of their delinquent values correlated significantly with the delinquent values of the boys who chose them as best friends (r = .31, p < .01). On the assumption that friendship more often develops among people with similar values, this correlation shows that the values they expressed to our interviewers were not merely responses to questions but characterize them as individuals in other settings as well.

Subscription to a group counterculture. Residents' subscription to a group counterculture of opposition to institutional authority was estimated by presenting them with seven hypothetical but plausible situations of potential staff–student conflict. Boys were asked to choose whether they would oppose the staff, support the staff, or remain neutral. For example, "Some guys are going to set up another guy so that he'll get into trouble. They ask you to help them with their plan. What would you do: help them, tell the staff, or not help them but keep quiet about it?" Presumably, students who subscribe to a counterculture would not be known to their peers as ones who "go along with the staff." That proved to be the case (r = .12, p < .04), indicating that boys' reports of their countercultural commitment reflected their actual behavior to some degree.

Boys' responses to these measures indicate that, in terms of delinquent values and behavior, most boys adjusted fairly well during their residence. On the average, they reported breaking rules or committing delinquent acts about four times during the third and fourth months after their admission. Most boys did not seem to value delinquency much after four months' residence. From 60 to 80 percent said they admired any of the various delinquents acts "not at all." For example, only 3 percent expressed "a lot" of admiration for someone who steals cars. The average commitment to delinquent values was to admire about half of the delinquent acts "a little." Here too, there was wide variation among the boys, from those who admired almost all the delinquencies "a lot" to those who admired none. Similarly, boys did not by and large display strong support for a counterculture. When presented hypothetical opportunities to join others in breaking rules or undermining the program, 60 to 90 percent said that they would inform the staff. The next most popular option was to take some middle ground, not participating but keeping quiet. Overall, boys said that they would give passive support to antisocial behavior in about one third of the vignettes. The highest commitment, displayed by only a few boys, was usually to keep quiet, sometimes to participate, and never to inform the staff.

Measuring Satisfaction with the Institution and Its Program

Another aspect of boys' adjustment to the institution was their own satisfaction with the experience. Of course, these boys were not placed in the training schools for their pleasure. Some authorities might suppose, to the contrary, that the boys' rehabilitation depended upon the deterrent effect of an unpleasant experience. Later, we will report data testing the relationship between satisfaction with the institution and post-release adjustment. In this chapter we examine to what degree boys' characteristics at intake predicted their satisfaction with the institutions and an acceptance of the treatment program.

Satisfaction with the institution. This variable was assessed with four questions concerning boys' feelings about whether their residency was a worthwhile experience. An example is, "When you are older and think back about the time you spent here, will you think it was a happy or an unhappy time?" After four months' stay, 55 percent of the boys believed they would think theirs was a happy time. Modal answers to the other questions indicated that most boys believed that being at the institution was helpful for them.

Acceptance of treatment. The focus of this variable is the extent to which boys felt that they needed treatment to help them solve their problems and stay out of trouble. Most boys accepted the program as worthwhile in this regard. When we asked them, for example, whether a delinquent friend would be helped if he were sent to the institution, 86 percent said he would. The four questions measuring this variable were asked only during the interim interview, not at the release interview.

Interest in school. After four months' stay and again at the threshold of their release, we asked boys three questions about their attitudes toward school—whether they liked school "more, about the same, or less" than most of the other boys in their group; how interested they were in the subjects they were studying at the institution's school; and how much of the time they did their best work at school. About half of the boys believed that they liked school about the same, and about a third, more than the others in their group. Three-fourths of them expressed more than a little interest in school and said that they usually did their best work.

General adjustment. We created a summary variable to reflect several facets of boys' adjustment taken together. It is composed of respondents' reports of their delinquent behavior at the institution, their delinquent values, subscription to a peer counterculture, acceptance of the program (these last two included only in the interim measure), satisfaction with the institution, and interest in school. The scores on these scales were standardized and then summed, with appropriate reversals of signs so that a high score indicates better adjustment.

The typical responses to our interviews indicate relatively positive institutional adjustment. One might wonder how well this reflects their true adjustment. It may well be that boys put on good faces for their interviews. We believe, however, that most boys did actually behave fairly well during their residence and did not hold extremely antisocial attitudes. In any case, it is most important for our investigation that boys' adjustment varied a great deal. Thus, we were able to ask the data what factors differentiated boys with better or worse adjustment, no matter what the average adjustment might be.

PERSONAL CHARACTERISTICS AND
INTERIM ADJUSTMENT

As we pointed out earlier, some criminologists hold that youths' adjustment to institutionalization is determined at least in part by the kinds of people they are when they are admitted. This is the "importation" hypothesis. We tested it by assessing boys' personal characteristics within days of their admittance and then attempting to predict their subsequent adjustment from these characteristics. We found some support for the importation hypothesis in that boys' personal characteristics measured at intake were predictive of later adjustment.

We gathered information about four types of different characteristics of the focal students at the time of their arrival: their delinquent involvement, their functioning at school, their relations with other people, and their personal adjustment. In some of these areas, information from the initial interview was augmented by data we obtained from the institutions' records and from justice system records.

Data Analysis

Before considering the relationship to institutional adjustment of each of these personal characteristics, we will describe briefly the way we analyzed our data and the meaning of the statistics we will use to report our results. Our basic tool for assessing the strength and statistical significance of the relationship between a measure at intake and a measure of institutional adjustment is the correlation coefficient (specifically, the Pearson product-moment correlation coefficient [Pearson, 1896]). This statistic is quite useful because it provides a simple, standardized index of the degree of relationship between any pair of variables.

Our analysis also uses multiple regression for two purposes. The first is to obtain an index of the overall relationship of the entire set of intake measures to each measure of institutional adjustment. We expected that many of the intake measures are interrelated. For example, boys who engaged in the most delinquent behavior were likely to have more delinquent values and more arrests for prior offenses. Thus, if one of these is significantly correlated with an index of institutional adjustment, such as support for the counterculture, then it is likely that others will be as well. Because of this redundancy among the explanatory measures (the measures at intake), their predictive strength is not simply additive; so it is useful to have a separate index of the strength of relationship of the whole set of these measures to each measure of institutional adjustment. Multiple regression provides this in terms of R^2, which corresponds to the proportion of the differences in adjustment among the boys that can be accounted for by the entire group of explanatory variables.[2]

Our second use of multiple regression is to choose a subset of the intake measures to stand in for the entire set in explaining an outcome measure. This set controls for the portion of the outcome attributable to characteristics present at arrival increasing the accuracy of later analyses of the effects of institutionalization. We have winnowed down the full set of intake measures to a limited set, each of which is a significant explanatory variable in the regression equation. Eliminating the remaining measures from the regression equation yields a set of predictors that is less redundant, so chance will play a smaller role in the statistical controls in the later analyses.

It may be tempting to interpret the regression coefficients as indicating the relative importance of the measures in explaining an outcome, and in many analyses it would be appropriate to do so. In the present circumstance, however, that would be unwise. While we have sought the smallest set of variables with the most explanatory power, for many measures of institutional adjustment the choice was somewhat arbitrary. Other combinations would have produced almost identical results. Furthermore, determining relative importance requires a good understanding of the causal relations among the explanatory variables. Otherwise we may fail to recognize the contribution of variables whose effects are mediated by other variables. Thus, we will concentrate on correlation coefficients as the indicator of the strength of relationship between intake variables and outcomes. The regression coefficients should be viewed as a weighing of the intake variables that efficiently captures the predictive power of the entire set.

Institutional Adjustment and Prior Delinquent Involvement

We obtained four measures that are relevant to boys' involvement in delinquency at the time they arrived at the institutions. At intake, we measured their delinquent behavior in the most recent four months that they were not incarcerated, as well as their delinquent values. The measure of delinquent values was identical to the one used to measure institutional adjustment. The measure of delinquent behavior included items concerning the frequency of committing twenty-six different delinquent acts. We also checked the institutions' records for prior institutionalization as a result of delinquent behavior, and we coded the number of prior arrests for felony charges from justice system records. We counted only felony arrests because we found that juvenile arrests for misdemeanors were not recorded consistently by law enforcement agencies.

In the intake interview, boys reported recently committing an average of at least one delinquent act every third day. This level was not unexpected for boys who eventually were incarcerated. Their values were somewhat more delinquent than they would be after four months at the institutions. At intake, the average respondent expressed some admiration for someone committing five out of eight delinquent acts, which would later fall to three out of eight.

Forty-four percent of the boys had previously been placed in residential institutions, and 18 percent had been placed two or more times. While it was technically possible for boys to be committed to the public institutions for a single misdemeanor and to the private institutions for a single status offense, all but 6 percent had been charged with at least one felony, and 60 percent had been arrested at least three different times. Note that this counts only distinct arrests, not multiple charges arising from a single event.

Table 4.1 shows the relationships between characteristics at intake and adjustment to the institution after four months of stay. At least one measure

Table 4.1
Relationship of Personal Characteristics at Intake with Adjustment to the Institution After Four Months

Characteristics at Intake	Measures of Institutional Adjustment					
	Delinquent Behavior		Delinquent Values		Counterculture	
	r	beta	r	beta	r	beta
Delinquent Involvement						
Delinquent Behavior	.12*	.15*	.09		.08	
Delinquent Values	.16*		.46*	.42*	.17*	.17*
Felony Arrests	-.07		-.02		-.05	
Prior Placements	.22*	.17*	.13*		.16*	.12*
Functioning at School						
Interest in School	-.21*		-.17*		-.20*	-.15*
Standardized Achievement	.02		-.18*		.00	
Relations with Others						
Value for Friendships	.05		-.03		.08	.12*
Success at Friendships	-.16*	.15*	-.20*	-.12*	-.17*	-.15*
Affection from Mother	-.13*		-.05		-.13*	
Autonomy from Mother	.07		.07		.18*	
Personal Adjustment						
Besetment	.15*		.12*		.11	
Conscious Self-Esteem	.04		-.03		.00	
Unconscious Self-Esteem	.05		-.01		.02	
Well-being	-.04		-.21*	-.15*	-.11	
Age at Entry	-.17*	-.14*	-.02	-.03	-.16*	-.14*
R-Squared	.163*	.118*	.269*	.255*	.129*	.098*

*p < .05

Characteristics at Intake	Measures of Institutional Adjustment							
	Satisfaction with Institution		Acceptance of Treatment		Interest in School		General Adjustment	
	r	beta	r	beta	r	beta	r	beta
Delinquent Involvement								
Delinquent Behavior	-.02		.03		-.06		-.08	
Delinquent Values	-.17*	-.13*	-.05		-.16*		-.28*	-.18*
Felony Arrests	.04		-.07		-.02		.02	
Prior Placements	-.12*		.00		-.09		-.18*	-.12*
Functioning at School								
Interest in School	.12*		.07		.27*	.27*	.25*	.15*
Standardized Achievement	.05		-.04		.05		.06	
Relations with Others								
Value for Friendships	.06		.07		-.04		.00	
Success at Friendships	.12*		.13*	.15*	.09		.21*	.14*
Affection from Mother	.11*		.07		.21*		.17*	
Autonomy from Mother	-.09		-.15*		-.17*		-.17*	
Personal Adjustment								
Besetment	-.12*		-.01		-.07		-.14*	
Conscious Self-Esteem	-.08	-.14*	-.08	-.14*	.03		-.01	
Unconscious Self-Esteem	-.01		-.08		-.04		-.03	
Well-being	.18*	.16*	.13*	.15*	.14*	.11*	.19*	.13*
Age at Entry	.12*	.22*	-.02	-.03	.08	-.03	.13*	-.10
R-Squared	.170*	.121*	.086*	.051*	.130*	.094*	.210*	.181*

*p < .05

Note: For Table 4.1 and other tables like it, the columns headed with "r" present the correlations between each intake characteristic of boys in the column at the left and the indicator of boys' interim adjustment at the head of the column. The beta column presents beta weights, the standardized regression coefficients for the multiple regression of the reduced set of intake variables. The R^2s at the foot of the table indicate how well the whole set of intake characteristics predict the indicators of adjustment. They represent "variance accounted for," expressed as the proportion by which the variation in adjustment among the boys would be reduced if they were equal in all the personal characteristics. We have given R^2 both for the entire set of intake measures and for the reduced set that will be used as control variables in subsequent analyses.

We use asterisks to indicate statistical significance. We invoke the customary standard of designating a relationship as significant if its *chance* occurrence has a probability of only five times out of a hundred or less—p<.05. Relationships with chance probabilities between .05 and .10 are regarded as "borderline," their reality somewhat suspect unless they are supported by other findings.

of prior delinquent involvement was significantly related to each measure
of institutional adjustment except acceptance of treatment. Delinquent values and prior institutional placement were most consistently associated with
the indices of boys' functioning after they had spent four months in the
institutions. It appears that the less a boy's values favor violating the law,
the more positively he will adapt to the institutional setting. Repeated institutional placement does not bode well. Either the experience of repeated
institutionalization provokes a more negative response, or the sort of boy
who is repeatedly placed is more prone to adapt poorly.

Note that neither the officially recorded number of times boys had been
arrested nor their self-reports of delinquent behavior in the months prior
to intake reliably predict their adjustment after four months. The only
significant correlation is a modest correlation of .12 for continuity between
prior self-reported delinquency and the same measure during residency.
These findings have some practical importance because the level of prior
delinquent activity is often taken to be prognostic of institutional adjustment, and decisions about placement and treatment are often made on this
basis. It appears that differences in the prior delinquency of these boys (who
had all been heavily delinquent by the time they were referred to a training
school) did not distinguish between those who were likely to adjust well
or poorly.

Institutional Adjustment and Prior Functioning
at School

We measured boys' interest in school before coming to the institution
using the questions with which we would measure interest in the institutional school. The average level of interest in school at intake fell slightly
below the mid-point of the scale, indicating that the typical boy was neither
bored nor interested in his school work and that he was not especially prone
to do the best he could. This is well below the level of interest in school
during residency. We also assessed boys' academic functioning through
standardized tests administered at the institutions. The four institutions used
a variety of tests, but each provided a score for overall scholastic performance in terms of grade level. Our index of functioning was the measured
grade level minus the expected grade level for someone of that age. The
average respondent performed at 4.2 years below grade level. Thus, this
group was remarkably unsuccessful at school, and many of them rarely, if
ever, attended.

Prior interest in school was significantly correlated with all of the measures of institutional adjustment except acceptance of treatment. We suspect
that this relationship arises because interest in school reflects acceptance of
organized activities and institutional authority.

It is interesting that standardized achievement is less closely associated with institutional adjustment, significantly correlating only with delinquent values. There is a great deal of research showing that scholastic performance and intelligence are associated with delinquent behavior (Hirschi & Hindelang, 1977). It appears that this does not generalize to institutional adjustment among this highly delinquent group where poor scholastic performance is typical. This may be partly due to a lack of variation in scholastic performance, and also due to the institutions' school programs, which are designed for students with serious learning problems.

Institutional Adjustment and Relationships with Others

As part of the intake interview, we asked about our respondents' relationships with parents and with peers. In relation to parents, we asked questions concerning the affection and autonomy that the boys felt they received from both their mother and father (or whoever they reported to be their primary caregivers). The questions with regard to peers pertained to how much value they put on friendships and how successful they felt at having friends.

Despite the image of severe conflict between heavily delinquent adolescents and their parents, the focal students as a group reported fair to excellent relations with their parents or primary caregivers. When we asked them at intake if they felt, for example, that their mothers and fathers gave them "the right amount of affection" and whether they felt "close" to their parents, 73 percent of those with parents or parent surrogates replied that these were at least "sometimes true" of their fathers and 89 percent of their mothers.

As Table 4.1 shows, boys' relationships with their mothers correlated significantly to some indices of boys' behavior and values at the institution: The more affection boys reported, the less misbehavior they admitted to in the early months of their residence, the less they subscribed to a student counterculture, the more satisfied they were in the institution, the more interest they expressed in school, and the more positive their adjustment in general. Boys' reports of greater autonomy from their mothers was also related significantly to greater support for a counterculture, less acceptance of treatment, less interest in school, and poorer general adjustment.

Boys' reports of relationships with their fathers (or father surrogates) did not predict reliably to any facet of interim institutional adjustment. These data are not presented in Table 4.1 because the number of boys who could be included in this analysis is only about half of the number for the other prior characteristics. This is because only about half of the boys could name *any* male adult as being responsible for their care during the past two years. To have included them in the analysis would have required that we omit entirely the many boys without fathers or father-surrogates.

Because the programs at the training schools were so heavily group-centered, we decided to measure boys' views about peer relations when they were admitted. We were interested in how much they valued peer relations and how well they thought they had got along with peers in the recent past. In order to measure their values, we asked such questions as how much they depended on their friends and whether they would go out of their way to be with friends. Boys varied widely in these matters. The modal responses indicate that most of the focal students would rather have been in the company of friends than alone, although they did not depend on friends a lot, nor would they go out of their way for friends' company.

The value our respondents placed on friendship was not significantly correlated with any of the seven measures of adjustment in the four months after admission to the institutions. This measure did, however, have a significant regression weight for predicting support for the counterculture. This indicates that, once other significant predictors are taken into account (prior placements, interest in school, and success at friendships), placing greater value on friendship is associated with more support for the counterculture.

The focal students generally regarded themselves as competent in peer relations. Over half agreed, some strongly, that they made "new friends more quickly than most people do" and over 85 percent reported that they were "well-liked" and "get along well with other people." Table 4.1 shows that the boys who considered themselves most successful in relating to peers had more successful adjustment to the institutional setting. This measure correlated significantly with six of the seven measures of adjustment.

Institutional Adjustment and Personal Adjustment at Intake

We also measured certain components of boys' psychological adjustment when they arrived. Our measure of boys' feelings of well-being at intake ("How happy are you these days?" and "How are you feeling about your life as a whole these days?") was designed to establish a baseline against which change would be assessed as we followed boys through their institutionalization and after. Well-being is itself a facet of adjustment.

We measured boys' self-esteem, primarily to test the proposition that their unconscious self-esteem would have to rise before they abandoned their delinquent way of life. Our measure of this was a projective test created by Ziller and his associates (1969). Boys were presented a horizontal array of six circles and asked to assign one of five kinds of people (e.g., "someone who is happy," "someone who is failing") and "yourself" to each circle. A boy's unconscious self-esteem was regarded as higher the more circles he put between himself and "someone who is failing." Our measure of conscious self-esteem was based on ideal-self/present-self discrepancies. Boys described "How I would like to be now" in terms of fourteen polarities (e.g., "tall–short," "gentle–harsh") and then, "How I am now." The lower the sum of the differences between ideal and real self descriptions, the higher the boy's self-esteem was scored.

We also measured the levels of boys' anxiety and depression when they were admitted to the institution. We used a composite scale of fifteen items, some adapted from the Center for Epidemiological Studies depression scale (e.g., "How often do you feel that you can't shake off the blues?") and some from the State-Trait Anxiety Index (e.g., "How often do you feel nervous and tense?"). Additional items asked about somatic symptoms of anxiety ("How often have you had a stomach ache or an upset stomach?"). This scale was designed to distinguish between the two types of delinquents we discussed previously, the beset and the buoyant. We expected that the beset delinquents would not adjust as well as the buoyant would to the group-centered treatment programs of the participating institutions, and that they would respond to different facets of the program than the buoyant delinquents would.

Table 4.1 presents the correlations between measures of psychological adjustment at intake and adjustment to the institution at the interim interview. In general, better psychological adjustment was a precursor to more positive institutional adjustment. Besetment and well-being were associated with several aspects of institutional adjustment. Greater besetment at intake was significantly correlated with more misbehavior over the third and fourth month of boys' residence, more delinquent values, less satisfaction with the institution, and poorer general adjustment. (Chapter 6 discusses besetment as a criterion for typing the boys as delinquents and the relationship of types of adjustment.) Boys' feelings of well-being predicted significantly to more favorable adjustment in terms of boys' delinquent values, their satisfaction with the institution, their acceptance of treatment, their interest in school, and their general adjustment four months after their arrival. The degree of boys' conscious self-esteem gauged at intake also predicted to boys' greater satisfaction with the institution and acceptance of treatment, but only after controlling for other intake measures. The measure of unconscious self-esteem was unrelated to adjustment to the institution.

Age at Intake and Institutional Adjustment

At the time of their arrival at the institutions, the average age of our respondents was 16.0 years, the youngest was 12.6, and the oldest was 17.9. Younger boys made poorer interim adjustments in several respects. As Table 4.1 shows, they behaved worse, gave more support to a peer counterculture, were less satisfied with school, and had poorer general adjustment.

There are two plausible interpretations of this finding. Authorities are ordinarily reluctant to institutionalize children and early adolescents. Thus, the few who are selected present especially severe problems, and they adapt less well to the institutional setting just as they did to other settings. The other interpretation is developmental: Separation from the family is more traumatic for younger people, so being in the institution is more stressful.

A methodological comment should be made with regard to the relationship between age and outcome measures. One of the significant differences among the four institutions participating in this study was the age range of their students. Some of the institutions admitted boys at an age that was considered too young for placement in the others. Moreover, these boys were usually placed in groups especially designated for younger students. This was one of the major sources of noncomparability of boys and groups across institutions and one of the reasons some groups were not comparable to others within the same institution. Mere differences in the ages of their students created apparent but spurious differences in the effectiveness of institutions and groups. Because of this and other differences, we refrain from making comparisons across residential settings that did not draw students at random from the same pool of delinquents.

Summary of Institutional Adjustment and Prior Characteristics

Thus far we have examined one link in our general model of institutional adjustment from Figure 4.1—the influence of their personal characteristics measured at intake on boys' adjustment to the institution. From the foregoing findings we can see that the boys did not enter the institutions altogether malleable to the remedial program. Boys brought with them patterns of behavior, attitudes, and values that affected their adjustment, setting some limits on the influence of the institutional experience. Nevertheless, these limits were not narrow, even though the predictive power of the variables measured at intake was highly reliable ($p < .001$ for all regressions, except for acceptance of treatment, where $p < .03$). Boys' characteristics at intake accounted for 21 percent of the variance in our global index of interim adjustment and 9 percent to 27 percent of the variance in the individual measures. Only one correlation exceeded .30, and that reflected the continuity of boys' delinquent values across the four months.

Boys' characteristics at intake were more relevant to some aspects of institutional adjustment than to others. Boys' delinquent values after four months' stay were most accurately predicted by variables we measured at intake ($R^2 = .269$ for the full set of intake measures), primarily because those values were quite stable across the four months ($r = .46$). The intake measures least successfully predicted acceptance of treatment, explaining only 8.6 percent of variation in the outcome. That was the only facet of adjustment uncorrelated with prior delinquent involvement and functioning at school.

Comparing the correlations in Table 4.1 across the outcome measures, we find more consistency than variation. Delinquent values, prior institutional placement, interest in school, success at friendships, affection from mother (or female caregiver), and well-being each reliably predicted at least four of the six individual outcome measures, and autonomy from mother (or female caregiver), besetment, and age at intake reliably predicted three of the six. Naturally, these are the nine intake measures that are significantly correlated with the measure of general adjustment, which is a composite of the individual measures.

Thus, the treatment programs had to work with the boys as they came, dealing with inertial personal forces, some inimical and some favorable to adjustment. A more complete understanding of how intervention can work constructively with delinquent boys requires an investigation of the interaction between the boys' personal characteristics and those elements of the program that the institution can control. We will report the findings of our inquiry into these interactions after reporting the effects of group properties on boys' adjustment, independent of boys' character.

GROUP PROPERTIES AND BOYS' INTERIM ADJUSTMENT

One of the central questions of correctional research is how much of inmates' attitudes and behavior, often antagonistic to correctional goals, flows from the conditions of incarceration and how much is simply a continuation of the antisocial patterns that led to incarceration. The previous section concerns the effects of personal characteristics, testing the importation hypothesis that the determinants of poor institutional adjustment reside within the residents themselves. The alternative position is that the nature of life at correctional institutions, with the consequent "pains of imprisonment" (Sykes, 1958), provokes opposition to institutional authority. We were in a good position to sort out the situational from the preexisting determinants of adjustment because we were able to assess boys' characteristics shortly after their admission to the institution, presumably before institutionalization had any effect on them. Of course, institutional adjustment need not be simply a function of either personal or situational characteristics; it may well be a joint product of the two. The findings that we report here have to do with both the additive and interactive effects of institutional conditions and boys' characteristics.

We studied situational influences in terms of characteristics of the groups in which the boys reside because life at the participating institutions is group life. Because groups are together almost all of the boys' waking hours, group membership is the context of virtually all possible situational influences at the institutions. The group characteristics we studied were selected on the basis of theory and research from social psychology, organizational psychology, corrections, and criminology.

As we pointed out in Chapter 2, several social psychological theories led us to investigate certain institutional conditions as potential determinants of institutional adjustment. Theories of group dynamics and reference groups suggest that boys should behave better in groups with norms that favor such behavior rather than favoring breaking institutional rules and resisting the treatment program. Thus, we begin here with an examination of the relationship of norms to individual adjustment. Further, a well-established principle of these theories is that individual members will conform to the norms of a group to the degree that they are attracted to the group. Therefore, we also tested whether the norms of the group about delinquency combined with a boy's feelings about his group to determine for better or worse his own behavior and values. We found that the conditions of group membership prevailing in the settings of this research qualify the oft-supported principle in an interesting and important way.

In addition to group norms, we investigated several aspects of the climate of the groups. One theme we concentrated on was residents' feelings of autonomy and involvement in decision-making. The absence of independence and control over one's life is central to the pains of imprisonment articulated by Sykes (1958). In social psychology, research and theory concerning coercive power, leadership style, and reactance predict that greater autonomy and decision-making generate more positive institutional adjustment, provided that the staff actively interact with the residents and that the program encourages active participation by the residents (Martin & Osgood, 1987). Our observations of these institutions led us to expect that these conditions generally hold there. The potential importance of these variables is also suggested by findings from organizational psychology that demonstrate that autonomy and participation in decision-making result in more positive feelings about the workplace (Mosley, 1987; Pollock & Colwill, 1987). These variables were particularly important in our research because we were able to study them under conditions seldom if ever encountered in previous organizational and social psychological research. That is, we observed group membership, participation, and autonomy under the extremely coercive conditions of involuntary incarceration.

It should also be kept in mind that the focal students were adolescents growing up in American culture, where increasing autonomy from adult care and supervision is developmentally normal (Allen, Aber, & Leadbetter, 1990; Gold & Douvan, 1969; Schaeffer, 1959). The students' incarceration substantially interfered with their progress in this respect, however. One might suppose that they valued whatever autonomy was granted them.

The other aspect of the group climate that we studied was the closeness of interpersonal relations, both among the boys and between the boys and the staff. We reasoned that boys would be influenced most strongly, for better or worse, by those to whom they felt most close. We also expected that boys' satisfaction with the institution and their sense of well-being while there would depend on whether they developed close relationships with others there.

We also drew general hypotheses about institutional adjustment from criminology. We reasoned that positive adjustment—reasonably close conformity to institutional rules, adoption of more prosocial values, and so on—were in a sense a reduction in delinquency. According to the theories and findings of criminology, this should be a consequence of a favorable change in the balance between provocations for delinquent behavior, or strains, and social control. We therefore weighed the joint effects of such provocations as scholastic failure with sources of social control such as feeling close ties to staff members and liking one's group.

Group Norms and Institutional Adjustment

Our measures of group norms came from questionnaires administered to the groups between four months before boys' arrival at the institution and two months after. We defined norms as the average response of group members to questions concerning how "most members" in the group would feel or act. We measured norms concerning delinquent values, support for the counterculture, and program acceptance. Each measure included the same questions as the corresponding measure of focal students' institutional adjustment, but instead asked in reference to most members of the group rather than the student himself. The measure of program acceptance combines the items from the measures of satisfaction with the institution and acceptance of treatment. Our index of the effect of group characteristics on institutional adjustment is the partial correlation coefficient, controlling for characteristics at intake (see Table 4.1).

The norms of the group to which boys happened to be assigned made a significant difference in their self-reported delinquent behavior, support for the counterculture, and general adjustment after four months of residency (see Table 4.2). The difference groups made, albeit real, was not substantial, accounting for no more than 3 percent of the variation among the boys. There was more delinquent behavior and greater support for the counterculture by boys assigned to groups with norms favoring the counterculture, and boys' support for the counterculture also coincides with norms favoring delinquent values. All three norms were significantly related to general adjustment.

Boys' delinquent values were not reliably affected by the groups' norms, nor was acceptance of treatment or interest in school. While satisfaction with the institution was significantly correlated to the most relevant normative dimension (program acceptance), the set of norms as a group failed to account for significant variation in this facet of institutional adjustment.

Table 4.2
Partial Correlations of Group Properties and Adjustment to the Institution After Four Months, Controlling for Boys' Characteristics

Group Properties	Delinquent Behavior	Delinquent Values	Counter-culture	Satisfaction with Institution	Acceptance of Treatment	Interest in School	General Adjustment
				Measures of Institutional Adjustment			
Group Norms							
Delinquent Values	.10	.08	.15*	-.06	-.06	-.10	-.14*
Counterculture	.18*	.08	.15*	-.05	-.03	-.09	-.15*
Program Acceptance	-.09	-.04	-.10	.14*	.11	.10	.14*
R-squared: norms	.029*	.005	.023*	.018	.012	.011	.022*
Group Climate							
Autonomy	-.10	-.03	-.10	.08	.09	.07	.11
Decision-Making	.04	.06	.06	-.02	.02	-.01	-.04
Ties to Staff	-.09	.01	-.08	.03	.01	.02	.05
Cohesiveness	-.12*	-.06	-.11*	.11	.04	.12*	.14*
R-squared: climate	.019	.008	.021	.012	.010	.013	.022
R-squared - all group properties	.039	.009	.029	.022	.021	.016	.028
R-squared - total, personal and group properties	.159*	.284*	.128*	.142*	.070	.118*	.029*

*p <.05

Note: With the exception of R-squared: total, all figures for R-squared represent increases in R-squared after controlling for personal characteristics.

Group Climate and Institutional Adjustment

The measures of group climate also came from the group questionnaires. Feelings of personal autonomy were measured by seventeen items that were divided into four subscales. Autonomy was greater to the extent that group members reported having more independence and responsibility and being subject to less control by the staff and by their group. We assessed participation in decision making with regard to eight issues of concern in daily life at the institution, such as rules about smoking, destinations for off-campus trips, and when residents are ready for release (which Positive Peer Culture designates as the joint prerogative of the group and the staff). For each of these, we asked boys how much say they had, how much say their group had, and how much say the staff had. Responses to these questions revealed that boys in most groups felt that the staff had "a lot" of say in these decisions (an average of 3.70 on a 4.00 point scale), that the group had "some" say (an average of 2.97), and that individuals had "a little" to "some" say (an average of 2.65). A group's participation in decision making was scored as the sum of the ratings about the individuals' and the group's say in decisions minus the ratings for the staff's say. (Whenever our measures were a composite of subscales, the subscales were standardized before being combined.)

Three questions assessed personal ties to the staff: "How many staff people here do you like?" "How many staff people you have met here would you like to see after you get out?" and "How close are you to the staff people here you know best?" There were five questions concerning cohesiveness of groups (or the average level of attraction of members to a group), such as "Are the guys proud of this group?" and "How many of the guys in this group are close friends of yours?" In the average group, responses about both the staff and the group fell at about the mid-point of the response scale, indicating positive feelings about more than a few, but fewer than half, of the other boys and the staff. While there was little active animosity, neither was there a lot of warmth and closeness.

On the whole, our data fail to show that the group climate was an important influence on adjustment to the institution. When the four measures of group climate were considered as a set, they did not account for a significant amount of individual variation in any of the seven measures of institutional adjustment. For autonomy and cohesiveness, however, the pattern of relationships was quite consistent in that both group properties were positively associated with members' favorable adjustment. Because cohesiveness is significantly related to four of the seven outcome measures, we consider it to be a reliable and meaningful correlate of positive institutional adjustment. While several of the partial correlations for autonomy approach statistical significance ($.05 < p < .10$), these results must be considered merely suggestive rather than trustworthy.

The next to last row in Table 4.2 shows the total amounts of variance (R^2) in boys' interim adjustment accounted for by the properties of the group to which the boy was assigned. These are considerably smaller than the comparable figures on boys' personal characteristics at intake (the figures to the right at the bottom of each column in Table 4.1). The last row of Table 4.2 indicates the total amount of variance in boys' interim adjustment that is accounted for when the properties of the group to which they were assigned are combined with boys' characteristics at intake. The two components are additive, inasmuch as boys' assignments were virtually independent of their personal characteristics, especially when we exert controls over the non-random factors of institution and age. Thus, their combination accounts for from 28 percent of the differences among the boys' commitment to delinquent values after four months' stay to a statistically insignificant 7 percent of the differences in their acceptance of the treatment program.

Two features of these data on accounting for the differences among the boys should be noted. One is that our theories and measures are considerably better at identifying the important characteristics that boys bring with them than they are the adjustment-relevant properties of their group. The second is that a lot of the interindividual differences remain unaccounted for. These data have several implications.

It is possible that groups are considerably more effective in determining boys' adjustment than we have found, both absolutely and relative to boys' personal characteristics. We may simply have not been clever enough in our use of theory and measures to measure the effective group properties. On the other hand, these data may reflect the reality that the differences among the groups in this study actually mattered little for boys' adjustment, particularly in comparison to boys' personalities. Perhaps a great deal more needs to be learned about group-oriented treatment before group properties contribute much to boys' rehabilitation.

This is not to say that this group-oriented program was weak compared to other programs. This study makes no such comparison. It is conceivable that the residents adjusted considerably better in this program than they might have in another. We are focusing here on the finding that what group boys were in made little difference in their adjustment, absolutely or relative to their personal characteristics at intake. When we consider mediating factors, we discover some of the reasons why this was so.

Withal, groups made some difference. Boys adjusted better if they were placed in a group that devalued delinquency, lent less support to a student counterculture, accepted the program more, and liked its staff more. The data point to these specific group norms that, if enhanced, would probably weigh more heavily than they did here to encourage boys' prosocial adjustment against the antisocial attitudes and values that boys brought with them. We will return to this point in the last chapter.

FACTORS MEDIATING THE INFLUENCE OF
GROUP NORMS

Perceptions of the Group

Inasmuch as group norms made some significant difference in boys' adjustment, we were prompted to investigate the social psychological processes by which the norms affected the individuals and how the institutions might encourage prosocial norms. That norms accounted for little variance does not concern us very much at this point for several reasons. The reliability of the effect is theoretically important, because it replicates, under field conditions, laboratory findings about normative influence and, moreover, under conditions of involuntary membership. That is, we have found that the effect is not limited to laboratory studies of voluntary groups. The effect of group norms, small as we have found it to be, has practical implications as well. For the effect need not be small; it might be amplified in prosocial ways if greater normative consensus were built and if the norms were made more clear to members. Identifying the conditions for prosocial norms and their influence on group members might suggest ways for institutions to strengthen their effects in the service of treatment.

Our model (see Figure 4.1) suggests that the effects of staff and group on boys' adjustment were mediated by boys' perceptions of their group. It is conceivable that boys were only dimly if at all aware of their group's norms. These perceptions may have affected boys' adjustment but, because they were inaccurate, they may have muted the effects of actual group norms. We would expect the boys' institutional adjustment to be affected by their perceptions of the groups' norms and climates, which would in turn be partly, but not completely, determined by the group norms and climates reflected in the average reports of the entire group.

To explore this possibility, we assessed boys' perceptions of several aspects of the group when we interviewed them four months into their stay. We asked the focal students not only about their own subscription to the group's counterculture and delinquent values, but also how they thought "most of the other guys in the group" would respond to these questions. These are the same questions we used in the group questionnaires to assess group norms on these two issues. We also interviewed the focal students about their perceptions of the delinquent behavior of the other group members. For each of the items in the measure of individual delinquent behavior, we also asked "How many out of ten of your group members [do] you think have done these things in the last two months they've been here?" Perceived autonomy was measured by a slightly reduced version of the group measure, with fifteen items instead of seventeen, and the individual measures of ties to staff contained the same items as the group measure. The three-item measure of individual attraction to the group overlaps with the measure of group cohesion, but the former is limited to personal feelings about the group where the latter also includes reports of other group members' feelings about each other. Attraction to the group was not expected to affect boys' adjustment independent of group norms but rather was expected to amplify the effects of the norms. That is, group norms, whether pro- or antisocial, would have stronger positive or negative effects the more attracted boys were to their group.

We assume that boys' perceptions about their groups are not simply a reflection of the actual nature of the groups but are also influenced by the personal characteristics the boys bring with them to the institution. Table 4.3 presents the relationships between boys' characteristics measured upon their arrival at the institutions and their later perceptions of their group and institution. Indeed, boys entered the institutions predisposed to perceive their fellow group members in certain ways, regardless of how they really were. For instance, after four months of living in their groups, boys believed them to be more delinquent the more delinquent they themselves had been, the more prior out-of-home placements they themselves had experienced prior to intake, the less they were interested in school, the less success they felt at making friends, the more beset they felt, and the higher their unconscious self-esteem.

The personal characteristics that most consistently foretold perceptions of the groups tended to be those that predicted institutional adjustment as well (see Table 4.1). Delinquent values, prior institutional placements, interest in school, success at friendships, and well-being were each significantly correlated with several of the measures of perceptions. The full set of measures of characteristics at intake explained from 8.5 percent to 15.8 percent of the variation among the boys in their perceptions of their group. Though the intake measures were somewhat more strongly related to the measures of institutional adjustment, the difference is not substantial. We will not dwell on interpreting these influences on perceptions because we are mainly interested in perceptions as mediators of the influence of group properties.

Though perceptions of their group were in part a function of the boy, these perceptions were not entirely autistic. We found that the other group members' descriptions of their group, given at about the time when a focal student was admitted, also shaped the focal students' assessments of their groups' characteristics made about four months later. As Table 4.4 shows, four of the six dimensions of perceptions about the group were significantly correlated with the conceptually related group properties. Focal students tended to recognize the degree to which their group held delinquent values, supported a counterculture, and felt autonomous, and they perceived other group members to be involved in delinquent behavior when the group norms favored delinquent values and the counterculture. Contrary to our expectation, individuals' attraction to their group was not correlated with

Table 4.3
Relationship of Personal Characteristics at Intake and Perceptions of the Group After Four Months

	Perceptions of the Group					
	Delinquent Behavior		Delinquent Values		Counterculture	
Characteristic at Intake	r	beta	r	beta	r	beta
Delinquent Involvement						
Delinquent Behavior	.12*	.15*	-.04		.06	
Delinquent Values	.03		.20*	.13*	.02	
Felony Arrests	-.07		.12*		.07	
Prior Placements	.14*	.12*	.15*	.12*	.14*	.14*
Functioning at School						
Interest in School	-.13*		.05		-.06	
Standardized Achievement	-.08		-.07		.08	
Relations with Others						
Value for Friendships	.06		-.09		-.04	
Success at Friendships	-.16*	-.13*	-.13*	-.11*	-.10	
Affection from Mother	-.08		-.03		-.04	
Autonomy from Mother	.06		.00		.06	
Personal Adjustment						
Besetment	.13*	.12*	.05		.03	
Conscious Self-esteem	-.06		.02		.07	
Unconscious Self-esteem	.11*	.12*	.05		.13*	.15*
Well-being	-.03		-.05		.05	
Age at Entry	-.10	-.04	.01	-0.04	-.05	-.09
R-Squared	.158*	.124*	.132*	.099*	.085*	.048*

*p < .05

Table 4.3 (continued)

| | Perceptions of the Group | | | | | |
| Characteristic at Intake | Autonomy | | Personal Ties to Staff | | Personal Attraction to Group | |
	r	beta	r	beta	r	beta
Delinquent Involvement						
Delinquent Behavior	.03		-.05		.03	
Delinquent Values	-.12*		-.07		.00	
Felony Arrests	-.02		-.02		-.07	
Prior Placements	-.06		-.02		-.04	
Functioning at School						
Interest in School	.15*		.13*	.13*	.07	
Standardized Achievement	-.03		-.12*	-.15*	-.06	
Relations with Others						
Value for Friendships	.07		-.03		.10	
Success at Friendships	.21*	.20*	.13*	.14*	.12*	.13*
Affection from Mother	.10		.15*		.07	
Autonomy from Mother	-.02		-.06		.00	
Personal Adjustment						
Besetment	-.19*		-.08		-.10	
Conscious Self-esteem	.02		-.02		.14*	
Unconscious Self-esteem	.04		.07		-.01	
Well-being	.25*	.23*	.15*		.18*	.13*
Age at Entry	.01	.01	.09	.13*	.00	.06
R-Squared	.136*	.108*	.151*	.126*	.129*	.091*

*p < .05

the group's cohesion, but rather with its autonomy. Personal ties to the staff were not a function of group ties to the staff (or any other group property), which may explain why that facet of groups failed to influence institutional adjustment.

The relative strength of personal characteristics and group properties in determining boys' perceptions of their group is found in comparing the next to last row of Table 4.4 with the last row of Table 4.3. Boys' predilections weighed more heavily in their attachment to their group and its staff. Personal and group factors figured about equally in shaping boys' perceptions of how delinquent the group was, how much group norms favored delinquent values, and how autonomous the group and its members were. The group shaped its members' perceptions of its counterculture more than its members' personal characteristics did.

The last row of Table 4.4 shows that together the boys' characteristics and the group norms at the time they were admitted account for 12 percent to 23 percent of the differences among boys' perceptions of their groups.

Thus, four of the six dimensions of boys' perceptions of their group would be potential mediators between group properties and institutional adjustment. Perceptions of delinquent behavior, delinquent values, counterculture, and autonomy are not only significantly correlated with group properties, but the correlations are considerably stronger than any correlations between those group properties and measures of institutional adjustment. Our next step is to examine the relationship of these perceptions to institutional adjustment.

Before doing so, however, it is worth considering the implications of the strength of relationships between group properties and perceptions. If group properties influence institutional adjustment only indirectly, through their influence on how boys perceive the group, then any inaccuracy (or disagreement) in perceptions about the group will dilute its influence. Group properties accounted for 9.3 percent to 11.9 percent of variation in these four measures of perceptions, after controlling for personal characteristics measured at intake. This indicates that much of the variation in perceptions was idiosyncratic to the individual and remains unexplained. Though the correlations between group properties and perceptions about the group are strong compared to most others we have considered so far, they are far short of perfect. If perceptions do mediate the influence of the groups (as we shall see below), then inaccuracy in perceptions does reduce group influence.

Table 4.5 addresses the role of perceptions about the group in mediating the influence of the group properties. The upper half of the table shows that perceptions about the group are highly related to institutional adjustment. Virtually all of these correlations are statistically significant, and many are quite strong. Perceptions about the group explained from 10.5 percent to 36.0 percent of the variation in measures of institutional adjustment (after

Table 4.4
Partial Correlations Between Group Properties and Perceptions of the Group, Controlling for Boys' Characteristics at Intake

	Perceptions of the Group					
Group Properties	Delinquent Behavior	Delinquent Values	Counter-culture	Autonomy	Personal Ties To Staff	Personal Attr. to Group
Group Norms						
Delinquent Values	.25*	.32*	.28*	-.09	-.01	-.08
Counterculture	.34*	.29*	.29*	-.06	-.05	-.10
Program Acceptance	-.18*	-.23*	-.25*	.13*	.08	.09
R^2: norms	.100*	.098*	.095*	.016	.011	.010
Group Climate						
Autonomy	-.15*	-.16*	-.14*	.27*	.07	.14*
Decision-Making	.04	.10	.13*	.15*	.02	-.04
Ties to Staff	-.10	-.11	-.13*	.04	.10	.05
Cohesiveness	-.16*	-.12*	-.15*	.09	.09	.11
R^2: climate	.033*	.053*	.060*	.087*	.012	.030*
R^2: all group properties	.102*	.117*	.119*	.093*	.021	.033
R^2: total, personal and group properties	.229*	.216*	.170*	.197*	.146*	.123*

*$p < .05$

Note: With the exception of R-squared: total, all figures for R-squared represent increases in R-squared after controlling for personal characteristics.

Table 4.5
Partial Correlations of Perceptions of Groups and Actual Group Properties to Institutional Adjustment, Controlling for Boys' Characteristics at Intake

	Institutional Adjustment					
	Delinquent Behavior		Delinquent Values		Counterculture	
Control Variables	Boys' Chars.	Boys' Chars. & Group Prop.	Boys' Chars.	Boys' Chars. & Group Prop.	Boys' Chars.	Boys' Chars. & Group Prop.
Perceptions About Group						
Delinquent Behavior	.62*	.60*	.15*	.13*	.38*	.36*
Delinquent Values	.26*	.23*	.34*	.34*	.23*	.20*
Counterculture	.24*	.21*	.13*	.11*	.46*	.44*
Autonomy	-.18*	-.17*	-.16*	-.16*	-.29	-.29
Ties to Staff	-.17*	-.16*	-.15*	-.15*	-.29*	-.29
Attraction to Group	-.14*	-.11*	-.09	-.08	.11*	-.09
R-Squared - perceptions	.360*	.330*	.105*	.104*	.310*	.291*

	Delinquent Behavior		Delinquent Values		Counterculture	
Control Variables	Boys' Chars.	Boys' Chars. & Perceps. of Grp.	Boys' Chars.	Boys' Chars. & Perceps. of Grp.	Boys' Chars.	Boys' Chars. & Perceps. of Grp.
Group Properties						
Norms						
Delinquent Values	.10	-.07	.08	-.03	.15*	-.01
Counterculture	.18*	-.06	.08	-.03	.15*	-.04
Program Acceptance	-.09	.04	-.04	.05	-.10	.05
Cohesiveness	-.12	-.01	-.06	-.01	-.11*	.00
R-Squared: group	.032*	.006	.006	.004	.024	.005
R-Squared: total	---	.478*	---	.380	---	.408*

*p < .05

Note: With the exception of R-Squared: total, all figures for R-Squared represent increases in R-Squared after controlling for personal characteristics (and any other control variables)

Table 4.5 (*continued*)

	Institutional Adjustment						General Adjustment	
	Satisfaction with Institution		Acceptance or Treatment		Interest in School			
Control Variables	Boys' Chars.	Boys' Chars. & Group Prop.	Boys' Chars.	Boys' Chars. & Group Prop.	Boys' Chars.	Boys' Chars. & Group Prop.	Boys' Chars.	Boys' Chars. & Group Prop.
Perceptions About Group								
Delinquent Behavior	-.18*	-.18*	-.23*	-.24*	-.24*	-.23*	-.44*	-.42*
Delinquent Values	-.16*	-.15*	-.22*	-.21*	-.10	-.08	-.31*	-.29*
Counterculture	-.26*	-.25*	-.29*	-.28*	-.18*	-.16*	-.39*	-.37*
Autonomy	.40*	.39*	.41*	.40*	.23*		.41*	.40*
Ties to Staff	.33*	.32*	.32*	.32*	.30*	.30*	.38*	.38*
Attraction to Group	.33*	.32*	.17*	.17*	.20*	.19*	.24*	.22*
R-Squared - perceptions	.229*	.217*	.246*	.247*	.138*	.128*	.346*	.328*

	Satisfaction with Institution		Acceptance or Treatment		Interest in School		General Adjustment	
Control Variables	Boys' Chars.	Boys' Chars. & Perceps. of Grp.	Boys' Chars.	Boys' Chars. & Perceps. of Grp.	Boys' Chars.	Boys' Chars. & Perceps. of Grp.	Boys' Chars.	Boys' Chars. & Perceps. of Grp.
Group Properties								
Norms								
Delinquent Values	-.06	.05	-.06	.08	-.10	-.03	-.14*	.05
Counterculture	-.05	.07	-.03	.14*	-.09	.01	-.15*	.09
Program Acceptance	.14*	.02	.11	-.03	.10	.03	.14*	-.04
Cohesiveness	.11	.01	.04	-.06	.12*	.05	.14*	.01
R-Squared: group	.019	.007	.013	.012	.014	.004	.024	.005
R-Squared: total	--	.355*	--	.311*	--	.240*	--	.524*

*p < .05

Note: With the exception of R-Squared: total, all figures for R-Squared represent increases in R-Squared after controlling for personal characteristics (and any other control variables)

controlling for intake measures), and in five out of seven cases the figure was above 20 percent.

In each case, boys' own behavior and attitudes seem to have been especially responsive to the matching group norm. That is, the perceived group property most closely related to boys' delinquent behavior during their early months of residence was their own perception of the group's delinquency; to their delinquent values, their perception of the group's delinquent values; and to their support for the group's counterculture, their perception of the group's support for it. Furthermore, the effects of boys' perceptions of their group on their adjustment were intertwined: the more actively delinquent they perceived their group to be, the more they valued delinquency; the more they supported a group counterculture, and the less interest they showed in school; the stronger they believed the group's counterculture to be, the more they admired delinquency. Their perceptions of the group's delinquent behavior had the most negative effect on boys' global adjustment.

Boys' reports of their adjustment to the institution were significantly related to their feelings about their staff and their group, and their assessment of their personal autonomy. We believe that a feeling of personal autonomy reflects a diminution of the "pains of imprisonment" that go with living in the institution. Boys who felt more autonomous reported better interim adjustment on every indicator, and feeling closer ties to staff had a positive effect almost as strong. Greater attraction to their group correlated with better adjustment for all but one of the measures, but it was somewhat less related to institutional adjustment, on the whole, than the other perceptions about the group.

The lower half of Table 4.5 allows us to determine whether the relationship between perceptions about the group and institutional adjustment is sufficient to account for the impact of group properties on adjustment. If perceptions mediate the impact of group properties, then controlling for perceptions will eliminate the relationship between group properties and adjustment. This is precisely what happens. All significant correlations are eliminated. In fact, the perceptions appear to "overexplain" the relationship a bit, in that the signs of many of the correlations are reversed after controlling for perceptions. In the upper half of the table we can see that controlling for group properties has virtually no impact on the relationship between perceptions and adjustment. Thus, it is clear that perceptions mediated the influence of group properties, and not the other way around.

Note that taking boys' perceptions into account "explains" more of the interindividual differences in adjustment than merely combining boys' characteristics and group properties. (Compare the last rows of Tables 4.2 and 4.5.) Combining personal characteristics with perceptions accounts for almost a quarter to almost half of the differences in the several facets of boys' adjustment, and more than half of the differences in the general index of adjustment. This underscores the importance of boys' perceptions of their group.

Attraction, Cohesiveness, and Group Influence

Based upon established findings of studies of group dynamics, we hypothesized that the norms of a group would influence its members to the degree that the group was attractive and had a strong consensus about its norms (Festinger, Schachter, & Back, 1950; Sakurai, 1975). Social psychologists have long believed that more attractive or cohesive groups have more power to control the behavior of their members and that members who are attracted to a group would have more interest in following the group's norms. We also had thought that groups whose members were in greater agreement pro or con would make a stronger impression on newcomers.

This did not prove to be the case. After extensive analysis, we were forced to conclude that neither a group's attractiveness nor its consensus increased the impact of group norms on institutional adjustment. Using multiple regression analyses with interaction terms, we could find no evidence that the impact of norms varied significantly (or even consistently) with either of these group properties. Apparently consensus was at best loose. This is probably one reason that group norms did not account for much more of the variance in the focal students' interim adjustment. While their group's central tendency had some effect on their behavior, boys could find support for a wide range of pro- and antisocial attitudes and behavior in most groups.

Our findings suggest an important qualification to these hypotheses when they are applied to ongoing groups in natural settings rather than to groups created in a laboratory for experimental purposes. In experimental research, the hypothesis about group attractiveness has typically been tested by deliberately creating more and less attractive groups with clear norms and then measuring the degree to which members conform to the norms. Conformity has been significantly greater among members of attractive groups, which have high consensus about their norms as well.

Apparently, we have not confirmed these hypotheses about these interactive effects of group properties because neither of the conditions for the hypothesis were firmly established in this natural setting. Group consensus about delinquent behavior, delinquent values, a counterculture, and other matters was not strong, so group norms were not clear. Furthermore, differences in consensus among the groups were not large or consistent. When we scored groups for their consensus (in terms of the standard deviation of individual ratings of perceived norms), there was little correlation across normative topics or across time. Moreover, boys in any particular group varied widely in their attraction to that group.

Thus, it was not at all certain that any particular boy in a group perceived the group norm accurately, nor was it certain how attractive the group was to *that* boy no matter how attractive the group was to the rest of its members. Under these weak conditions, it was necessary to test the hypothesis by taking into account each boy's perceptions of the group norm and the degree to which he was attracted to the group. Stated on this individual level, the hypothesis is that boys will be influenced by the group norm as they perceive it, to the degree that they are personally attracted to their group.

Actually, stating the hypothesis in terms of individual members is implicit in the theories underlying the hypotheses. Lewinian field theory (Lewin, 1943/51), reference group theory (Newcomb, 1950; Sherif, 1948), balance theory (Heider, 1958; Newcomb, 1953), and symbolic interactionism (Mead, 1934) all state that it is the individual's perception of social reality, rather than social reality itself, that influences his or her attitudes and behavior. The strength of the conditions created in the laboratory has permitted the hypothesis to be tested with groups as units, ignoring individual differences in perceptions and attractions.

From the results we reported in the preceding section, we can conclude that perceived norms mediate between actual group norms and institutional adjustment. This is the basis for the path model we used to determine whether attraction to a group increases the subjective influence of perceptions on adjustment (Osgood, Gold, & Miller, 1986). A path model is useful here because it allows us to take into account a potential confounding factor that we ignored in our earlier analysis of perceived norms. The strong relationship between perceived norms and adjustment may not result from the influence of perceptions about the group; instead it may arise from the focal students imagining their groups in their own image.

Our path model is shown in conceptual terms in Figure 4.2. Osgood has written elsewhere about how such a model is a considerable improvement over the standard methods of assessing interpersonal influence (Jussim & Osgood, 1989). If a path model includes all of the influences that lead the variables to be related to one another, then it will generate meaningful estimates of the strength of influence for each path (like regression coefficients). In this model, institutional adjustment is a function of stability (influence of prior standing on the same dimension of adjustment), subjective influence (influence of current perceptions about the group norm), and social control (if attraction to the group leads to more positive adjustment). According to the model, perceptions about the group are influenced by the actual group norms, a path that would generate agreement about the norms. The model also allows for two sources of divergence between perceptions and norms. Perceptions about the group may result, in part, from respondents assuming that the group is more similar to themselves than is in fact the case, and people who are attracted to the group may be biased to report more prosocial norms. The reciprocal paths between perceptions and in-

Figure 4.2
Conceptual Model of Normative Influence

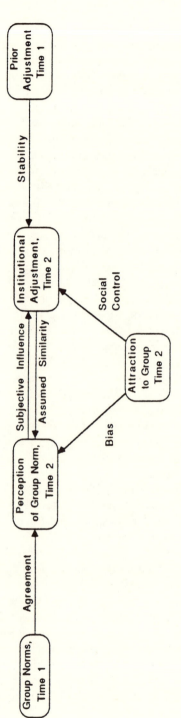

stitutional adjustment can be separated because we assume that perceptions mediate the influence of group norms and that institutional adjustment mediates the impact of prior adjustment on perceptions about the group.

We used the LISREL statistical program (Joreskog & Sorbom, 1983) to implement our path model for three of the measures of institutional adjustment: delinquent behavior, delinquent values, and support for the counterculture. Because this book is directed at a nontechnical audience, many features of this analysis are not discussed here. The original source (Osgood, Gold, & Miller, 1986) provides full details. A few important features not included in the figures bear mentioning here. All variables were standardized to have equal variance in measures of institutional adjustment, but not to have equal variance over time or reference target (e.g., norms vs. perceptions vs. individual adjustment). The three measures in each vertical column in Figure 4.3 were assumed to be correlated. The measurement model was based on using alpha reliability estimates to determine error of measurement. Age, race, and state versus private institutional affiliation were included as control variables.

The major results appear in Figures 4.3 and 4.4. The numbers on the paths represent the amount of change in the target variable produced by one unit of change in the source variable. The first important result is that the model fits the data quite well (chi^2 = 60.50, 72 df, p = .83), which means that the correlations among these variables are quite consistent with our causal model.

Some features of the model reflect what we have already seen. Earlier delinquent values are related to institutional adjustment, and norms influence perceptions about the group. (The latter estimates are larger than the corresponding correlations because there is more variance in perceptions than in group norms.) The degree to which respondents project their own attitudes onto the rest of the group varies across the topics. The tendency is strong for delinquent values (.55), moderate for delinquent behavior (.39), and weak for support for the counterculture (.13).

Perceptions of the group had a stronger influence on the institutional adjustment of boys who were more attracted to their groups. This was true for delinquent behavior, delinquent values, and support for the counterculture, and the overall difference in the amount of influence was statistically significant (chi^2 = 23.57, 3 df, p < .001). Attraction made the biggest difference for influence of the perceived counterculture of the group on individual adjustment (.38 for low attraction and .81 for high attraction). Considering both the pattern of results for subjective influence and assumed similarity, we see that assumed similarity accounts for most of the relationship between perceptions and individual adjustment for delinquent values, while subjective influence predominates for support for the counterculture, and both are important for delinquent behavior. Thus, after taking into account a potential bias to perceive others as more similar to

Figure 4.3
Paths Among Norms, Perceptions, and Adjustment

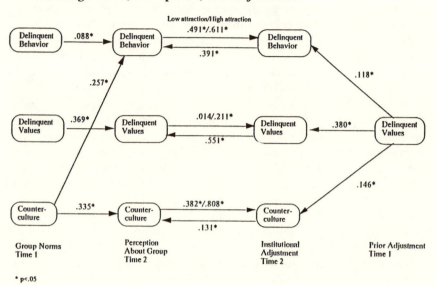

Group Norms
Time 1

Perception
About Group
Time 2

Institutional
Adjustment
Time 2

Prior Adjustment
Time 1

* p<.05

Figure 4.4
**Effects of Attraction on Institutional Adjustment and Perceptions
About Group**

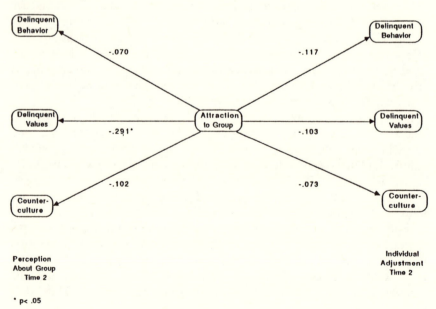

Perception
About Group
Time 2

Individual
Adjustment
Time 2

* p< .05

oneself than is actually the case, there remains a substantial amount of subjective influence on institutional adjustment, though the level of influence varies considerably across measures of adjustment.

Figure 4.4 shows the direct effects of attraction on both institutional adjustment and perceptions about the group. In each case, greater attraction to the group leads to more favorable institutional adjustment or more pro-social perceptions about the group. Taken as a set, these paths are definitely statistically significant (chi^2 = 24.40, df 6, p < .005), though only two of the individual paths are significant. Attraction has the strongest effect of leading respondents to see the group as less delinquent and reducing their own delinquent behavior. Thus, we have some indication of a social control effect of attraction reducing deviance from the rules, presumably because attraction to others leads to a desire to maintain a more prosocial reputation (Hirschi, 1969). Furthermore, attraction has an additional indirect effect on institutional adjustment by generating a bias toward more prosocial perceptions about the group, which in turn enhances boys' own adjustment.

THE IMPACT OF STAFF PROPERTIES ON GROUP NORMS AND INSTITUTIONAL ADJUSTMENT

In the preceding sections we have demonstrated that group norms and the group climate affected individuals' adjustment to the institutions. These group properties in part determined boys' perceptions of their groups, and their influence on boys was mediated by these perceptions. We now turn to a likely source of the differences among the groups in their norms and climates: the staff teams who were responsible for them.

Though all of the institutions were nominally using the same treatment program, Positive Peer Culture, the implementation of that program varied substantially from group to group within each institution. We believe that these differences were due largely to differences among the staff teams. We have not done a systematic study of the backgrounds and personalities of individual staff members or of relationships within staff teams and between the teams and their supervisors. Rather, we have tried to describe potentially relevant differences among the staff teams without explaining their origins.

The conditions of fairly stable inter-group differences in treatment and virtual random assignment of boys to groups created the opportunity for the quasi-experimental design of this study. It is "quasi-" rather than purely experimental because we researchers did not have control over variations in staffs' treatment. Differences occurred naturally and we recorded them. One disadvantage of this was that we might have created greater variations among groups and among staff teams to observe more clearly the differences certain variables would have made. On the other hand, because the research did not alter the treatment program, its findings more plausibly generalize to the participating institutions and to similar places in their natural states.

Measures of Staff Team Properties

Theory, previous findings, and the advice of the participating institutions led us to study certain characteristics of the staff teams. These were their morale, the relative emphasis they placed on addressing the boys' socio-emotional problems versus controlling their antisocial behavior, how much autonomy they said they gave to boys, and how much they said the group participated in day-to-day decision making.

The relevance of staff morale to boys' adjustment was suggested by organizational psychology. If boys' positive adjustment is the goal of the institution, then adjustment should be positively related to morale, as organizational psychology has shown that other kinds of productivity are.

Our original plans for the study were to measure several different aspects of staff morale rather than a single global construct. To our surprise, we found that this was not practical because the correlations among answers to the different scales were so high that the measures were essentially indistinguishable. This applied not only to variables we considered conceptually relevant to morale, such as team cohesion, team involvement, and belief in program success, but also to a wide variety of other staff properties, such as success at reaching various goals, group functioning, and group autonomy. It seems that a wide variety of opinions about treatment methods, staff relations, and program success are strongly clustered together into a general syndrome of positive or negative feelings about the program and the job. For that reason, we formed a single index of staff morale as a composite of the four subscales we considered conceptually appropriate: team cohesion, team involvement, belief in program success, and pessimism about reform. The four subscales had a total of twenty items.

The issue of treatment versus custodial orientation has been prominent in discussions of correctional practice (e.g., Street, Vinter, & Sarri, 1966). Inadequate research design has hampered discovery of the differential consequences of these orientations, however. Differences in orientation have been systematically confounded with differences among the delinquents selected for the various treatments and other differences between the programs. Our quasi-experimental design permitted us to compare the effects of the two orientations on randomly assigned students.

In order to investigate the differential effects of these orientations, we computed a measure of relative emphasis, which was the difference in the importance given to treatment and control. However, treatment versus custodial orientations were not antithetical among the participating staff teams. As we measured staff orientations, the more that staff expressed concern for boys' problems, the more they also resolved to control boys' behavior. In response to such statements as "How important is maintaining order and discipline?" and "How important is developing students' emotional maturity?" staff members who found one important tended to find

the other important as well. For the three times we collected this information, the correlations between individual staff members' responses to the
two measures were .30, .34, and .40 (p < .01 in all three cases). This initial
result led us to suspect that contrasting the goals of treatment and control
would not yield an important dimension of difference among the staff teams.

Autonomy given to the group is another important aspect of staff members' orientations to working with incarcerated youths. It reflects the absence
of authoritarian staff control over students, and was measured by the same
questions that were administered to the boys to measure group autonomy.

Our interest in the groups' participation in day-to-day decision making
was prompted by the literature in group dynamics and organizational psychology. An early study in group dynamics by Lewin, Lippitt, and White
(1939) showed that boys' groups were more productive, members were
happier, and boys behaved better when the group participated regularly in
democratic decision making. Other studies of natural and experimental
groups (e.g., Misumi & Nakano) some in the workplace (e.g., Baumgartel,
1957; D'Angelo, 1973) replicated these findings. Participation seemed particularly important to us because we had a rare opportunity to study it
among individuals living under extremely coercive conditions of involuntary incarceration. We measured the staffs' assessment of boys' participation
in decision making through the same questions used to assess the groups'
reports of this variable.

Stability of Group and Staff Properties

We are interested in variables characterizing staff teams as potential influences on the groups. It is also possible, however, that the properties of
the groups, and even of the staff teams, were responsive to particular boys
assigned to the groups. One reason that the staff team was a more plausible
influence, however, was the stability of its membership. One or two new
students joined a group each month as others were released, an annual
turnover rate of about 75 percent. In contrast, the median annual staff
turnover was 30 percent, with a substantial proportion of the staff staying
with a single group for many years.

Table 4.6 shows the correlations across time of the properties of the staff
teams and boys' groups for the two six-month intervals between our questionnaire administrations. Notice that the group properties evidence a substantial level of stability, with the exception of cohesiveness. This is
encouraging for the analysis of the effects of group properties on institutional
adjustment, which we reported in the previous section. If these properties
varied markedly from month to month, then any given assessment would
be a poor characterization of any particular boy's experience as a member
of that group. Instead, these properties were relatively stable, so it is meaningful to assess their influence on individuals.

Table 4.6
Cross-Time Correlations of Properties of Staff Teams and
Students' Groups

	Time1-Time2	Time1-Time3	Time1-Time3
Staff			
Morale	.78	.62	.82
Treatment/Custodial Emphasis	.41	.64	.63
Autonomy for Group	.80	.45	.62
Group Decision-Making	.80	.82	.76
Group			
Norms			
Delinquent Values	.50	.35	.60
Counterculture	.64	.26	.55
Program Acceptance	.43	.34	.58
Climate			
Autonomy for Group	.66	.37	.57
Group Decision-Making	.80	.56	.63
Ties to Staff	.52	.22	.31
Cohesiveness	.35	.15	.36

Time 1 = Fall 1982; Time 2 = Spring 1983; Time 3 = Fall 1983

Turning to the relative stability of staff and group properties, Table 4.6 attests that properties of the staff teams were more highly correlated over time than were properties of their groups. Staff teams high in morale and other properties at one point in time tended to be high at another point. Some properties of boys' groups were almost as stable, notably the autonomy and decision-making opportunities the boys felt they had. These relatively high correlations may also reflect the influence of the staff, for these properties were the ones most directly reflecting the staffs' management of their groups. Even so, the stability of these properties was not as great as the comparable staff properties. It is probable, therefore, that associations between properties of staff teams and of students' groups originate in the staff.

Still, it is likely that sometimes one or two new students so altered the dynamics of their group that the staff's handling of that group changed radically. The level of stability seen in Table 4.6 indicates that this did not often occur during the year we observed these groups, or perhaps that changes resulting from new students were short-lived, and staff teams reverted to their accustomed treatment as soon as they could. Thus, despite student turnover, stability in staff treatment prevailed enough so that we can consider the properties of staff teams as consistent conditions of group life and individual experience.

The Relationship of Staff Team Properties to Group Properties

Table 4.7 shows the correlations between the four staff properties and seven group properties that we have focused on in this chapter. These correlations are based on the average scores for each group and its staff team across the three time periods.

The state and private institutions differed on many of these measures, sometimes markedly. Because these differences might have been due to the somewhat different populations served by these two types of institutions, Table 4.7 also includes partial correlations that control for state versus private institutional affiliation.

Note that many of the correlations among group and staff variables are much stronger than we have seen for measures about individuals, sometimes ranging up to about .8. This is in large part a reflection of the reduction in error in measures that are aggregations of the responses of several individuals. Typically, the correlation between two variables measured for individuals will be considerably lower than the correlation between the same two variables when the individual responses are combined into meaningful subgroups (such as classrooms, neighborhoods, or census tracts).

The level of staff team morale was strongly and significantly correlated with many of the group properties. When teams enjoyed higher morale, their group reported less delinquent norms, norms favoring acceptance of the program, more group autonomy, and greater cohesiveness. After controlling for state versus private affiliation, the relationships of morale to less countercultural norms and closer ties to staff approach statistical significance ($p < .10$), while without that control the former had been insignificant and the latter had been very highly significant. On the whole, there is considerable evidence that when staff members feel better about their jobs, their group has more prosocial norms and a more positive group climate.

Relative treatment versus custodial orientation initially showed no reliable zero-order correlations with any of the group norms. Controlling for the private/public character of the institution, however, yielded a statistically significant relationship between staffs' orientation to treatment and the group's personal ties to the staff. The more relative emphasis staffs gave to addressing boys' emotional problems rather than their behavior, the less close to staff boys reported their group was. With this exception, however, the staff's emphasis on treatment rather than control had little bearing on group norms or the climate of the group.

It might be reasonable to suppose that staff teams granted more autonomy

Table 4.7
Correlations of Properties of Staff Teams with Group Properties

	Staff Variable							
	Morale		Treatment Orientation		Autonomy		Group Decision-Making	
Group Variable	r	Partial r	r	Partial r	r	Partial r	r	Partial r
Norms								
Delinquent Values	-.44*	-.39*	-.21	-.08	-.43*	-.35*	.25	.22
Counterculture	-.17	-.28	-.12	-.14	-.22	-.27	.21	.21
Program Acceptance	.60*	.49*	.29	.09	.49*	.34*	-.14	-.08
Climate								
Autonomy	.39*	.42*	.02	-.08	.35*	.30	.14	.18
Decision-Making	-.26	.08	-.07	.17	-.17	.07	.78*	.79*
Ties to Staff	.72*	.28	.16	-.45*	.57*	.22	-.25	-.17
Cohesiveness	.62*	.51*	.14	-.11	.51*	.35*	-.18	-.12

N = 43 groups and staff teams

*p < .05

Note: Partial r's are correlation coefficients controlling for state vs. private affiliation of the institutions.

to their groups when the boys behaved better. But the data in Table 4.6 suggest that the cause–effect relationship ran in the reverse. The level of autonomy that staff said they gave their groups was much more stable over the period of our observations than the norms of the groups were, and we have found that the actual delinquent behavior of groups was considerably less stable than the norms. Thus, it appears that the ways staffs handled their groups affected the groups' behavior more than the other way around.

The autonomy that staff reported giving to their groups was very closely related to the staffs' morale; the higher the one, the higher the other (r = .89, partial r controlling for state/private = .86). This correlation is so strong that the measures of these two concepts are not truly distinct from one another. For these institutions, apparently the staff's positive versus negative feelings about their jobs, which comprise the measure of morale, so strongly overlap with their reports about issues of independence and control for the boys that the two become almost identical. Accordingly, the pattern of relationships of staff-reported autonomy with group properties is almost identical to that of staff morale. Staff-reported autonomy coincides with norms for less delinquent values and more program acceptance and with more group cohesiveness. Note that group-reported autonomy is somewhat more strongly correlated with staff morale than with staff-reported autonomy for the group.

As Table 4.7 shows, staffs' ratings of their groups' participation in decision making had little bearing on group properties. The sole exception is the groups' reports of participation in decision making. Apparently there was a clear consensus between the boys and staff on this issue, which indicates that this dimension is well-measured. Given this finding, and the lack of relationship between individuals' institutional adjustment and group reports of decision making, we can conclude with confidence that giving boys a greater role in decision making had no beneficial (or detrimental) impact. In fact, it did not even lead the boys to report that they felt that they had more autonomy, a measure that includes freedom from coercive control by the staff and group and a greater sense of independence. It seems that feelings of autonomy must be more a function of ongoing informal relationships than of structured participation in explicit decisions, which is assessed by our measure of decision making.

Thus, two of the staff properties, morale and autonomy, affected group norms and group climate, while the others, treatment orientation and group participation in decision making, did not.

It is also worth noting that group properties differed in their relationships with the properties of staff teams. Norms concerning delinquent values and program acceptance were influenced by the variables concerning the staff team, as were group autonomy and cohesiveness. In contrast, personal ties to the staff was associated with a staff team's emphasis on treatment versus control rather than with the staff team's reports of morale and group autonomy. Group reports of involvement in decision making correlated only with staff reports of the same variable, and group norms about the counterculture were only marginally related to staff morale and staff-reported autonomy for the group.

Staff Team Properties and Individual Institutional Adjustment

Our conceptual model of the influences on institutionalized boys, shown in Figure 4.1, specifies that the properties of the staff team will influence individual boys' adjustments by their effects on group properties, which in turn influence perceptions of the group. Thus, the influence of the staff on individuals would be indirect, and correlations between staff properties and individual adjustment should be eliminated by controlling for group properties and individual perceptions about the group. Table 4.8 reports the results of analyses testing this hypothesis.

The upper third of Table 4.8 contains partial correlations between staff properties and measures of institutional adjustment, controlling only for intake characteristics (which should be irrelevant to the impact of the staff). Few of these correlations are statistically significant, indicating that there is little relationship between these variables. The only significant correlations that are consistent with the general pattern of findings we have reported throughout this chapter are the negative relationships of individual support for the counterculture with staff morale and staff-reported autonomy for the group. The two remaining significant correlations are more idiosyncratic: positive correlations between staff-reported participation by students in decision making and delinquent behavior and between staff emphasis on treatment and individual interest in school. In neither of these cases did the set of four staff properties explain significant variance in the measure of adjustment, so there is a substantial possibility that the correlations are actually due to chance.

The weak relationships between staff properties and individual adjustment are understandable in the context of the larger conceptual model. By the basic tenets of path analysis (Kenny, 1979), when the impact of one variable on another is mediated by one or more stages of intervening variables, the correlation between those variables is the product of the intervening paths. Thus, the distal relationship may be quite weak even if each intervening step were a significant and strong relationship. For instance, the partial correlations (controlling for intake) were $-.44$ for the path from staff morale to norms supporting delinquent values, $.32$ from those norms to perceptions of the group as delinquent, and $.34$ from the perceptions to individual delinquent values. Treating those partial correlations as standardized path coefficients (which they approximate), we should find that the correlation between staff morale and individual delinquent values falls to $-.05$. The

Table 4.8
Partial Correlations of Properties of Staff Teams with Individuals' Institutional Adjustment

	Measure of Institutional Adjustment						
Controlling for Intake Measures	Delinquent Behavior	Delinquent Values	Counter-culture	Satisfaction w/ Institution	Acceptance of Treatment	Interest in School	General Adjustment
Staff Property							
Morale	.00	-.03	-.16*	.03	.08	.03	.10
Treatment Orientation	.08	.00	.00	-.03	.06	.15*	.04
Autonomy	.02	-.03	-.14*	.02	.09	.06	.10
Decision-Making	.12*	.08	.06	.03	.01	.05	-.04
R-Squared: Staff Properties	.017	.001	.033*	.002	.011	.025	.015
Controlling for Intake Measures and Group Characteristics							
Staff Property							
Morale	.06	-.01	-.12*	-.03	.06	-.03	.03
Treatment Orientation	.09	-.01	.00	.03	.05	.16*	.05
Autonomy	.08	-.01	-.09	-.01	.07	.01	.04
Decision-Making	.12*	.08	.05	.01	.00	.04	-.04
R-Squared: Staff Properties	.019	.007	.017	.002	.008	.031*	.007
Controlling for Intake Measures, Group Properties, and Individual Perceptions about Group							
Staff Property							
Morale	.07	-.04	-.11	-.01	.06	-.03	.04
Treatment Orientation	.02	-.06	-.05	.07	.10	.24*	.16*
Autonomy	.10	.01	-.03	-.06	.01	-.03	-.04
Decision-Making	.09	.05	.07	-.01	-.02	.05	-.05
R-Squared: Staff Properties	.007	.005	.013	.008	.010	.050*	.015
R-Squared: Total	.483*	.390*	.420*	.360*	.314*	.296*	.538*

*p< .05

Note: With the exception of R-Squared: total, all figures for R-Squared represent increases in R-Squared after controlling for personal characteristics (and any other control variables)

actual correlation of $-.03$ is actually closer to this value than we would expect by chance, though it is far too small to be statistically significant.

The lower portions of Table 4.8 report the partial correlations between the same variables, but with the addition of controls for group properties and individual perceptions about the groups. These would allow us to determine whether the correlations between staff properties and individual adjustment are attributable to those factors. The lack of relationship found in the upper part of the table renders the remaining figures largely irrelevant. Note, however, that the significant correlations of support for the counterculture with staff morale and staff-reported autonomy are eliminated by the control variables.

Thus, properties of the staff teams have at best only indirect effects on the adjustment of the boys in their groups. The effect of staff on an individual is qualified by the properties of the whole group (and by the characteristics of the individual student).

ADJUSTMENT AT RELEASE

The boys in our study were incarcerated for an average of one year. Some were released as early as four-and-a-half months after admission, and some not until more than two years later. Actually, some of the boys we interviewed upon their admission left the institution in less than four months, but we excluded those from the study because we could not collect any more data about them. Most of these boys were judged to be inappropriate for the programs at these institutions, and they were transferred to another placement, usually less than two months after their arrival.

Of the 306 boys whom we interviewed at release, 77 percent (236) "graduated" normally; that is, they were released upon the recommendation of their group and staff team. Ten percent (32) were granted "administrative release"—either the institution released a boy because it appeared he could not further benefit from the program, even though his progress was less than adequate, or the referring juvenile court (which pays for his stay) decided that a boy had been incarcerated long enough. These boys stayed an average of fourteen months. Seven percent (20) of the boys were sent to a more secure institution after an average of 8.4 months. Another 4 percent (12) were released for miscellaneous idiosyncratic reasons. And 2 percent (six) ran away and did not return, but remained in the study nevertheless because we were able to locate them for further interviews.

The boys who graduated normally evinced better adjustment on the threshold of their release than they had after only four months' stay. Presumably, these changes led to their release. Figures 4.5 to 4.7 display significant declines in boys' delinquent behavior and values, and significantly greater satisfaction with the institution. Boys told us that in the third and fourth months of their residency they had broken rules more than four

Figure 4.5
Change in Delinquent Behavior from Interim to Release by
Type of Release

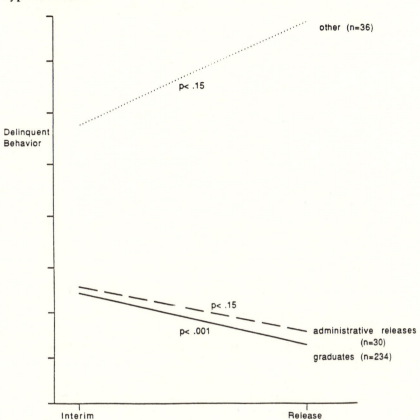

times on the average; but in the two months prior to their release, they had broken rules less than three times. The percentage who said that they would look back on their institutional experience as a "happy time" climbed from 55 to 63. The boys who were released administratively showed parallel improvements, although their changes were statistically less reliable because of the smaller number of boys. In contrast, the other boys, including the ones who had run away or who had been sent to a more secure institution, increased their delinquent behavior significantly, and their satisfaction with the institution improved only negligibly; at the same time, their subscription to delinquent values weakened in parallel with the other groups of boys.

This contrast between the boys who ran away or were placed more securely versus the other boys raises our confidence in the validity of our data. It is notable that the former already looked worse as a group four

Figure 4.6
Change in Delinquent Values from Interim to Release by Type of Release

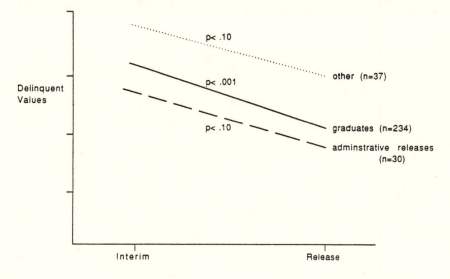

Figure 4.7
Change in Satisfaction with the Institution from Interim to Release by Type of Release

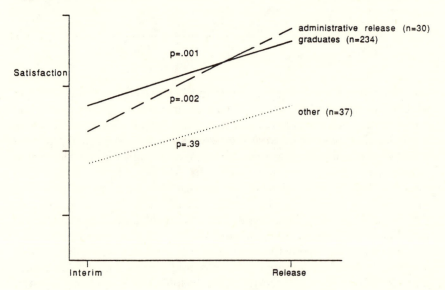

months into their stay. They admitted to breaking more rules and showed greater admiration for delinquent behavior, and they were less satisfied with the institution. Furthermore, the changes they evinced were the kind one would expect of boys who did not graduate normally. These findings validate our data because the boys' responses to our interviews are meaningfully related to an independent measure, their form of release.

The Relationship of Prior Personal Characteristics and Adjustment at Release

We have found it more difficult to detect the correlates of institutional adjustment at the point of boys' release than the correlates of their interim adjustment. This is due to the greater homogeneity of boys' adjustment at release. As we have seen, most of the boys graduated normally from the institutions, and they had to reach certain levels of adjustment to do so. They were released when staff and their group judged that they were ready. Thus, the adjustment of graduates varied less at release than it had after four months' stay (see Table 4.9). Differences in adjustment also declined from interim to release among boys who were placed more securely or ran away, but generally not as much as among the graduates, and it remained relatively high. We had expected that the graduates would be the most homogeneous in adjustment at release, but in fact the boys who were granted administrative releases were the most alike. Not only were they more alike, but we have already seen that their adjustment was about as good as that of the graduates. Apparently, administrative judgment about boys' readiness for release was in this respect as good as the staffs' and the groups'. Overall, then, smaller variation in adjustment at release meant that we could not as readily detect the conditions that caused boys to differ in their adjustment at that time.

The measures of adjustment taken at the time of release were somewhat different from those taken after four months at the institutions. The measures of support for the counterculture and acceptance of treatment were not administered because boys about to leave the institution found it difficult to respond to questions about issues that they were about to leave behind them. The measure of general adjustment at release is, therefore, a composite of the remaining four measures: delinquent behavior, delinquent values, satisfaction with the institution, and interest in school. The length of boys' residency and the type of their release provided additional measures of their adjustment to the institutional setting, as judged by the institutional staff and group. We limited our analysis of length of stay to boys who graduated, because the measure does not bear the same interpretation for the other boys. A shorter term indicated better adjustment among the graduates but not among those who ran away or were remanded to a more secure institution. We were also able to gather measures of three aspects of personal

Table 4.9
Changes in Variance of Scores of Institutional Adjustment, Interim to Release, by Type of Graduation

	S.D. int	S.D. rel	F-ratio of variances
Delinquent Values			
All (n=301)	2.82	2.17	1.69*
Grad (n=234)	2.68	1.99	1.82*
Adm Grad (n=30)	2.78	1.84	2.30*
Others (n=37)	3.59	3.17	1.28 .
Adm Grad & Others (n=67)	3.27	2.69	1.48*
Delinquent Behavior			
All (n=298)	4.60	4.25	1.17
Grad (n=232)	4.30	3.26	1.73*
Adm Grad (n=30)	3.08	2.79	1.22
Others (n=36)	6.36	6.28	1.02
Adm Grad & Others (n=66)	5.34	5.83	0.84
Satisfaction with Institution			
All (n=301)	2.43	1.87	1.69*
Grad (n=234)	2.28	1.79	1.64*
Adm Grad (n=30)	2.56	1.66	2.37*
Others (n=37)	3.10	2.25	1.89*
Adm Grad & Others (n=67)	2.85	2.11	1.82*

*$p < .05$

adjustment (not especially pertaining to the institution) at the time of departure. These were besetment and well-being, as measured in the intake interview, and scholastic gains, in terms of improvement in performance on a standardized achievement test since arriving at the institution.

Prior characteristics and institutional adjustment. To what degree was boys' adjustment to the institution at release predictable from the kinds of people they were at intake? Tables 4.10 to 4.12 present the relationships of boys' characteristics when we first met them to these indicators of their adjustment at the time they left the institution an average of a year later. Table 4.10 has the same structure as Table 4.1: it presents the bivariate correlations with no other variables controlled, as well as the betas for variables used as controls in later analyses. Table 4.11 presents comparable information for the type of release as an outcome measure. Because this variable is dichotomous (graduation or administrative release versus truant, escalation, or other), correlations and ordinary multiple regression are inappropriate. Therefore Table 4.11 contains comparisons of means and logistic regression coefficients.

We call attention first to the finding that what boys were like when they were

Table 4.10
Relationship of Boys' Characteristics at Intake with Adjustment to the Institution at Release

Characteristics At Intake	Institutional Adjustment				Length of Stay (grad only)	
	Delinquent Behavior		Delinquent Values			
	r	beta	r	beta	r	beta
Delinquent Involvement						
Delinquent Behavior	.16*	.15*	.07		.00	
Delinquent Values	.16*		.38*	.37*	.04	
Felony Arrests	.02		-.08		-.19*	
Prior Placements	.27*	.22*	.14*		.09	
Functioning At School						
Interest in School	-.12*		-.20*		-.19*	
Standardized Achievement	-.07	-.15*	-.12*	-.13*	-.02	
Relations With Others						
Value for Friendships	.13*		-.11		-.05	
Success at Friendships	-.07		-.05		-.18*	-.14*
Affection from Mother	-.06		-.06		-.09	
Autonomy from Mother	.08		.11		-.10	
Personal Adjustment						
Besetment	.09		.05		.05	
Conscious Self-Esteem	.00		.00		-.02	
Unconscious Self-Esteem	-.02		-.02		-.05	
Well-being	.01		-.03		.05	
Age At Entry	.02	-.06	-.03	-.02	-.30*	-.27*
R-Squared	.131*	.116*	.170*	.160*	.145*	.131*

* p < .05

Table 4.10 (*continued*)

Characteristics At Intake	Institutional Adjustment					
	Satisfaction with Institution		Interest in School		General Adjustment	
	r	beta	r	beta	r	beta
Delinquent Involvement						
Delinquent Behavior	.03		.00		-.07	
Delinquent Values	-.06		-.07		-.24*	
Felony Arrests	.05		.02		.05	
Prior Placements	-.18*	-.19*	-.10		-.25*	-.21*
Functioning At School						
Interest in School	.11		.17*	.17*	.21*	.19*
Standardized Achievement	.12*		.04		.12*	.15*
Relations With Others						
Value for Friendships	-.01		-.09		-.12*	
Success at Friendships	.06		.07		.09	
Affection from Mother	.14*		.15*		.15*	
Autonomy from Mother	-.01		-.09		-.10	
Personal Adjustment						
Besetment	-.12*		-.02		-.10	
Conscious Self-Esteem	-.01		.01		.00	
Unconscious Self-Esteem	.15*	.14*	.04		.09	
Well-being	.07		.13*		.08	
Age At Entry	-.05	-.02	.05	.03	.02	.04
R-Squared	.115*	.079*	.080	.030	.152*	.116*

* p < .05

Table 4.11
Relationship of Boys' Characteristics at Intake with Type of Release

| Characteristics at Intake | Type of Release | | | | Logistic Regression Coefficient |
| | Graduate or Administrative | | Truant, Escalate or Other | | |
	Mean	Variance	Mean	Variance	
Delinquent Involvement					
Delinquent Behavior	64.70	488.20	66.40	394.00	
Delinquent Values	13.12	10.08	13.84	10.74	.26*
Felony Arrests	3.75	8.50	3.42	5.20	
Prior Placements	.58	.78	1.07*	1.32	.51*
Functioning at School					
Interest in School	7.37	5.36	6.89	4.68	
Standardized Achievement	-4.12	5.40	-4.46	4.34	
Relations with Others					
Value for Friendship	30.40	28.40	30.90	28.70	
Success at Friendship	15.63	3.88	15.32	4.24	
Affection from Mother	27.40	24.70	25.90*	45.20	
Autonomy from Mother	15.80	15.20	16.50	21.40	
Personal Adjustment					
Besetment	40.20	96.30	39.90	107.70	
Conscious Self-Esteem	64.40	85.50	64.00	60.00	
Unconscious Self-Esteem	7.18	10.52	7.04	7.81	
Well-being	6.12	4.46	6.44	5.40	
Age at Entry	15.97	.92	15.95	.76	.22

chi-squared = 37.2, 5 df
Fraction explained = .032

*p < .05 for difference between means or for logistic regression coefficient.

admitted did not predict as well to their adjustment at release as it did to their adjustment after only four months residence. Though the value of R^2 for delinquent values at release is only slightly lower than that at four months, the values for delinquent behavior, satisfaction with the institution, and general adjustment are only 60 percent to 70 percent of those in Table 4.1. Part of this is probably due to the greater similarity in adjustment at release that we mentioned earlier, and part is because an average of eight months more of life and exposure to the institutional program had created greater change.

One or more of the measures of delinquent involvement correlated significantly with each of the measures of institutional adjustment at release except for interest in school. Prior institutionalization foretold less favorable adjustment on five of the seven measures. Initial delinquent values predicted greater delinquent behavior, more delinquent values, and poorer general adjustment at release. Both of these measures were consistent predictors of adjustment at four months, but the relationships have become somewhat stronger for prior placements and weaker for delinquent values. Prior delinquent behavior predicted only later delinquent behavior.

Felony arrests prior to coming to the institution have predicted few outcomes in this study. Here they were significantly correlated with length of stay, but in the opposite direction from what might have been expected. Boys with more prior arrests for felonies had shorter lengths of stay.

Both interest in school and standardized achievement were significantly correlated with several aspects of positive adjustment at the institution, the former with all but satisfaction with the institution and type of release, and the latter with all but interest in school, length of stay, and type of release. Interest in school had been an equally potent predictor of adjustment after four months at the institution, but standardized achievement is a considerably stronger predictor for adjustment at release.

Turning to prior relations with others, recall that affection and autonomy from one's mother and success at friendships correlated with several measures of adjustment at four months. Relationships were more sparse at the time of release. Feeling more successful at making friends predicted a briefer institutional stay. Boys who had reported greater affection from their mothers at intake displayed better institutional adjustment at release in several ways: satisfaction with the institution, interest in school, general adjustment, and a positive status at termination (graduation or administrative release). Autonomy from their mother was not significantly related to any of these measures at release.

Prior personal adjustment also was less related to institutional adjustment at release than at four months. Both besetment and well-being had been relatively consistent predictors, but each correlated with only one of these outcomes at release. Similarly, being younger at entry foretold only a shorter length of stay, while it had been correlated with all but two of the seven measures of interim adjustment.

As with the interim findings, there was considerable variation in how well facets of institutional adjustment could be predicted by boys' characteristics at intake. The pattern was similar, with delinquent values being the most predictable ($R^2 = .170$) and interest in school being the least predictable ($R^2 = .080$). Note that the level of prediction and the pattern of relationships for length of stay, type of release, prior placements, and standardized achievement test scores are similar to those for boys' reports of institutional adjustment at release, even though the former were taken from records and staff reports. This is encouraging because it once again indicates that the boys were not merely giving us spurious reports during the interviews. Instead, those measures are consistent with several other sources of information.

There is some practical as well as methodological significance to the predictive powers of boys' achievement test scores and the number of their prior placements. These are data ordinarily available to institutional staff at boys' intake. Our findings suggest that they are indicative of higher risk and should alert staff to consider devoting more attention to boys with low achievement scores and a history of several out-of-home placements. Note in Tables 4.1, 4.10, and 4.11 that boys' official delinquency records predicted no better than chance to their adjustment while at the institutions, except for predicting *shorter* institutional stays. It is our impression that more consideration is typically given to boys' delinquency records when planning intervention than is warranted by these data.

Thus, what the focal students were like when they arrived was prognostic of their adjustment on the threshold of their release. Two characteristics were relatively stable, their besetment and their delinquent values. Less profession of delinquent values, along with other indicators of less involvement in delinquency, was significantly predictive of relatively better adjustment generally. So was the degree to which boys had played their role at school well, both in terms of higher achievement and greater interest. Their delinquent values upon arrival were most predictive of boys' adjustment at release. Of more immediate practical value is that the more commonly available indicators of what boys are like at intake—having been placed out of their homes before and their scholastic achievement scores— were also predictive. The facet of their adjustment least well foreshadowed by our observations at intake was the interest in school that boys expressed when they left the institution.

Prior characteristics and personal adjustment at release. These measures of personal adjustment do not refer to the institutional setting itself, and presumably they have broader relevance beyond the institution. The relationships of characteristics measured at intake to these indicators of adjustment are presented in Table 4.12. All were reliably foreshadowed by what boys were like when they were admitted.

Boys' besetment and well-being demonstrated significant stability over about a year, although they were not as beset or as unhappy throughout their residence. Understandably, boys felt significantly less beset and expressed greater well-being on the threshold of their release than they had a intake (p < .001). What the significant autocorrelations show is that boys who ranked high at intake tended also to rank high at release. Apparently the institutional experience between the interviews improved boys' feelings, but certain predispositions persisted. Well-being, which presumably reflects one's current life situation, is considerably less stable than besetment, which reflects levels of anxiety and depression.

As with many of the measures of institutional adjustment, both besetment and well-being were reliably predicted by the number of boys' prior placements: the fewer placements, the less beset and the happier boys felt at release. In addition, boys with higher achievement test scores at intake felt less beset at release, and boys who felt more affection from their mothers

Table 4.12
Relationships of Boys' Characteristics at Intake with Personal Adjustment at Release

	Measures of Personal Adjustment at Release					
	Besetment		Well-Being		Academic Growth	
Characteristics at Intake	r	beta	r	beta	r	beta
Delinquent Involvement						
Delinquent Behavior	.07		-.01		-.04	
Delinquent Values	.11		-.02		-.14*	-.17*
Felony Arrests	-.09		.03		.11	
Prior Placements	.22*	.17*	-.17*	-.18*	-.07	
Functioning at School						
Interest in School	-.20*		.09		.00	
Standardized Achievement	-.12*	-.12*	.02		.06	
Relations with Others						
Value for Friendship	.10		-.03		.19*	.17*
Success at Friendship	-.14*		-.03		.09	
Affection from Mother	-.03		.17*		-.02	
Autonomy from Mother	.04		-.02		.08	
Personal Adjustment						
Besetment	.36*	.32*	.02		-.12*	
Conscious Self-esteem	-.07		.07		.02	
Unconscious Self-esteem	-.11		.09		-.06	
Well-being	-.03		.13*	.11*	.07	
Age at Entry	-.08	-.04	-.02	-.03	.09	
R-Squared	.219*	.179*	.087*	.048*	.110*	.071*

*p < .05

reported greater well-being at release. Boys who had at intake valued delinquency less, valued friendship more, and felt less beset made greater gains in achievement test scores.

Relationship Between Interim and Release Adjustment

To what degree does adjustment after a four-month stay foreshadow adjustment at release? Would an interim assessment of boys' adjustment be useful for identifying those students who, because they will otherwise probably adjust poorly throughout their stay, need more concerted or different treatment? The correlations in Table 4.13 and 4.14 reveal that a wide array of indicators of adjustment at release are predicted by many indicators of interim adjustment. All of the indicators of release adjustment except length of stay are predicted by at least three of the seven indicators of interim adjustment.

In each case the best predictor of a facet of adjustment at release was the earlier measure of the same variable, though virtually all of the other correlations were significant as well. To express the strength of these relationships another way, 70 percent of the boys whose interim general adjustment had been above average showed above average general adjustment at release as well; and 70 percent of those whose adjustment had been below average remained below average at their release.

Part of our success in predicting this particular set of variables is due undoubtedly to their duplication in the interim and release interviews. Thus, since there were no measures of besetment or well-being taken at four months, the interim measures were less closely related to them than to other release measures. Even so, those outcomes were significantly predicted by interim measures of delinquent behavior, support for the counterculture, satisfaction with the institution, interest in school, and general adjustment.

The interim variables less consistently predicted the outcome measures that did not come from the interviews. Length of stay correlated significantly only with less interest in school. There were greater scholastic gains for boys who had reported less delinquent values, greater interest in school, and better general adjustment. A favorable release status (graduation or administrative release) was more likely for boys who had engaged in less delinquent behavior, expressed greater interest in school, and had better general adjustment after four months' stay.

Though there was some variability in how well the measures of adjustment at release were predicted by interim adjustment, evidence indicates that more favorable adjustment at four months predicted more favorable adjustment at release, and there are no reversals of this pattern. Even so, it should be remembered that predictions of adjustment on the basis of the interim scores would be far from perfect. The correlations over time are highly reliable, but the interim scores never account for more than 37 percent of the variance in scores at release.

Table 4.13
Correlations Between Adjustment at Release and Adjustment Four Months After Arrival

Adjustment After Four Months	Adjustment at Release								
	Delinquent Behavior	Delinquent Values	Satisfaction with Inst.	Interest in School	General Adjustment	Length of Stay	Besetment	Well-Being	Academic Growth
Delinquent Behavior	.47*	.18*	-.15*	-.25*	-.37*	.09	.25*	-.13*	-.11
Delinquent Values	.24*	.53*	-.18*	-.19*	-.40*	-.01	.16*	-.04	-.16*
Counterculture	.33*	.27*	-.23*	-.29*	-.40*	.07	.21*	-.14*	-.07
Satisfaction with Institution	-.20*	-.26*	.50*	.25*	.44*	-.08	-.20*	.15*	.08
Acceptance of Treatment	-.09	-.14*	.21*	.20*	.23*	-.09	-.04	.04	.03
Interest in School	-.26*	-.29*	.37*	.46*	.49*	-.15*	-.24*	.25*	.13*
General Adjustment	-.38*	-.40*	.40*	.40*	.56*	-.12	-.25*	.18*	.14*
R-squared: interim	.240*	.303*	.285*	.226*	.366*	.033	.140*	.081*	.036
R-squared: interim, controlling for intake	.172*	.259*	.260*	.192	.307*	.028	.078*	.064*	.018
R-squared: total	.290*	.345*	.339*	.228*	.387*	.154*	.268*	.117*	.088*

*p < .05

106

Table 4.14
Interim Adjustment and Type of Release

Adjustment at Four Months	Type of Release			
	Graduate or Administrative		Truant, Escalated or Other	
	Mean	Variance	Mean	Variance
Delinquent Behavior	14.50	16.40	17.60*	40.80
Delinquent Values	11.02	6.93	11.32	11.57
Counterculture	9.64	7.93	10.46*	13.45
Satisfaction with Institution	12.72	5.27	12.48	8.22
Acceptance of Treatment	12.91	6.88	13.30	6.11
Interest in School	9.65	3.67	8.84*	4.54
General Adjustment	.06	.38	-.17*	.80
Logistic Regressions	Chi-squared		df	Fraction explained
Interim only	28.52*		6	.029
Interim, control for intake	18.71*		6	.020
Total	46.49*		11	.048

*p< .05 for comparison between means or logistic model.

To summarize our analysis of adjustment at release to this point, we have found that certain characteristics of boys when they first entered the institutions were predictive of their institutional adjustment after they had been there for four months and were still predictive of their adjustment at release after about a year. Among those predictive characteristics are two that the staff ordinarily has access to: the number of boys' previous out-of-home placements and their standard scholastic achievement test scores—but, it is worth noting again, not the number of their arrests. Our interviews yielded other statistically significant predictors, chiefly boys' delinquent values as reflected in their admiration for others' delinquent behavior, the interest they showed in school, and the amount of affection they believed they received from their female caregivers. We have also seen that boys' adjustment at four months is prognostic of their adjustment at release, notably their earlier subscription to a student counterculture, their expressed interest in school, and their satisfaction with the institution.

What can staff who are aware of these signs do to improve the adjustment of boys who show a poor prognosis? What changes in the students' groups would enhance the boys' adjustment and reentry into the community when they are released? In order to answer these questions, we inquired about which properties of the groups were most conducive to boys' adjustment at release, and about what properties of the staff teams affected those group properties.

Group Properties, Staff Team Properties, and Adjustment at Release

We related properties of boys' group and staff team measured from two to eight months after the boys' arrival at the institutions to boys' adjustment at release. Assessments of groups and staff teams came only shortly before departure for a few of the boys who had the shortest stays. For the vast majority, however, at least four months had elapsed since these assessments, and a year or more had gone by for many of them. Thus, there should be very little confounding between the measures of adjustment and the measures of group and staff properties.

The effects of group properties on boys' adjustment at release appear in Tables 4.15 and 4.16. The results are quite similar to those in Table 4.2, relating group properties to interim adjustment. In both cases delinquent behavior was more common for boys in groups that had norms supporting the counterculture and groups that were less cohesive. At release, correlations with more delinquent values and less program acceptance also became significant, but there was little change in the actual magnitude of the correlations. On both occasions greater autonomy for the group predicted more satisfaction with the institution, and all three measures of norms significantly predicted general adjustment. Delinquent values and interest in school had little relationship with group properties at release, as was true in the interim

Table 4.15
Partial Correlations of Group Properties and Adjustment at Release, Controlling for Measures at Intake

Group Property	Delinquent Behavior	Delinquent Values	Satisfaction with Inst.	Interest in School	General Adjustment	Length of Stay	Resetment	Well-being	Academic Growth
					Adjustment at Release				
Norms									
Delinquent Values	.19*	.05	-.06	-.04	-.14*	.02	.02	-.02	-.11
Counterculture	.18*	.04	-.03	-.11	-.15*	.03	.03	-.01	-.16*
Program Acceptance	-.12*	-.09	.11	.11	.18*	.00	.00	.05	.09
R-Squared: norms	.036*	.008	.014	.022	.033*	.007	.001	.003	.025
Climate									
Autonomy	-.09	-.01	.14*	.08	.11	-.05	-.05	.14*	.10
Decision-making	.08	.08	.01	.02	-.04	.01	.01	.04	-.01
Ties to Staff	-.05	-.03	.06	.03	.05	.03	.03	.20*	.04
Cohesiveness	-.15*	.01	.00	.05	.07	.00	.00	.09	.15*
R-Squared: climate	.030	.009	.041*	.007	.022	.011	.008	.041*	.022
R-Squared: all group properties	.044*	.022	.049*	.025	.046*	.029	.009	.046	.033
R-Squared: total, group and intake	.173*	.192*	.131*	.058	.121*	.160*	.196*	.095*	.116

*p < .05

Note: With the exception of R-squared: total, all figures for R-squared represent increases in R-squared after controlling for personal characteristics.

Table 4.16

Group Properties and Type of Release (Adjusted Means), Controlling for Intake Characteristics

	Type of Release			
	Graduate or Administrative		Truant, Escalated or Other	
Group Properties	Mean	Variance	Mean	Variance
Norms				
Delinquent Values	13.84	4.50	13.59	4.21
Counterculture	11.62	3.67	11.57	4.08
Program Acceptance	19.12	.50	19.20	.47
Climate				
Autonomy	.06	1.85	.24	1.30
Decision-making	10.20	1.67	10.19	2.28
Ties to Staff	8.19	.60	8.09	.61
Cohesiveness	12.09	2.32	12.14	2.54

Logistic Regression	Chi-squared		df	Fraction explained
norms, controlling for intake	1.18		3	.001
climate, controlling for intake	4.61		4	.005
all group properties, controlling for intake	5.67		7	.006
total: group and intake	39.45*		13	.041

*p < .05

analysis. Thus, the relationships of group properties to these measures of institutional adjustment were not strong, but they were consistent and statistically significant.

Relationships between the remaining measures of adjustment at release and group properties are scattered. There was very little relationship between the group measures and measures of adjustment based on staff and group decisions: length of stay and type of release. None of the pertinent correlations even approached statistical significance. Similarly, besetment (feelings of anxiety and depression) was not related to these properties of the groups. Groups did have some impact on well-being and scholastic gains. Feelings of well-being were enhanced by being in groups with more autonomy and with closer personal ties to the staff. Scholastic gains were greater in groups that gave less support to the counterculture and groups that were more cohesive.

Consistent with our findings about the staffs' influence on boys' adjustment after four months' stay, staff team properties have little direct impact on adjustment at release. The findings for adjustment at release are presented in Tables 4.17 and 4.18, and they can be compared to the findings for adjustment at four months, which are presented in Table 4.8. Boys engaged in more delinquent behavior during the two months immediately preceding their release when their staff team had poorer morale and reported giving them more say in decisions. The staff teams that placed greater emphasis on both custodial and treatment goals generated greater interest in school and more favorable general adjustment, and they decreased levels of besetment. The correlation between treatment orientation and interest in school also appeared in the interim analysis. Graduates from the program had shorter lengths of stay in groups whose staff teams had better morale and who reported that the groups had greater autonomy. Note that there were no significant relationships between staff properties and many of the measures of adjustment at release: delinquent values, satisfaction with the institution, well-being, scholastic gains, and type of release.

It is plausible that the cause–effect relationships we are inferring here—that properties of the staff teams affected boys' adjustment at release—are in fact opposite, that actually staff morale went up and staffs favored treatment over custody when the boys in their group adjusted better. But we have seen that these properties of staff teams remained relatively stable over the year of our observations, regardless of changes in the membership of their groups and in the way their groups functioned. We believe that staff teams did have the effect inferred.

Perceptions of the Institution and Adjustment at Release

Our model of the process by which boys' institutional experience affected their adjustment interposes boys' perceptions of their staff and group be-

Table 4.17
Partial Correlations of Staff Team Properties and Adjustment at Release, Controlling for Measures at Intake

Staff Team Property	Measure of Adjustment at Release			
	Delinquent Behavior	Delinquent Values	Length of Stay	Satisfaction with Inst.
Morale	-.14*	-.06	-.15*	.05
Treatment vs. Custodial Emphasis	-.06	-.09	.12	.10
Autonomy for Group	-.05	.00	-.14*	-.01
Group Decision-making	.16*	-.10	-.07	-.04
R-Squared: staff	.052*	.024	.037	.019
R-Squared: total, staff and intake	.189*	.189	.168*	.100*

*p < .05

Note: R-squared: staff represents the increase in R-squared after controlling for personal characteristics.

Staff Team Property	Measure of Adjustment at Release				
	Interest in School	Academic Growth	Besetment	Well-being	General Adjustment
Morale	.03	.00	.07	.09	.08
Treatment vs. Custodial Emphasis	.13*	.07	-.16*	-.01	.15*
Autonomy for Group	.00	.03	.10	-.01	.00
Group Decision-making	.02	-.04	.10	-.01	-.09
R-Squared: staff	.019	.010	.037*	.026	.046*
R-Squared: total, staff and intake	.046	.086*	.224*	.074*	.120*

*$p < .05$

Note: R-squared: staff represents the increase in R-squared after controlling for personal characteristics.

Table 4.18
Staff Team Properties and Type of Release (Adjusted Means), Controlling for Intake Characteristics

Staff Team Property	Type of Release			
	Graduate or Administrative		Truant, Escalate or Other	
	Mean	Variance	Mean	Variance
Morale	20.69	4.90	20.57	4.79
Treatment vs. Custodial Emphasis	-.05	1.03	.17	.90
Autonomy for Group	2.05	.85	2.18	.79
Group Decision-making	9.77	1.44	9.95	1.91
Logistic Regression		Chi-squared	df	Fraction explained
Staff, controlling for intake		5.59	4	.006
Total. staff and intake		39.19*	10	.042

*$p < .05$

tween the reality, as defined by the staff and other group members, and adjustment (see Figure 4.1). We hypothesized that staff teams affected their groups significantly, that boys perceived their groups with some but not perfect accuracy, and that boys' adjustment was affected by what they believed their groups were like. For example, according to this model, the reason that staff morale had a significant effect on boys' delinquent behavior preceding release would be that the level of staff morale affected the development of a counterculture in the group, the strength of which was apparent to the group members, whose adjustment it then affected.

Our data support this model. We have already seen that certain properties of staff teams, particularly their morale, affected their groups (Table 4.7). Table 4.19 shows the relationship between perceptions about groups at release and the group properties. These results are quite comparable to those from the interim interview (see Table 4.4) for the four measures of perceptions about the group that were included in the release interview. (Unlike the interview at four months, the release interview did not include measures of perceptions about the counterculture or about autonomy.) Data collected at the time boys were about to be released show that the properties of their groups were apparent to them: if the group reported stronger support for a counterculture, departing members reported that the group had been breaking more rules recently; if the group reported more admiration for delinquent behavior (i.e., endorsed delinquent values), boys described the group as valuing delinquency; and boys tended to report closer ties to the staff when the rest of the group did so. Perceptions about delinquent behavior and delinquent values were consistently influenced by the norms of the groups. Personal ties to the staff and attraction to the group were only modestly influenced by the set of group properties.

Boys' perceptions were not altogether accurate, however. As we have seen, they were shaped partly by group properties, but they also varied a great deal among members of the same or comparable groups. As Table 4.20 shows, boys' perceptions are to some degree a function of their personal characteristics when they arrived at the institutions. A comparison of these data to those in Table 4.3, however, shows that prior characteristics came to have less impact on boys' perceptions of their groups over time. Intake characteristics consistently account for less of the variation in perceptions at release than of perceptions four months after arrival.

Boys' perceptions of their group in turn affected their adjustment. For example, perceptions accounted for 27.5 percent of the variance in boys' global adjustment at release (see Table 4.21), compared to less than 5 percent accounted for by staff or group properties alone. If boys perceived that their group was breaking a lot of rules, then they reported more misbehavior of their own over the two months prior to their release, they expressed less satisfaction with the institution, and consequently, their global scores on adjustment at release were lower. Similarly, boys who believed that their

Table 4.19
Partial Correlations of Group Properties and Perceptions of the Group at Release, Controlling for Measures at Intake

	Perception of Group			
Group Property	Delinquent Behavior	Delinquent Values	Ties to Staff	Attraction to Group
Norms				
Delinquent Values	.21*	.27*	.06	.11
Counterculture	.21*	.18*	-.05	.03
Program Acceptance	-.14*	-.31*	.05	.04
R-squared: norms	.045*	.105*	.028*	.032*
Climate				
Autonomy	-.14	-.13*	.05	.09
Decision-making	.02	.11	.02	.04
Ties to Staff	-.07	-.06	.16*	.14*
Cohesiveness	-.20*	-.14*	.01	.09
R-Squared: climate	.040*	.048*	.026	.021
R-Squared: all group properties	.056*	.138*	.050*	.057*
R-Squared: total, personal and group properties	.159*	.186*	.116*	.102*

*p < .05

Note: With the exception of R-squared: total, all figures for R-squared represent increases in R-squared after controlling for characteristics at intake.

Table 4.20
Relationship of Personal Characteristics at Intake and Perception of the Group at Release

Characteristics at Intake	Perception of Group							
	Delinquent Behavior		Delinquent Values		Ties to Staff		Attraction to Group	
	r	beta	r	beta	r	beta	r	beta
Delinquent Involvement								
Delinquent Behavior	.08		.12*		-.05		-.01	
Delinquent Values	-.01		.09		-.09		.00	
Felony Arrests	-.06		.13*		-.12*		-.11*	
Prior Placements	.12*	.11*	.12*		-.15*	-.15*	-.11	
Functioning at School								
Interest in School	-.05		-.05		.09		.02	
Standardized Achievement	.02		.09		.02		-.04	
Relations with Others								
Value for Friendships	.12*		.06		.06		.05	
Success at Friendships	-.10		.01		.03		.07	
Affection from Mother	.00		-.03		.18*		.06	
Autonomy from Mother	.03		-.03		-.10		-.07	
Personal Adjustment								
Besetment	.20*	.19*	-.04		-.04		-.08	
Conscious Self-Esteem	-.05		.02		.01		.09	
Unconscious Self-Esteem	.00		.03		.04		.03	
Well-being	-.04		.03		.11*		.13*	
Age at Entry	-.09	.02	.12*	.09	-.11	-.04	-.02	.07
R-Squared	.121*	.098*	.071	.042*	.088*	.064*	.083	.037*

*p < .05

Table 4.21
Partial Correlations of Perceptions of Group to Institutional Adjustment at Release, Controlling for Measures at Intake

Perceptions of Group	Adjustment at Release			
	Delinquent Behavior	Delinquent Values	Length of Stay	Satisfaction with Inst.
Delinquent Behavior	.53*	.06	.05	-.19*
Delinquent Values	.17*	.40*	.01	-.18*
Ties to Staff	-.18*	-.15*	.03	.33*
Attraction	-.04	-.02	-.07	.13*
R-Squared: perceptions, controlling for intake	.277*	.153*	.008	.141*
R-Squared: group properties controlling for intake	.044*	.022	.029	.049*
controlling for intake and perceptions	.010	.005	.028	.040*
R-Squared: staff team properties controlling for intake	.052*	.024	.037	.019
controlling for intake and perceptions	.020	.012	.036	.008

*p < .05

| | Adjustment at Release | | | | |
Perceptions of Group	Interest in School	Academic Growth	Besetment	Well-Being	General Adjustment
Delinquent Behavior	-.11	-.03	.20*	-.08	-.33*
Delinquent Values	-.07	-.01	.07	.08	-.32*
Ties to Staff	.38*	.07	-.08	.22*	.39*
Attraction	.20*	.11	-.08	.04	.14*
R-Squared: perceptions, controlling for intake	.148*	.012	.037*	.058*	.275*
R-Squared: group properties controlling for intake	.025	.033	.009	.046	.046*
controlling for intake and perceptions	.011	.028	.011	.040	.011
R-Squared: staff team properties controlling for intake	.019	.010	.037*	.026	.046*
controlling for intake and perceptions	.008	.011	.034*	.018	.016

*p < .05

group endorsed more delinquent values subscribed more to those values themselves, behaved worse, were less satisfied with the institution, and taken all together, showed poorer global adjustment at release. Believing that they had been in a group that misbehaved more was related to boys feeling more beset on the threshold of their release.

The relationships boys formed with other people at the institutions were also related to their adjustment. As Table 4.21 shows, closer personal ties to the staff discouraged delinquent behavior and values, and they enhanced boys' satisfaction with the institution, their interest in school, their feeling of well-being, and consequently, their overall adjustment. Being more attracted to the group coincided with being more satisfied with the institutional experience, being more interested in school, and showing better general adjustment.

Boys' perceptions of their group and their feelings about their staff also affected the nature of their release (see Table 4.22). Boys who perceived their groups to be more delinquent were more likely to run away or be sent to a more secure placement. Boys with closer ties to staff were more likely to graduate or receive an administrative release. Scholastic gains and graduates' lengths of stay at the institutions were not influenced by perceptions of the group, however.

Tables 4.21 and 4.22 also demonstrate that the actual group and staff team properties accounted somewhat less well for boys' adjustment at release when we took boys' perceptions into account. The variance in general adjustment accounted for by group properties falls from 4.6 percent to 1.0 percent, and variance accounted for by staff team properties falls from 4.6 percent to 1.6 percent. A large share of the decline in the direct influence of group properties on adjustment is attributable to the diminished direct effect of the group counterculture on group members: Boys' perceptions of the degree to which their group supported delinquent values and broke institutional rules mediated between the counterculture and members' adjustment. Perceptions about the group explained the bulk of the association between adjustment at release and the variations among groups and staff teams. In some cases significant relationships remained after controlling for perceptions (e.g., group properties and satisfaction with the institution or well-being). It appears likely that this is because of the limited set of measures of perceptions that was obtained in the release interview, which did not include autonomy and perceptions of the counterculture.

SUMMARY

Though the correlates of adjustment at release were somewhat more difficult to determine (because of reduced variation), they were on the whole similar to those of adjustment four months after arrival. Indeed, we found that interim adjustment was strongly related to adjustment at release. Our

Table 4.22
Relationships Between Perceptions of Groups and Type of Release (Mean Adjusted, Controlling for Personal Characteristics)

| | Type of Release | | | |
| | Graduate or Administrative | | Truant, Escalated or Other | |
Perceptions of Group	Mean	Variance	Mean	Variance
Delinquent Behavior	16.08	165.10	26.99*	226.71
Delinquent Values	13.70	13.76	13.33	13.62
Ties to Staff	9.58	3.34	8.45*	6.83
Attraction to Group	6.41	3.32	6.30	4.42
Logistic Regressions		Chi-Squared	df	Fraction explained
Perceptions, controlling for intake		16.44*	4	.021
Group properties, controlling for intake and perceptions		11.89	7	.016
Staff team properties, controlling for intake and perceptions		3.27	4	.004

* $p < .05$

analyses produced strong evidence to support each link in our conceptual model. Adjustment is influenced by many features of both the boys' prior characteristics and the nature of their group. The influence of the groups is mediated by the individuals' perceptions about them, which are also somewhat influenced by prior characteristics. Staff teams have considerable impact on the properties of groups. Their influence on individual adjustment is diluted, however, because it is filtered by both the group itself and individuals' perceptions of their group.

We more carefully scrutinized the roles in the influence process of both attraction to the group and perceptions about the group in a causal model of adjustment after four months. This analysis revealed that both subjective influence and the projection of one's values onto others contribute to the relationship between perceptions and adjustment, and that attraction to the group tends to bring about more positive adjustment and more favorable views about the group.

In the next chapter we will address the adjustment of these boys six months after they returned to the open community. There we will consider the impact of many of the same factors: boys' characteristics when they arrived at the institutions, their adjustment while at the institutions, and the properties of their groups. In Chapter 6 we will turn to a dimension of individual differences in adjustment that has proved useful for differentiating responses to this setting and others, namely besetment, which is the extent of boys' anxiety and depression.

NOTES

1. It is our practice in this report to describe a measure of a variable when we first introduce a finding that involves it. The reader who wishes to find a description of a measure can do so through the subject index, under "[variable], measure of."

2. In developing these regression equations, we first considered the intake variables in conceptually related groups. We used variables from a group in the final model if a group explained a statistically significant amount of variance when considered as a set. This was done to reduce the possibility of erroneously treating chance relationships as meaningful, a danger when a large number of explanatory variables are considered. The sets of variables were (1) delinquent involvement, including prior out-of-home placements, (2) functioning at school, (3) relations with other people, and (4) personal adjustment. A small proportion of the prior placements were due to neglect and abuse rather than delinquency; nevertheless, we included this variable as an index of involvement in delinquency because it is primarily a gauge of the seriousness with which the juvenile justice system regarded the boys' antisocial behavior. We had no data concerning affection or autonomy from the mothers (or other female caregivers) of twenty-four of the boys because they could name no one who filled that role. Rather than lose those cases in later analyses that include intake variables as statistical controls, we did not include these two variables in the regressions. This is no reflection on the importance of boys'

relations with their caregivers but rather a statistical compromise. The effects of boys' relations with their female caregivers were investigated in simple correlational analyses. All regressions also included age at intake, race (black versus nonblack), and public versus private institution as predictors because these are factors that vary systematically across institutional centers.

5

ADJUSTMENT TO THE
OPEN COMMUNITY

We now consider what many readers may regard as the critical question for our research: What conditions shaped these youths' adjustment to the open community? We look mostly at the conditions that encouraged them to abandon their delinquent behavior, and also at factors that may have led the boys to return to school, to go to work, and in general to join the mainstream of our society.

We will present data that speak to this question and will report on the focal students' sense of well-being. This too is a important aspect of their adjustment. Were they satisfied with their lives in the six months after their release? Were they hopeful about their future? Did they feel good about themselves? Or were they beset with anxiety and depression? These practical questions guided our inquiry.

Here, as throughout this work, we also address underlying theoretical issues. One of these is the contemporary psychological effects of past experiences, represented in this chapter concretely by the effects of the institutional experience on post-release adjustment. If the institution had any lasting effect on these adolescents, by what processes was this achieved? This is an issue for personality theory.

By "personality," we mean more *enduring* motives, values, and skills. We thus look for psychological change that travels. Whatever remained of the institutional experience after the focal students left became part of their personality. What if anything of the institutional experience stuck, in this sense, and what were the characteristics of such transforming experiences?

The other theoretical issue that we address with these data on post-release adjustment concerns the effects of social conditions on the respondents' adjustment. Here we look for determinants of adjustment originating in the community to which they were released. The "community" includes the neighborhood to which a boy was released, the school he attended, the family or group home where he lived, the peers with whom he associated, his probation officer, and his opportunities for employment. All of these had some potential to shape his adjustment. The theoretical question we address is: If any of these social conditions proved to be influential, what distinguishes them?

We approached these practical and theoretical questions with some guiding hypotheses. Concerning personality change induced by the institution, we looked particularly at those experiences that might have altered the respondents' beliefs in their potential to play important social roles adequately—specifically, as workers and as friends. Did they discover during their institutionalization that they could achieve in social institutions like school, and did they discover that they could establish good relationships with others? During this analysis of our data, we were mindful of Sigmund Freud's response when asked what a well-adjusted adult should be able to do: "Leiben und Arbeiten"—love and work (Erikson, 1963). We employed the concept of *reference group* to guide our search for the social conditions that might have had enduring effects on these youths' adjustment. A person's self-evaluation is affected by the evaluation of a reference group (or person). Whether a group is a reference depends on how much one cares about the others' opinion of oneself and how much control the others have over one's fate (Kelley, 1952, 1956; Sherif, 1948; Newcomb, 1943, 1950). Our inquiry focused on the availability of reference groups in the community, respondents' commitments to them, and whether the reference groups encouraged pro- or antisocial adjustment.

We assumed that focal students' adjustment in the community, like their institutional adjustment, was shaped by the encounters of their personalities with their social environment. The personal and the social are inextricably tied. The boys took part in shaping their social environments. This raises questions as to whether the institutional experience so altered respondents' images of themselves that they sought out prosocial rather than antisocial reference groups, whether they became more hopeful of acceptance and so reached out to others more, and whether personality change actually rendered them more acceptable to schools, employers, and other reference groups, and thus encouraged positive adjustment.

DATA COLLECTION

Six months after they left their respective institutions, the focal students were scattered widely about the state of Michigan, and a few beyond. So we did not try to interview each of them face to face, but instead contacted most of them by phone. The last decade's research on survey methodology supports the validity of telephone interviewing as a means of studying even sensitive topics (Judd, Smith, & Kidder, 1991). Also, the interviewing task was simplified by our respondent's experience with most of the measures in the earlier interviews. We had asked boys upon their release for an address and phone number where they could probably be reached for a forty-five minute interview during the months immediately ahead, and the institutions and the Department of Social Services also helped us to find respondents we could no longer reach with the information they had given us. Unfortunately, some were found in the state's monthly census of prison and jail populations. Most of the youths in secure placement could not be interviewed by phone, so these interviews were taken in person. We offered the focal students ten dollars for the interview, which greatly encouraged cooperation.

We tried to follow up as many as we could find of the 306 focal students from whom we obtained release interviews. We limited our follow-up to that population because what respondents were like upon release was hypothetically a major condition of their post-release adjustment. We ultimately obtained 247 interviews, or 81 percent of those we sought. This corresponds to 66 percent of the 372 residents we asked to participate in the study and who remained at the institutions for at least four months. Table 5.1 compares the 247 respondents whom we interviewed with the 59 that we failed to find.

There are two statistically significant differences between respondents to the post-release interview and those we missed. The former are on the average three months younger than the latter. A larger (though still small) proportion of those we found experienced a different kind of release: 8 percent of the respondents we found had actually been sent to a more secure institution rather than having been released, compared to only 2 percent of those we missed. Conversely, 7 percent of the focal students we missed had actually absconded rather than been released, compared to only 1 percent of the boys we found. Naturally, it was easier to locate the former residents who were in secure placements than those on the run.

There were two other small differences, of borderline significance, between the characteristics of boys interviewed and boys not found. The former had on the average fewer arrests for felonies on their official records prior to institutionalization and had stayed at the institution a month longer on average.

MEASURES

Adjustment

As we have stated, our conception of adjustment to the open community includes desisting from antisocial behavior; enacting conventional, age-

Table 5.1
Comparison of Focal Students Interviewed in Six-Month Follow-up with
Those Who Were Not Interviewed

Variables	Interviewed n=247	Not Interviewed n=59	Pdiff
Measured at intake			
age	15.9	16.2	.03
(var)	(1.1)	(0.8)	
race			.72
% white	52	49	
% black	44	49	
% other	4	2	
delinquent behavior	65.1	68.2	.34
(var)	(485.6)	(481.2)	
institution			.30
% public: Maxey/Adrian	66	65	
% private: Starr	28	29	
% private: Boysville	7	5	
arrests for felonies	3.5	4.2	.06
(var)	(7.4)	(9.5)	

Measured at release			
length of stay (in days)	395	365	.06
(var)	(12,977)	(9,647)	
delinquency at institution	14.1	13.4	22
(var)	(18.4)	(15.2)	
institutional satisfaction	13.3	13.7	.21
(var)	(3.6)	(3.1)	
well-being	8.6	8.7	.76
(var)	(2.3)	(2.2)	
type of termination			.02
% graduated	77	74	
% administrative release	10	14	
% escalated	8	2	
% absconded	1	7	
% other	4	3	
delinquent values	10.2	10.3	.91
(var)	(4.2)	(6.4)	
besetment	34.5	33.6	.46
(var)	(73.0)	(53.7)	
staff rating (public only)	5.5	5.4	.72
(var)	(1.9)	(2.1)	

appropriate roles such as attending school and working; relating comfortably with adults and peers; and having a sense of well-being. In order to take stock of these, we asked respondents whether they had committed any offenses in the six months since their release and, if they had, whether their offenses had been detected by any law enforcement authority. We also obtained arrest and court records from the juvenile and adult justice systems (including records on the fifty-nine focal students whom we were not able to interview). We asked respondents whether they had attended any school or training program since their release and, if they had, how successful they were, and whether they had found or had looked for employment during that time. Our interviewers asked them to identify the people with whom they were living and how well they were getting along with them, as well as who, if anyone, they "hung around with" regularly. We also asked whether they had maintained any contact with their staff team or group at the institution, and whether they were seeing a probation officer or aftercare worker. We measured respondents' well-being by administering the besetment and quality of life scales with which they had become familiar in earlier interviews at the institution.

Reference Groups

After we had identified the major actors in their lives since release to determine the quality of their social relations, we explored with the respondents the extent to which any of these served as reference groups. How much were they attached to each of these others? Did they believe that these others approved of them? Were these evaluations important to them? We also tried to determine whether, from the respondents' perspective, these others supported pro- or antisocial behavior. At another point in the interview, we asked respondents if they felt accepted or rejected by people they wanted to associate with, and particularly if they attributed any rejection they had experienced to the stigma of their institutionalization.

Personality

In order to test hypotheses about the effect of focal students' personality on their post-release adjustment, we invoked measures from the interviews we had conducted when the focal students entered the institution and when they were about to be released, six months before. We focused on two indices: besetment and delinquent values. Note that these two factors are also considered indices of adjustment when measured during the post-release interview. In a sense, then, the question we posed here is, to what degree did the boys' personality change after their release?

Table 5.2
Descriptions of Focal Students at Follow-up

Living arrangements

With parent(s)	47%
With other relative	13
With friends	6
Alone	3
Half-way home or group home	7
Foster home	3
Secure placement	20

Arrested	20%

Occupation

School	24%
Job	20
School and job	19
Idle	17

DATA ANALYSIS AND FINDINGS

As before, our data analysis consists mainly of correlations and multiple regressions. The dependent variables are measures of post-release adjustment. There are three sets of independent variables or predictors: personality factors, adjustment at release, and social conditions in the community. These three sets are first treated separately, then together, to determine their interdependence and joint influence.

The Focal Students, Six Months After Release

Table 5.2 reports some important facts about the respondents when we found them six months after they left the institution. We found 60 percent of the young men living with parents or relatives. The next most frequent living arrangement was secure placement, where 20 percent resided. The rest were scattered in other living arrangements.

In retrospect, most of the boys judged that their institutional experience had been satisfactory. Out of a possible range of scores on institutional satisfaction from 4 to 16, the median score was 13, and the mean was 12.4. Though this indicates a positive view of the institutional stay, it is somewhat less strongly positive than at the time of release, when the mean score was 13.4.

Note that we found 20 percent of the young men in some kind of secure placement again. This includes adult jails, juvenile detention homes, and training schools. Eighteen of our focal students had gone directly from one secure placement to another and had remained there throughout the following six months. Another 7 percent told us that they had been in secure placement sometime during the sixth months, although we found them in the community. Of those not in secure placement, 89 percent reported some contact with an aftercare worker since they had been released. Twenty percent reported having been arrested at least once during the six months.

Arrests and placements do not by any means reflect all of the respondents' delinquency after their release. Their own reports of their delinquent behavior revealed that all of them had committed at least one chargeable delinquent act in the subsequent six months. Seventy-nine percent reported that they used or sold illegal drugs; 75 percent admitted to assault, threatening assault, or fighting; 73 percent committed some sort of status offense like running away from a placement or drinking; 56 percent said they had destroyed property; and 42 percent said that they had stolen something. The frequency and seriousness of their delinquent behavior varied widely, from well within the range of normal adolescent acts to a continuation and even amplification of the pattern that had gotten them incarcerated in the first place.

Of those who were living freely in the community 17 percent said they were idle, neither going to school nor holding a job. Only 5 percent had been idle throughout the whole six months, however, On the other hand, 63 percent of the young men were either going to school, holding a job, or both. Eighty percent of the boys said that they were "somewhat" or "quite satisfied" with their lives at the moment.

Clearly there is sufficient variation in the respondents' subsequent integration into the open community to warrant a search for the conditions that accounted for the differences in their adjustment.

The Relationship of Prior Personal Characteristics to Adjustment in the Community Six Months After Release

An average of eighteen months elapsed between our focal students' arrival at the institutions and their first follow-up interview. During this time they had undergone the major disruptions of leaving their home communities, adapting to a new setting, and then, in most cases, returning to a world of adolescent and family life that had been proceeding apace without them. A substantial number of these young men had experienced even more disruptions of their normal lives, such as placements in group or foster homes following release, being jailed, and so on. Eighteen months is a long time in any teenager's life and for the boys in this study especially, many significant changes had occurred.

Given these changes, it is questionable whether the focal students' personal characteristics, measured when they arrived at the institutions, would predict to their adjustment upon returning to the community. On the one hand, most of them returned to an open environment, typically the same setting they were in before coming to the institution. For that reason, one might expect that how they functioned before would be the best indication of how they would adapt once they had returned home. On the other hand, it would not be surprising if otherwise stable personal characteristics were greatly altered by their experience of institutionalization.

Our analysis of the relationship of prior personal characteristics to adjustment in the community takes the same form as the comparable analyses for institutional adjustment. We have used the same set of personal characteristics gathered from the initial interview and from institutional records, and we have subjected them to the same kind of statistical analysis.

Note first the evidence for continuity of personal characteristics in the data of Table 5.3. The correlations of measures taken at intake with measures of the same characteristics taken six months after release are among the strongest in the data. These are partial correlations, controlling for the age, race, and institutional placement of the boys. The correlations indicate that, over an average of eighteen months, the boys tended to maintain their order in regard to delinquent behavior and delinquent values, their interest in school, besetment, and feelings of well-being. The number of times they were arrested in the six months after their release was also related to the number of their arrests prior to their incarceration, after controlling for besetment.

That the intercorrelations of repeated measures are the most significant in the data raises the question of whether we have merely captured behavior for responding to questions or have measured stable characteristics that would be manifest in settings other than an interview as well. Did the boys simply respond to the first post-release interview in the same way that they had responded earlier, or were they revealing something really pervasive about themselves? One indication that the respondents were not simply exhibiting consistent respondent behavior would be that the measures of their personal characteristics are also related to other measures. The data on how well personal characteristics at intake predicted to various facets of post-release adjustment provide such evidence.

Adjustment to the community. First we consider the focal students' behavior and relationships to conventional institutions in the open community—family, school, work, and law enforcement. Then we report on more internal facets of the respondents' personal adjustment—their feelings of well-being and besetment.

In analyzing the post-release data, we had to make a number of decisions about which focal students to include in the analysis for particular outcome measures. When following up on their delinquent behavior and felony ar-

Table 5.3
Relationship of Personal Characteristics at Intake to Adjustment Six Months After Release

Characteristic at Intake	Adjustment Six Months After Release							
	Delinquent Behavior		Delinquent Values		Felony Arrests		Interest in School	
	r	β	r	β	r	β	r	β
Delinquent Involvement								
Delinquent Behavior	.26*	.20*	.04		.05		-.13	
Delinquent Values	.23*	.19*	.34*	.36*	.03		.03	
Felony Arrests	-.03		-.12		.11		.12	
Prior Placements	.09		-.02		.08	.13*	.02	
Functioning at School								
Interest in School	-.13		-.13*		.02		.19*	
Standardized Achievement	.18*	.15*	-.03		-.08		-.09	
Relations with Others								
Value for Friendships	.08		.07		-.09		-.02	
Success at Friendships	-.03		-.05		-.02		.05	
Affection from Mother	-.07		-.01		.01		.16*	
Autonomy from Mother	.04		-.04		-.11		-.14	
Personal Adjustment								
Besetment	.03		.10		.16*	.16*	.01	
Conscious Self-Esteem	.02		-.02		.03		.02	
Unconscious Self-Esteem	.01		.00		.02		-.04	
Well-Being	-.01		-.08		-.07		.10	
Age at Entry	-.05	-.02	-.13*	-.08	-.06	-.07	.09	.06
R²	.126*	.126*	.154*	.153*	.073	.049*	.111	.034

	Caregiver Rating		Besetment		Well-Being	
	r	β	r	β	r	β
Delinquent Involvement						
Delinquent Behavior	.07		-.04		-.15*	
Delinquent Values	.11		.06		-.09	
Felony Arrests	.13		-.08		-.08	
Prior Placements	-.19*	-.18*	.14*		-.06	
Functioning at School						
Interest in School	-.07		-.16*		.11	
Standardized Achievement	.08		-.06		-.20*	-.24*
Relations with Others						
Value for Friendships	.01		.04		.01	
Success at Friendships	.13		-.11		.09	
Affection from Mother	.06		-.04		.13*	
Autonomy from Mother	-.03		-.07		-.02	
Personal Adjustment						
Besetment	-.09		.46*	.44*	-.26*	-.20*
Conscious Self-Esteem	-.02		-.08		.03	.21*
Unconscious Self-Esteem	-.01		-.02		.02	
Well-Being	-.03		-.10		.29*	
Age at Entry	.13	.06	-.16*	-.10	.01	-.05
R^2	.125	.092*	.282*	.242*	.189*	.158*

*p < .05

135

rests, we excluded the eighteen respondents who had spent the entire six months in one or more institutions. We reasoned that the restricted opportunities for delinquent behavior and their negligible chances of arrest would distort the findings. Of course, many other boys spent at least some of the period in an institution; we decided to include them because it is likely that their detention resulted from their illegal behavior. Also, we did not seek answers to questions about interest in school from the fifty-six respondents who had not attended school since leaving the institutions. The others answered these questions in reference to the specific schools they were attending, which was of course not possible for these fifty-six.

The set of measures at intake, taken as a whole, explains 12.6 percent of the variance in later delinquent behavior. The significant predictors were prior delinquent behavior, delinquent values, and standardized achievement.[1]

The delinquent values expressed by the focal students when they arrived at the institution foreshadowed their delinquent values six months after their release, as did a lack of interest in school. Younger boys held more delinquent values after they were released into the community. Intake characteristics accounted for 15.4 percent of the differences in the boys' delinquent values.

Twenty-two percent of the focal students were arrested for felonies within six months of their release, one for as many as eight offenses. How many times the boys were arrested was related significantly to two characteristics measured at intake, the number of felonies already on their records and the degree of their besetment. Only about 7 percent of the variance in arrests was accounted for by intake measures, meaning that a prediction of a boy's post-release recidivism from his intake characteristics, while significantly better than chance, was still not very accurate. One should not expect that boys' personal characteristics would predict very well to their arrests, because getting arrested depends on so many other conditions as well. That the number of arrests on the official records has a moderately high and highly reliable correlation ($r = .31$, $p < .001$) with focal students' reports of their post-release delinquent behavior testifies to the validity of the self-reports of delinquency.

The respondents we found in institutional placements had reported more delinquent values, perceived themselves as less successful at friendships, and felt more beset (anxious and depressed) at the time of the intake interview (see Table 5.4). Taken as a set of variables, intake measures did not predict very well whether or not focal students would be found in secure placement six months after their release. Since reincarceration depends heavily on rearrest, it is not surprising that it is not very predictable from boys' personal characteristics measured over a year before.

Turning now to other indicators of integration into the open community, the only factor at intake that differentiated the youth who were idle from

Table 5.4
Means on Prior Characteristics in Relation to Placement and Work and/or School Status Six Months After Release

Characteristic at Intake	Placed Out of Home?				Working or Attending School?			
	No		Yes		Yes		No	
	$\bar{x}$	(Var)	$\bar{x}$	(Var)	$\bar{x}$	(Var)	$\bar{x}$	(Var)
Delinquent Involvement								
Delinquent Behavior	64.50	(493.00)	67.80	(398.00)	65.50	(500.00)	64.10	(393.00)
Delinquent Values	13.00	(10.00)	14.20*	(10.60)	13.20	(11.00)	13.50	(8.00)
Felony Arrests	3.40	(7.40)	3.70	(6.00)	3.40	(6.61)	3.70	(8.80)
Prior Placements	.60	(.88)	.86	(.78)	.65	(.92)	.67	(.72)
Functioning at School								
Interest in School	7.39	(5.43)	6.80	(4.65)	7.19	(5.05)	7.51	(6.14)
Standardized Achievement	-4.20	(4.92)	-4.00	(5.89)	-4.09	(4.87)	-4.37	(5.88)
Relations With Others								
Value for Friendships	30.80	(25.20)	29.60	(41.30)	30.50	(30.10)	30.80	(24.20)
Success at Friendships	15.58	(4.21)	14.94*	(4.30)	15.30	(4.39)	15.93*	(3.67)
Affection from Mother	27.00	(27.60)	26.70	(42.50)	27.00	(30.20)	26.80	(31.40)
Autonomy from Mother	15.80	(16.60)	15.50	(23.20)	16.00	(17.20)	14.90	(18.80)
Personal Adjustment								
Besetment	39.80	(99.00)	43.50*	(94.60)	40.20	(97.00)	41.80	(109.00)
Conscious Self-Esteem	64.10	(86.00)	64.00	(63.00)	64.30	(70.00)	63.30	(116.00)
Unconscious Self-Esteem	6.90	(9.50)	7.20	(9.30)	7.00	(9.50)	7.00	(9.50)
Well-Being	6.13	(4.53)	6.02	(5.16)	6.18	(4.43)	5.86	(5.31)
Age at Entry	15.94	(.98)	15.79	(.68)	15.81	(.92)	16.20	(.82)

Logistic Regression	χ^2	df	Fraction Explained		χ^2	df	Fraction Explained	
Full Model	24.77	15	.032		23.98	15	.030	
Final Model	8.82	4	.011		16.46*	3	.020	

*p < .05

those who were engaged either in work or in school was perceived success at friendships (see Table 5.4), a finding difficult to interpret. We should note that this measure of idleness is conceptually and empirically distinct from institutional placement, because boys in institutional placement often participated in work or school in those settings.

Boys' interest in school in the open community was less strongly related to their prior characteristics than were their antisocial behavior and values. Interest in school and affection from their mothers measured at intake were significantly correlated with interest in school after leaving the institution.

Personal adjustment. The strongest predictor of post-release besetment was, understandably, the intake measure of besetment, with a correlation of .46 (p < .001). A history of institutional placements, lack of interest in school, and younger age were also associated with greater post-release besetment—a pattern of relationships similar to the earlier findings on adjustment to the institution.

Among the intake variables, earlier well-being and affection from mothers correlated significantly with respondents' reports of their well-being six months after release. Boys' feelings of well-being in the open community were also negatively related to intake measures of their delinquent behavior, scholastic achievement, and besetment.

If the environment from which they had just been removed was critical to determining their personal characteristics at intake, then we should find that the measures taken at that time predicted better to boys' adjustment when they were returned to the open community than to their adjustment at the institution. This would suggest that personality, in the sense of enduring characteristics, has little independent influence, but, like adjustment, is a consequence of setting. In fact, comparisons of Table 5.3 with Tables 4.10 and 4.12 show that measures of personal characteristics taken at intake predicted to institutional adjustment assessed at release as well as they predicted similar measures of adjustment in the community (which was somewhat less well than they had predicted interim adjustment). Two exceptions to this are that intake measures were more strongly related to besetment and well-being six months after release than to the same measures taken at the time of release. The variance explained for besetment rose from 21.9 percent to 28.2 percent, and the variance explained for well-being rose from 8.7 percent to 18.9 percent. In predicting these two outcomes, it appears that the similarity of the settings is more important than proximity in time.

We also measured respondents' adjustment from phone interviews with a parent or other caregiver for 190 of the focal students. This measure is a composite of responses concerning topics such as difficulties in living with the focal student, his delinquent behavior, his self-esteem, and whether he was making constructive use of his time. Attempts to derive more specific indices proved fruitless. Caregivers apparently could provide only global assessments of boys' adjustment. The only prior characteristic significantly related to the caregivers' rating was the number of prior placements: the more his prior placements, the poorer the focal student's post-release adjustment, according to his post-release caregiver. It seems that the caregivers' criteria for adjustment either had been involved in earlier decisions to place boys out of their homes or the criteria bore little relationship to the characteristics of boys when they began their residential treatment. In any case, caregivers' assessments of their wards' post-release adjustment were hardly predictable from what we learned about the boys at intake.

Implications. According to several indicators, the quality of boys' post-release adjustment was partly attributable to their enduring characteristics. Continuity is especially evident in the auto-correlations of variables over time. The most stable characteristics, as indicated by the size of the auto-correlations, are besetment and delinquent values, and we treat these as important facets of personality in analyses to be presented later.

In addition, personal characteristics combine in various ways to predict to how well boys adjust to the open community. Thus, while respondents' feelings of well-being are not themselves so stable over time as their delinquent values, post-release well-being was somewhat better predicted than delinquent values because it was a function of other factors that had some continuity—besetment, relationships with the primary female caregiver, scholastic achievement, and delinquent behavior.

It is notable that the reliable predictors are not simply those that reflect prior delinquent behavior; boys' prior scholastic achievement as well as their delinquent behavior foreshadows both delinquent behavior and feelings of well-being six months after their release. This pattern suggests that treatment should not focus exclusively on antisocial behavior and values. Attention to aspects of adjustment like performance in school not only will directly affect the individual's welfare, but also contribute to better behavior.

That the personal characteristics of delinquent values and besetment, measured some eighteen months before drastic changes occurred in the conditions of their life, predict reliably to a variety of indicators of boys' adjustment demonstrates that some elements of their personalities had already crystallized for these youth before they encountered these circumstances. The treatment program and the focal students' other experiences did not wipe the psychological slate clean. The program did have its own influence on post-release adjustment, but its effects were constrained and shaped by the personalities with which it dealt.

The Relationship of Adjustment at the Institution to Adjustment Six Months After Release

In this section we turn to an issue that is a central concern for juvenile corrections: Do changes in adjustment during residency foretell adjustment after release? The boys in this study were sent to the institutions with the goal of improving their behavior, values, and personal adjustment. During their residency the staff was charged with monitoring their adjustment to maximize the gains they made from the program and to determine when they were ready for release. The decision to release a youth to the open community was based heavily on observations of his institutional adjustment, although factors such as the "normal" length of stay (about a year), costs, and the press of the waiting list also entered into the decision.

Even so, it would not be surprising if the relationship between adjustment in the institution and adjustment in the community were weak. Functioning well in the highly structured confines of an institution is hardly the same as adapting acceptably when facing the broad set of choices available in daily life outside.

We examined the relationship between institutional adjustment and post-release adjustment in several ways. The predictive power of institutional adjustment was assessed with and without taking intake measures of personal characteristics into account. The simple correlations indicate the usefulness of knowledge about institutional adjustment when considered in isolation, as if it were the sole information a decision maker had at his or her disposal. The other approach, by taking into account what the boys were like before their arrival, shifts attention to change during the institutional stay. The question addressed then becomes, does institutional adjustment provide any useful information beyond what we could have known about the focal students at the time of their arrival?

Another distinction to keep in mind is between our measures of institutional adjustment obtained from our interview with the focal students and information from other sources. By definition, decision makers cannot have access to data from confidential interviews. Therefore, we also consider other sources of information that decision makers are more likely to have at their disposal, such as staff ratings and improvement on standardized tests of scholastic achievement. Furthermore, we are interested in such records to determine the degree to which our findings are validated by different methods of data collection.

Measures of institutional adjustment. We obtained measures of the focal students' adjustment during residency from institutional records, from questionnaires administered to members of the participating groups and their staff teams, and from interviews taken with focal students both four months after their arrival at the institutions and at the time of their release. Here we will concentrate on the measures at or near the time of release because they should more completely represent the effect of the institutional experience than would measures taken part way through boys' stay. Indeed, additional analyses (not reported here) show that measures of adjustment taken with the release interview are more strongly related to post-release adjustment than are the interim interview measures. Nevertheless, we included in our analysis two important measures of institutional adjustment that appeared in the interim interview because they were not in the release interview: support for the counterculture and acceptance of the treatment program.

Table 5.5 shows both the simple correlations of adjustment during incarceration with post-release adjustment and the partial correlations controlling for relevant intake measures (age, race, state vs. private affiliation, and any other intake measures with significant beta weights in Table 5.3). These data came from interviews with the focal students. Table 5.6 shows the relationship of adjustment at release to the two categorical measures of post-release adjustment (with the same controls).

We also obtained a number of measures of institutional adjustment from sources other than personal interviews. Three of the non-interview measures of institutional adjustment are familiar in that we have treated them as outcomes at release in Chapter 4. These are release status (e.g., graduated, transferred to another secure institution), length of stay at the institution, and gains on standardized scholastic tests. An additional measure based on institutional records is the number of days truant (runaway) from the institution.

From the group-administered questionnaires we have also obtained several indicators of our respondents' reputations with their fellow group members. These include popularity, influence, leadership, and a general dimension of prosocial behavior or conformity to staff expectations versus antisocial behavior or disobedience (based on a series of eight items). Each of these measures reflects the proportion of other group members who named the focal student in response to questions, "Who in your group . . . " The final non-interview measure of institutional adjustment was a rating by the staff team of the likelihood that the respondent would be free from illegal behavior and trouble with the law.

Data on release status, length of stay, and days truant from the institution were available for all respondents. Standardized tests often were not administered upon departure to boys who left on negative terms (e.g., transfers or runaways), so information on scholastic gains was unavailable for thirty-three of the respondents to the post-release interview. The measures about reputation were obtained from the group questionnaire that fell between two and eight months after a focal student's arrival. For eighteen of the respondents to the post-release interview, these measures were not obtained because of early departure, transfers between groups, or insufficient data (i.e., going unmentioned in any of the peer nominations). Staff ratings of adjustment were a part of the release procedures only at the public institutions, and they were not required for youths who were transferred to other institutions or ran away. Therefore, we had this information for only 152 of the focal students.

Tables 5.7 and 5.8 present the relationships between these non-interview measures of release adjustment and outcomes six months after release, both

Table 5.5
Correlations of Adjustment Six Months After Release with Measures of Adjustment Taken at Release, with and without Controls for Intake Measures

Measures at Release	Measures Six Months After Release					
	Delinquent Behavior		Delinquent Values		Felony Arrests	
	r	β	r	β	r	β
Institutional Adjustment						
Delinquent Behavior	.28*	.27*	.26*	.25*	.01	.00
Delinquent Values	.19*	.10	.42*	.33*	.01	.01
Counterculture[1]	-.18*	.13	.21*	.18*	-.01	-.02
Satisfaction with Institution	-.09	-.10	-.19*	-.20*	.03	.06
Acceptance of Program[1]	-.15*	-.17*	-.16*	-.17*	.04	.03
Interest in School	-.20*	-.19*	-.09	-.06	-.09	-.09
General Adjustment	-.29*	-.25*	-.34*	-.30*	-.03	-.01
Personal Adjustment						
Besetment	.08	.06	.12	.06	.04	-.03
Self-Esteem	-.02	-.04	.02	.03	.03	.05
Well-Being	-.07	-.08	-.14*	-.14*	-.06	-.07
R^2, release adjustment	.123*	.091*	.220*	.135*	.021	.025
R^2, total, release adjustment and intake		.222*		.292*		.080

*p < .05

[1] Measured in the interim interview

	Measure Six Months After Release							
	Interest in School		Caregiver Rating		Besetment		Well-Being	
Measures at Release	r	β	r	β	r	β	r	β
Institutional Adjustment								
Delinquent Behavior	.05	.09	-.11	-.05	.26*	.22*	-.04	-.07
Delinquent Values	-.08	-.06	.01	.05	.16*	.13*	-.05	-.05
Counterculture[1]	-.23*	-.24*	.08	.13	.14*	.08	-.08	-.07
Satisfaction with Institution	.15*	.17*	.10	.11	-.18*	-.18*	.08	.07
Acceptance of Program[1]	.19*	.22*	.03	-.02	.09	.10	.09	.08
Interest in School	.29*	.29*	.03	.01	-.14*	-.12	.19*	.20*
General Adjustment	.17*	.16*	.09	.05	-.27*	-.24*	.14*	.14*
Personal Adjustment								
Besetment	-.03	.02	-.15*	-.07	.50*	.38*	-.16*	-.16*
Self-Esteem	.04	.06	-.04	-.01	-.17*	-.15*	.17*	.02
Well-Being	.17*	.16*	.02	.02	-.08	-.11	.19*	.19*
R^2, release adjustment	.155*	.171*	.061	.049	.282*	.145*	.081*	.056
R^2, total, release adjustment and intake		.214*		.163*		.372*		.199*

*$p < .05$

[1] Measured in the interim interview

143

Table 5.6
Means on Release Adjustment in Relation to Placement and Work and/or School Status Six Months After Release

Measures at Release	Standard Deviation	Placed Out of Home?				Working or Attending School?			
		Means		Adjusted Means		Means		Adjusted Means	
		No	Yes	No	Yes	No	Yes	No	Yes
Institutional Adjustment									
Delinquent Behavior	4.28	13.44	17.15*	13.51	16.58*	14.35	13.54	14.30	13.50
Delinquent Values	2.15	10.05	10.79*	10.14	10.57	10.26	9.98	10.30	10.00
Counterculture[1]	2.99	9.67	10.90*	9.72	10.81*	10.10	9.35	10.07	9.52
Satisfaction with Institution	1.89	13.45	12.94	13.44	12.89	13.25	13.66	13.76	13.89*
Acceptance of Program[1]	2.60	13.01	12.40	13.01	12.22	12.74	13.36	12.70	13.32
Interest in School	1.68	9.97	9.45	10.01	9.52	9.92	9.71	9.99	9.67
General Adjustment	.70	.07	-.37*	.06	-.31*	-.04	.06	-.04	.09
Personal Adjustment									
Besetment	8.28	33.69	37.38*	33.50	37.42*	34.80	33.30	34.60	33.40
Self-Esteem	7.79	68.24	69.75	68.19	69.67	68.60	68.20	68.60	68.00
Well-Being	1.53	8.82	7.81*	8.82	7.82*	8.60	8.68	8.61	8.67
Logistic Regression									
χ^2		37.19*		31.99*		9.68		13.25	
df		9		9		9		9	
Fraction Explained		.051		.044		.012		.017	

*p <.05

Note: Adjusted means control for relevant intake characteristics.

[1] Figure for logistic regression under the adjusted means column represent increases over models including the intake variables.

144

Table 5.7
Correlations of Adjustment Six Months After Release with Non-Interview Measures of Adjustment During Residency

Measure of Adjustment During Incarceration	Measures Six Months After Release					
	Delinquent Behavior		Delinquent Values		Felony Arrests	
	r	ß	r	ß	r	ß
Unfavorable Release Status	.04	-.01	-.12	.06	.08	.08
Length of Stay	.05	.03	.01	-.04	-.07	-.07
Days Truant from Institution	-.11	-.11	-.02	-.01	.05	.09
Academic Growth	-.15*	-.12	-.07	.00	-.17*	-.16*
Popularity	.02	-.03	-.09	-.08	-.09	-.08
Peer Nomination as Influential	.05	.01	-.09	-.08	-.01	.01
Peer Nomination as Leader	-.06	-.06	-.14*	-.08	-.05	-.03
Prosocial Peer Nominations	-.03	-.05	-.06	-.04	-.07	-.05
Staff Rating	-.06	-.10	-.16	-.15	.00	-.01

Note: Partial correlations control for relevant intake measures.

Table 5.7 (continued)

Measure of Adjustment During Incarceration	Measures Six Months After Release							
	Interest in School		Caregiver Rating		Resentment		Well-Being	
	r	β	r	β	r	β	r	β
Unfavorable Release Status	.04	.08	-.19*	-.11	.18*	.15*	-.07	-.11
Length of Stay	-.12	-.08	-.11	.00	.01	-.07	.13*	.15*
Days Truant from Institution	.08	.09	-.02	.02	-.04	-.01	.06	.03
Academic Growth	.02	.04	.07	.06	-.06	-.02	.01	.00
Popularity	-.04	-.06	.12	.09	-.16*	-.09	-.01	.01
Peer Nomination as Influential	-.03	-.05	.03	.01	-.09	.01	-.06	-.09
Peer Nomination as Leader	.01	-.01	.04	-.02	-.15*	-.06	-.06	-.07
Prosocial Peer Nominations	.00	.00	.03	.00	-.12	-.07	-.09	-.10
Staff Rating	-.01	.00	-.06	-.01	.02	.04	-.10	-.10

Note: Partial correlations control for relevant intake measures.

146

Table 5.8
Means on Non-Interview Measures of Adjustment During Incarceration in Relation to Placement Status and Work and/or School Status Six Months After Release

Measures of Adjustment During Incarceration	Standard Deviation	Placed Out of Home?				Working or Attending School?			
		Means		Adjusted Means		Means		Adjusted Means	
		No	Yes	No	Yes	No	Yes	No	Yes
Unfavorable Release Status	.42	1.07	1.45*	1.07	1.44*	1.12	1.15	1.13	1.15
Length of Stay	131.70	390.50	389.30	391.40	385.70	386.80	391.40	403.30	386.20
Days Truant from Institution	15.93	3.48	12.75*	3.50	12.65*	5.61	5.31	5.32	5.40
Academic Growth	1.23	1.29	.92*	1.27	.96*	1.10	1.28	1.06	1.29
Popularity	24.22	27.43	20.13*	27.38	19.34*	26.50	25.75	24.90	26.13
Peer Nomination as Influential	21.42	20.15	16.09	20.01	17.75	21.59	19.56	22.65	18.59
Peer Nomination as Leader	30.46	24.15	16.58	23.53	19.19	24.02	22.28	23.04	22.59
Prosocial Peer Nomination	17.25	53.10	48.14	52.99	49.60	48.91	53.18	48.60	53.28
Staff Rating	1.38	5.49	5.46	5.50	5.39	5.36	5.54	5.31	5.56

147

with and without controls for intake measures. Unlike most of our tables, these do not include indices of the explanatory power of the entire set of predictors. Because the pattern of missing cases varied considerably among the predictors, an analysis based on the entire set would include too few cases to be meaningful.

Antisocial adjustment. Delinquent behavior and delinquent values six months after release (see Table 5.5) and whether boys resided in secure placement at that time (see Table 5.6) were all predicted at better than chance levels by most facets of boys' reports of their institutional adjustment. In addition, absconding from the institution and an unfavorable type of release foreshadowed subsequent secure placement (see Table 5.8). There is a consistent pattern that poorer institutional adjustment was followed by indications of antisocial adjustment in the community, with the exception of arrests for felonies.

Controlling for characteristics assessed at intake made little difference for the correlations between release measures and later indicators of antisocial behavior and values. Although a few of the correlations were reduced below the level of statistical significance, most partial correlations were quite close to the zero-order correlations. The values of chi-squared and "fraction explained" in the findings of the logistic regression model presented in Table 5.6 indicate that the release measures were much more useful for predicting later institutional placement than were intake measures.

When considered without regard to the focal students' characteristics at intake, the set of release measures predicts these three measures of post-release adjustment as well or better than the intake measures do. For post-release delinquent behavior, release measures explained 12.3 percent of the variance, compared to the 12.6 percent explained by the intake measures. Adjustment at release predicted better to delinquent values, accounting for 22.0 percent of the variance compared to 15.4 percent. And, as we have seen, intake measures did not predict reliably at all to boys' reincarceration. Including respondents' personal characteristics in the regression equations shows that almost all of the variance is still explained by adjustment at release. (Note the similarities of R^2 attributable to release adjustment, with and without controlling for measures at intake.)

The figures in Tables 5.5 and 5.6 show that almost all aspects of boys' responses to the institution were implicated in how they adjusted after they left—changes in the level of their misbehavior, delinquent values, interest in school, and so on. It appears that differences in the residents' institutional experience made some difference in whether boys resumed their delinquent careers after they were released, independent from what they were like when they arrived. Indeed, only two indicators of post-release adjustment were not reliably related to the quality of the focal students' adjustment to the institution—the number of times they were arrested during their first six months out and whether they were idle rather than working and/or going to school when we interviewed them.

Interest in school. We have seen that respondents' interest in school after their release was in part continuous with the interest they had shown at intake. Table 5.5 shows that changes in interest during residency contributed further to interest among those going to school six months after their release. Scholastic performance during residency also predicted to these respondents' post-release adjustment. The gains they made in standard achievement test scores are relevant to several aspects of their post-release adjustment, specifically those reflecting delinquent behavior (see Table 5.7). Greater scholastic gains predicted less self-reported delinquent behavior, fewer felony arrests, and less likelihood of further institutional placement. This gives clear support for the value of strong school programs as an element of institutional programs.

Personal adjustment. Besetment and well-being were also foreshadowed at release. Not surprisingly, they were more closely related to the same facets of post-release adjustment than they were to others. In addition, general adjustment to the institution and changes in interest in school predicted post-release well-being; and many measures of institutional adjustment, including an other-than-normal "graduation" upon release, predicted the level of boys' post-release besetment. Controlling for intake measures did little to reduce the strength of these relationships.

While these relationships seem plausible and meaningful, one other is less easily interpreted (and perhaps due to mere chance). Well-being six months after release was greater for youths who had stayed longer at the institution (did their extended residency make them appreciate their freedom more? had they had more ample treatment?).

It appears that besetment is more consistent across settings than well-being is. Post-release besetment is as well-correlated with besetment measured just after boys had been removed from the open community as it is when measured after as many as fifteen months of institutionalization. Post-release well-being, on the other hand, is more highly correlated with well-being measured at intake than it is with the same, more proximal measure taken at release. (Compare Table 5.3 with Table 5.5). Furthermore, the whole set of characteristics describing the focal students as they entered the institution accounts for as much variance in post-release besetment as release (28.2 percent variance explained in both cases). Characteristics at intake, in contrast, were more predictive of post-release well-being than they were of well-being at release (19.9 percent versus 8.1 percent). These are the kind of findings that lead us to consider besetment more a trait of personality than well-being, which is more a reaction to the situation.

The last indicator of the focal students' post-release adjustment that we consider is the overall assessments made by their primary caregivers when we interviewed the boys six months after their release. (See Tables 5.5 and 5.7) Caregivers found their wards adjusting better to the open community if the boys had been less beset at their release and if they had behaved themselves better in their last few months of residency. Those boys who had been released in an unfavorable status were later rated as adjusting more poorly than those who had graduated normally.

Interview versus non-interview measures of post-release adjustment. It is notable that the three least well-predicted indicators of post-release adjustment are all more independent of respondents' reports of their adjustment than are the other indicators. Institutional adjustment bore little relationship to later felony arrests, the boys' involvement in school or work, and their caregivers' ratings of their adjustment. Of the sixty possible correlations and partial correlations of release adjustment to these post-release measures, only three reach the nominal .05 level of statistical significance. Given that we could expect three by chance alone, these correlations probably should not be treated as meaningful.

Perhaps our measures of these outcomes are weak. Six months may simply be too short a period for a meaningful assessment of arrests. The average number of arrests during this period was only .3, and the chance aspects of detection and of actions by the justice system are likely to contribute a large random component to the small variation observed over this period. Even so, the measure of arrests appears to be valid, because it correlates significantly with many of the other measures of post-release adjustment. The failure of the measure of involvement in school or work is likely to be the transience of these roles for many of our respondents. These youths frequently switched jobs and went to school off and on. It is likely that a large share of the 24 percent of our respondents who were idle at the time of the interview would not have been a month before or a month after.

Still, we should consider the possibility that our findings are heavily determined by response biases, that they mostly reflect whatever image of themselves respondents want to present to interviewers and to the world in general. We find evidence against this conclusion in that a fourth independent indicator, whether or not boys were again in secure placement six months after their release, was foreshadowed by several of boys' reports of their institutional adjustment in the interim and release interviews. This exception suggests that the interview measures have a reality beyond the boys' responses to an interview. The data from the interviews can succeed in predicting later institutional placement only if they measure aspects of the respondents' subsequent functioning that are observable to others and that thereby lead to a secure placement.

Interview versus non-interview measures of institutional adjustment. Another approach to assessing the validity of our findings and weighing the influence of response bias is to compare the predictive power of measures of institutional adjustment. Were respondents' reports at the time of their release more or less predictive than independent measures of how well respondents' adjusted afterward?

One independent measure is the number of days boys were truant during their residency, although this is not necessarily a gauge of their ultimate adjustment at release. It proved predictive only of an independent measure of post-release adjustment, whether or not a focal student wound up in secure placement, and not of any of the students' own reports of their adjustment. (See Tables 5.7 and 5.8.)

The length of boys' residency and the nature of their release reflect the institutions' assessments of boys' adjustment, although not purely. In some cases, the referring juvenile court decided the release date and thereby occasioned an administrative release. These two indicators did not predict very well to post-release adjustment as the boys reported it. Only besetment after release was greater among youths with unfavorable release status, and only their reports of well-being were predicted at a better than chance level by the length of their stay (see Table 5.7). An unfavorable release status is significantly related to two independent indicators of post-release adjustment, the parent rating (see Table 5.7) and secure placement (see Table 5.8).

We might expect that measures of focal students' reputations with their peers would be especially useful for predicting their adjustment. Their fellow group members observed their behavior every day and should have been able to report accurately whose adjustments were more and less problematic. We found that a more prosocial reputation (e.g., not lying to staff, really wanting to go straight, and caring about others) correlated with focal students' own reports of their adjustment. Prosocial reputations also appeared at first to predict to post-release adjustment: subsequently more beset youth had been less popular and less likely to be seen as leaders, and youths nominated as leaders came to have less delinquent values (see Table 5.7). Controlling for intake characteristics eliminates these relationships, however. So it appears that peer ratings predicted to focal students' later adjustment because peers were sensitive to their more enduring characteristics rather than to changes at the institution.

The predictive value of staff ratings at release is of special interest because this rating is most closely tied to actual decisions about release and is supposed to estimate future prospects. These staff members had been responsible for the respondents for an average of a full year, and they had at their disposal an enormous wealth of information from daily observations, discussions with coworkers, reports from school, and so on. It is therefore quite telling that these reports were essentially unrelated to post-release adjustment, whether that adjustment was reported by the boys themselves, by their caregivers, or assessed by boys' records (see Tables 5.7 and 5.8).

The gains that focal students made in scholastic skills were measured by standardized achievement tests given early and late in their residency. These scores can be assumed to be free of any response bias from the interviews. They proved predictive of students' antisocial orientation in the community as measured both by the students' own reports and by independent measures: Boys who made greater gains later reported less delinquent behavior and values (see Table 5.7), they were arrested less frequently (see Table 5.7), and fewer of them were found in secure placement six months later (see Table 5.8).

A survey of the findings reported in Tables 5.5 through 5.8 reveals many instances of statistically significant relationships across time periods and sources of data. Respondents' pre-release reports of their delinquent behavior and values, subscription to a peer group counterculture, besetment, and satisfaction with their institutional experience were variously predictive of these independent measures of post-release adjustment (their subsequent secure placement, idleness, and caregivers' ratings of their adjustment). Independent measures of boys' institutional adjustment—the duration of their institutionalization, the type of their release to the community, their reputation in their group, and their gain scores on scholastic achievement tests predicted significantly to their subsequent reports of delinquent behavior and values, besetment, and well-being. There seems to be ample evidence here that the findings regarding the effects of institutional adjustment on adjustment after release are not due merely to response bias.

Summary. The various post-release outcomes were not predicted equally well by the set of variables relating to institutional adjustment. Changes in psychological characteristics while they were in the treatment program predicted best to focal students' interest in school out in the community, accounting for 17 percent of the differences among the respondents (see Table 5.5). Almost as much variance, 14 percent, was accounted for in delinquent values and besetment. And change during residency accounted for 9 percent of the variation in respondents' post-release delinquent behavior.

The most powerful predictor of post-release adjustment among our measures of institutional adjustment is boys' reports of their delinquent behavior in the few months prior to their release. It predicted at significantly better than chance to subsequent delinquent behavior and values, besetment, and whether boys would be found in secure placement. Other relatively powerful predictors included boys' satisfaction with the institutional experience, delinquent values, and interest in school. These data suggest the kinds of changes a residential program should aim to effect in order to achieve more lasting rehabilitation.

Our findings attest to the difficulty of predicting post-release outcomes. Even the people most familiar with the focal students, their staff teams and fellow group members, provided little information that was useful. The most valuable information came from personal interviews.

To summarize: Over and above the stability of their personal characteristics, certain changes over the course of the focal students' institutionalization were predictive of their adjustment in the community six months later. The degree to which they behaved during those six months is indicated by whether or not they were returned to a secure institution, the number of times they were arrested, and their own reports of their delinquent behavior and delinquent values. A weakened commitment to delinquent values by the time they were released, gains in scholastic test scores, a greater interest in school, and less anxiety and depression were prognostic of better adjustment according to these indicators. The degree to which respondents out in the community felt better psychologically was indicated by their reports of well-being and their besetment. These were foreshadowed at release by better behavior in the months just prior to their release, reduction in besetment, and, again, improvement in scholastic test scores and a greater interest in schooling.

Thus, it appears that certain changes during their institutionalization facilitated boys' positive adjustment to the open community. The boys did not have to adjust to the same communities, however, and the differences in the conditions they encountered out there undoubtedly also affected their adjustment. In the next section we report these findings.

Experiences in the Community that Influenced Adjustment

The environments to which the focal students were released varied widely in many respects. Many of the staff members of institutions for delinquents believe that what they might be able to accomplish with youth at the institution is quickly negated by poor conditions in the communities to which boys return. These conditions include the destitution, crime, and disorganization of the neighborhoods; the poverty and disorganization of the boys' families; the poor quality of their schools; the lack of decent jobs; and the antisocial influence of the peer groups that they rejoin when they return home. We attempted to assess some of these characteristics of the communities to which the focal students were released in order to discover how much they determined the quality of focal students' adjustment. Additionally, and more important to the larger purpose of this study, we analyzed the degree to which community characteristics may have mediated between change at the institution and later adjustment. We inquired of our data whether what focal students took away with them from the treatment program by way of diminished delinquent values, greater scholastic ability, less besetment, and so on affected their later adjustment because they facilitated positive experiences in the community.

The measures we took of the communities and the respondents' reactions to them are listed in the leftmost columns of Table 5.9 and 5.10.[2] The *areal* measures are demographic indicators of environmental conditions in the census tracts where they resided during all or most of the six months after

Table 5.9
Correlations of Community Variables with Adjustment Six Months After Release

Community Conditions	Measures of Adjustment						
	Delinquent Behavior	Delinquent Values	Felony Arrests	Interest in School	Caregiver Rating	Besetment	Well-Being
Areal							
SES	.00	.01	-.05	.01	-.02	-.03	.03
Crowding	-.08	-.02	-.04	.06	-.11	-.04	.06
Transiency	.01	.07	.05	-.01	-.02	.12	-.01
% White	-.14*	-.04	-.07	.02	-.06	-.15*	.09
R²	.019	.006	.012	.005	.015	.028	.010
Family							
SES	.00	-.19*	.07	-.02	-.05	-.05	.18*
Number of Places Lived	.38*	.09	.38*	.19*	-.06	.14*	-.32*
Affection, Male	-.17	-.09	.12	.08	.26*	.03	.31*
Affection, Female	-.21*	-.07	.03	.17*	.18*	-.25*	.29*
Satisfaction, Male	-.19*	-.13	-.03	.24*	.33*	-.02	.42*
Satisfaction, Female	-.35*	-.18*	-.18*	.19*	.29*	-.31*	.39*
R²	.206*	.072*	.180*	.065	.101*	.099*	.219*
Peers							
Delinquent Behav., Peers	.54*	.32*	.16*	-.23*	-.05	.20*	-.12
Delinquent Values, Peers	.30*	.60*	.24*	.05	-.01	.11	-.01
Satisfaction with Friendships	-.13*	-.18*	-.14*	.16*	-.01	-.19*	.20*
Time Spent "Hanging Out"	.03	.01	.00	-.07	-.09	-.16*	.00
R²	.267*	.317*	.073*	.083*	.009	.071*	.054*

School							
Grade Point Average	-.02	.05	.03	.35*	.09	.11	.05
Attendance	-.16*	-.05	-.16*	.24*	.03	-.18*	.24*
Relationship with Teacher	-.01	-.17*	.03	.34*	.03	.01	.18*
Satisfaction with Teacher	-.16*	-.19*	-.04	.38*	.10	-.01	.19*
Satisfaction with Other Students	-.16*	-.12	-.17*	.32*	.03	-.11	.18*
Confidence as a Student	-.01	-.16*	.02	.13*	-.01	-.07	.01
R^2	.051	.063*	.061	.288*	.015	.059*	.076*
Employment							
Satisfaction with Job	-.12	.06	.11	.15	.08	-.10	.11
Importance of Job	-.06	-.19*	-.13	.14	-.03	.00	-.03
R^2	.014	.037*	.032	.034	.007	.008	.011
Institutional Ties							
Satisfaction with Inst.	-.19*	-.20*	.01	.15*	.21*	-.13*	.23*
Contact with Staff	-.06	.01	.10	.10	-.18*	-.01	-.04
Contact with Group	-.08	-.16*	.03	-.03	.12	.11	-.01
R^2	.042*	.062*	.010	.039	.093*	.024*	.047*
Reference Groups							
Adult Approval	-.23*	-.18*	-.04	.30*	.12	-.07	.22*
Adult Tolerance of Delinquency	.10	.14*	-.05	-.05	-.03	.05	-.08
Peer Approval	.03	-.07	-.02	.03	-.08	-.06	-.08
Peer Tolerance of Delinquency	.34*	.34*	.14*	-.18*	-.01	.17*	-.11
Stigma\Exclusion	.22*	.17*	.10	-.07	-.13	.25*	-.17*
R^2	.157*	.118*	.032	.110*	.035	.058*	.073*
Overall R^2 Increase	.500*	.430*	.324*	.435*	.252*	.246*	.336*
R^2 Total	.641*	.577*	.366*	.468*	.363*	.479*	.483*

*p < .05

155

Table 5.10
Means on Community Variables in Relation to Secure Placements and Work/School Status Six Months After Release

	Standard Deviation	In Secure Placement? Adjusted Means		Working and/or Attending School Adjusted Means	
		No	Yes	No	Yes
<u>Areal</u>					
SES	2.55	10.33	9.03*	9.92	10.23
Crowding	.17	1.04	1.08	1.05	1.03
Transiency	11.90	47.77	50.11	48.16	48.07
% White	37.66	59.69	58.14	58.77	59.71
χ^2		8.510* (4df)		1.616 (4df)	
Fraction Explained		.013		.002	
<u>Family</u>					
SES	20.97	32.82	24.80*	32.77	30.93
Number of places lived	1.24	1.17	2.88*	2.66*	1.79
Affection, male	6.01	24.26	24.50	23.78	24.43
Affection, female	5.41	25.90	24.88	25.19	25.91
Satisfaction, male	.82	3.12	3.13	3.03	3.14
Satisfaction, female	.76	3.31	3.22	3.09*	3.36
χ^2		47.410* (6df)		28.188* (6df)	
Fraction Explained		.060		.035	
<u>Peers</u>					
Delinquent behavior	25.14	41.95	60.46*	44.33	46.02
Delinquent values	3.76	12.92	15.67*	13.35	13.50
Satisfaction with friendships	.76	3.27	3.02*	3.12	3.25
Time spent hanging out	1.13	3.37	3.31	3.69*	3.25
χ^2		32.540* (4df)		8.613 (4df)	
Fraction Explained		.041		.010	
<u>School</u>					
Grade point average	.77	2.41	2.72*	2.57	2.47
Attendance	.67	2.50	2.36	2.39	2.48
Relationship with teachers	4.18	21.47	21.47	20.98	21.54
Satisfaction with teachers	.84	3.11	3.26	2.91	3.17
Satisfaction with students	.75	3.27	3.08	3.09	3.25
Confidence as student	.43	3.73	3.81	3.71	3.75
χ^2		14.825* (6df)		4.067 (6df)	
Fraction Explained		.023		.007	

Table 5.10 (*continued*)

	Standard Deviation	In Secure Placement? Adjusted Means		Working and/or Attending School Adjusted Means	
		No	Yes	No	Yes
Employment					
Satisfaction with job	.97	2.84	3.00	2.57*	2.96
Importance of job	.86	4.30	4.22	4.21	4.31
x^2		.801 (2df)		4.151 (2df)	
Fraction Explained		.002		.007	
Institutional Ties					
Satisfaction with Institution	2.30	12.54	11.70*	12.66	12.28
Contact with staff	1.88	2.23	2.58	2.59	2.21
Contact with group	1.76	2.06	2.01	1.95	2.08
x^2		6.550 (3df)		3.473 (3df)	
Fraction Explained		.008		.004	
Reference Groups					
Adult approval	1.63	10.82	10.45	10.78	10.73
Adult tolerance of delinquency	1.04	5.39	5.38	5.47	5.36
Peer approval	1.86	10.26	10.25	10.35	10.22
Peer tolerance of delinquency	3.47	11.05	12.36*	11.29	11.32
Stigma/Exclusion	.65	2.08	2.29*	2.19	2.10
x^2		10.577 (5df)		1.632 (5df)	
Fraction Explained		.013		.002	
x^2		170.350* (36df)		78.390* (36df)	
Total Increased		.252		.103	

*$p < .05$

their release. These include the average income of the households (SES), the average number of people per bedroom (crowding), the transiency of the population there (the proportion who had moved into the census tract by 1975), and the ethnic composition of the tract expressed as the proportion of the population that was white. These indicators have been prominent in social ecological studies of crime and delinquency; they have often been found significantly related to the proportion of the juvenile population that has been arrested and the proportion that are institutionalized.

In these data, however, almost none of these social ecological conditions are reliably related to any of our measures of adjustment after release. The only characteristic of the neighborhood to which focal students were released that relates reliably to any facet of post-release adjustment is the proportion of the population that is white: The larger the proportion, the less delinquent behavior and besetment the respondents reported. This was true regardless of the race of the boys. Apparently, residing after release in an area that was more heavily populated by people of color was conducive to more delinquent behavior and to more anxiety and depression.

The next set of measures of the community assesses characteristics of the *families* to which the focal students were released and their feelings about them. SES here measures the socioeconomic status of the primary bread-winner's occupation, a combination of the average, age-adjusted income and the average educational attainment of Americans who hold that kind of job. Also in this set are four measures of boys' feelings about their male and female caregivers, and a count of the number of places at which they lived for more than a week during the six months after their release. These familial variables, literally closer to home than characteristics of their neigh-borhoods, did account for significant portions of the differences in almost every measure of post-release adjustment.

Half of the focal students changed placements in the six months after their release, 28 percent more than once. The more times they changed placements during these six months, the more delinquency they reported and the more often they were arrested for felonies. It is not clear, however, what the cause–effect relationship is between the number of placements on the one hand and delinquent behavior and arrests on the other. These sig-nificant correlations can be interpreted as the negative effect of discontinuity in post-release care: the less stable a boy's placement, the worse his behavior. It is also plausible that delinquent behavior and consequent arrests occa-sioned more changes in placement. A greater number of placements also was associated with less interest in school, more besetment, and lower well-being.

Most notably, boys' relationships with their caregivers, most of these the respondents' parents, made a significant difference in the respondents' ad-justment in the community. Of the 217 respondents who lived with a female caregiver, 89 percent said that they were "pretty satisfied" or "very satis-fied" with their relationship; 82 percent of the 148 respondents living with a male caregiver felt the same way. Good relationships with caregivers enhanced the focal students' feelings of well-being and their interest in school, and they reduced the focal students' feelings of besetment. Positive feelings about their caregivers also diminished youths' delinquent behavior and values.

The higher the socioeconomic status of caregivers, the less respondents expressed delinquent values and the greater their well-being.

There is evidence in Table 5.9 that caregivers tended to be sensitive to the quality of their relationships with the boys. Their ratings of boys' adjustment correlate positively and reliably with boys' affection for and satisfaction with their caregivers.

Variables concerning our respondents' peer companions in the commu-nity also relate to their adjustment, although, again, cause–effect relation-ships are not clear. We discovered in our investigation of friendships in the institution that boys' reports of their friends' delinquent behavior and values were to some degree projections of their own. We found that in the community, focal students' reports of their friends' delinquent behavior and values are similarly related to their own. Projection was undoubtedly going on here as well, but we did not have the independent data from the friends necessary to separate projection from influence. This might also be the reason that the perceived delinquent behavior of their friends in the community seems to have had a negative effect on focal students' interest in school and increased their besetment; that is, interest in school and besetment may actually be related to focal students' own delinquent behavior. Similarly, the fifty-one respondents we found reincarcerated after six months reported more delinquency in their friends' behavior and values than did the respondents in the open community (see Table 5.10).

We found that 154 (62 percent) of the focal students were going to school when we interviewed them six months after their release. The data in Table 5.9 show that boys who attended school reported significantly less delinquent behavior, less besetment, and significantly greater well-being, and they were arrested less often. Satisfaction with their teachers was related to less delinquent behavior and less commitment to delinquent values. These youths tended also to eschew delinquent values if they expressed greater confidence in themselves as students. Their interest in school, not surprisingly, was related to the whole set of attitudes toward their teachers and classmates, to their attendance, and to their grade point average.

The data on how focal students were faring in school after their release includes a surprising finding: The respondents in secure placement had earned significantly higher grade point average in recent months than those we found going to school in the community. We suspect that the reason for this is that the schools in the closed institutions had their students on individualized programs that were tailored more closely to the youth's scholastic skills. Thus, these focal students earned better grades there than did those who, in conventional schools, had to compete for grades against their classmates and norms for their age.

Forty-nine percent of the focal students were employed and another 16 percent were actively looking for jobs when we first spoke with them after their release. Naturally, those currently employed expressed more satisfaction with their jobs than the respondents who had lost or quit their jobs (see Table 5.10). The more importance boys assigned to having a job, the less they cleaved to delinquent values. Otherwise, conditions of employment bore no reliable relationships to facets of their adjustment.

We asked the respondents to think back about the institution from which they had been released six months before. As we reported above, most of them were positive about that experience. The more satisfaction with the institution that focal students reported in retrospect, the better their post-release adjustment on several counts—the greater their satisfaction, the less delinquent behavior boys reported, and the less they subscribed to delinquent values. They also showed more interest in school and less besetment, and they felt greater well-being. Apparently these positive signs were not merely a rosy picture that some respondents painted for our interviewers; their primary caregivers tended also to rate their ward's adjustment better if he had reported greater satisfaction with his institutional experience. Furthermore, focal students whom we found in the open community six months after their release (rather than in secure placement) tended to look back more favorably on their residency.

Do these relationships indicate that leaving the institution with more positive feelings about the experience helped these adolescents to adjust better to the open community? Or did better adjustment persuade these youths in retrospect that the experience must have been a good one? We have already seen that boys who had said at their release that they were more satisfied with the institution later showed signs of better adjustment. Close analysis of the data (employing the LISREL technique of Joreskog & Sorbom, 1983) indicated that the enduring satisfaction that respondents felt upon their release, rather than any retrospective changes in their feelings, was related to their adjustment.

Two-thirds of the focal students had some contact with members of their staff team sometime during the six months and almost three-quarters had had some contact with members of their group. Caregivers apparently regarded their wards' continued contact with people at the institution with mixed feelings. On the one hand, they rated boys' adjustment as worse the more frequent contact boys had with staff members; but on the other hand, the more contact boys had with former group members, the better their adjustment appeared to their caregivers (though not to a statistically significant degree). Perhaps the caregivers felt that contact with staff occurred because of continuing problems, while contact with other youths was of no special significance. The data suggest that caregivers were in this respect misled, because boys' continued contact with their former groupmates was reliably associated with more delinquent values.

We investigated whether choices of reference groups in the open community related to adjustment there. We asked respondents to what degree "it was important" that their caregivers, their teachers (if they were going to school), the staff at the institution, and their friends "approved of what you do" and several other questions to this effect. We found that responses concerning all three of the kinds of adults clustered, but they were unrelated to the importance of friends' approval. So we built separate indexes for the degree of adult and peer reference. (The Cronbach alpha index of internal reliability for the adult scale = .75 and the peer scale = .65.)

We also asked focal students about how much these adults and peers would tolerate a variety of delinquent behaviors such as substance abuse, fighting, and stealing. Here, too, youths' beliefs about adult tolerance clustered and were independent of their judgments of peers' tolerance. So we created separate indexes of adult and peer tolerance for delinquent behavior. (Adult alpha = .79, peer = .84.)

Whether respondents looked to adults or peers as reference groups made a difference in their adjustment to the community. The more boys said they wanted adult approval, the less delinquent behavior they reported and the less they subscribed to delinquent values. They also expressed more interest in school and greater well-being. Conversely, focal students who thought their friends were more tolerant of delinquent behavior reported that they engaged in more delinquency themselves, demonstrated more admiration for others who engaged in delinquent behavior (our measure of delinquent values), showed less interest in school, and were more beset. We found significantly more of these youths in secure placement.

We asked the focal students several questions designed to get at the degree to which they felt that their institutionalization had stigmatized them. We asked if they believed that their caregivers, teachers, employers, and peers thought of them as "juvenile delinquents" and how strongly they preferred that these people did not know they had been institutionalized (alpha for the index of stigma = .69). By and large, they did not report feeling much stigma. Nevertheless, our composite index of these items related significantly and positively to delinquent behavior and values and to feelings of besetment. In addition, the more stigma they felt, the poorer their feelings of well-being. Boys who were returned to secure placement felt more stigmatized.

The "Overall R^2 increase" figures in Tables 5.9 and 5.10 reflect how much of the differences in boys' adjustment to the community our measures of conditions in the community account for, after controlling for their characteristics at intake. (The "R^2 total" figure includes the variation accounted for by intake characteristics as well.) For example, community conditions accounted for 50 percent of the differences in the amount of delinquent behavior reported by the focal students and 43 percent of the differences in delinquent values among them. "Accounting for" does not necessarily imply "caused by," however, so some interpretation of these figures is in order.

Substantial proportions of the differences among the respondents' self-reported delinquent behavior and values are accounted for by their reports of their friends' delinquent behavior and values. As we have noted already, projection as well as causation may be operating here. Respondents may appear similar to their friends partly because they are influenced by the friends and partly because they imagine that their friends were as delinquency-prone as they themselves were. Another consideration before interpreting these relationships as evidence for the influence of peers is that boys who were prone to be more delinquent after their release might have chosen to hang around with peers similarly delinquency-prone.

Perhaps more reflective of causal factors are the statistical relationships between these youths' feelings about the adults in their lives. The respondents' delinquent behavior was lower if they said that they had good relationships with their female caregivers and if they wanted adults rather than peers to approve of their behavior. Similarly, the 34 percent of the variance in reported feelings of well-being is accounted for substantially by their reported relationships with adults. The focal students' besetment was also diminished to the degree that they reported good relationships with their female caregivers. Thus, it appears that coming under the care of adults with whom the boys developed good relationships had positive consequences in terms of their behavior, values, and emotional state.

Community conditions accounted for 44 percent of the differences in the amount of interest in school expressed by the respondents. It is not surprising that conditions in school particularly contributed most to these differences. What is notable, however, is that again social relationships in the school setting seem to have been important. Relationships with teachers and with other students accounted for a substantial share of the variance, as did the focal students' scholastic success as reflected in their grade point average. Furthermore, relationships with adults outside the school setting also seemed to affect interest in school. Youths who expressed more interest tended also to report better relationships with adult caregivers.

The community conditions that were measured accounted for only 25 percent of the variation the respondents' besetment, one of the smallest amounts of variation attributable to these community conditions. Compare this, for example, to the differences community conditions seemed to have made in the youths' feelings of well-being, where 34 percent of the variance was accounted for. This finding reinforces our belief that feelings of well-being were more responsive to their current situation than their feelings of anxiety and depression were. Besetment appears to be a more stable characteristic, a component of personality.

What effects community conditions did have on this less malleable characteristic were found both at home and with peers. Good relationships with their female caregivers and peers seem to have ameliorated boys' feelings of besetment.

Measured community conditions accounted for less of the differences among respondents in the facets of their adjustment that were assessed by means other than their own reports. Twenty-five percent of the variance in their caregivers' ratings of their adjustment were accounted for, 32 percent for the number of their arrests for felonies, 25 percent for whether they were back in secure placement, and 10 percent for whether they had a job and/or were going to school. These findings may be partly due to "response bias," that is, a tendency for boys to present a consistently good or poor report of their adjustment throughout their interview. We believe that it is more likely that the findings are due to the greater validity of the respon-

dents' reports. We consider focal students' reports of their delinquent behavior and values to be more accurate gauges of their delinquency-proneness
than their arrest records, and we consider their reports of their well-being,
besetment, and interest in school to be more accurate reflections of their
psychological state than their caregivers' ratings.

Most prominent in these findings on how conditions there affected boys'
adjustment to the community after their release is the effects of adult reference groups. Boys behaved better and felt better about themselves if they
engaged in good relationships with their caregivers and other adults. Recall,
for example, that our respondents' post-release interest in school was relatively poorly predicted by their adjustment to the institution. Here we
have found that relationships with their teachers at the community school
(and with the other students) was a significant determinant of their interest.
If boys chose peer reference groups instead, especially peers who, they
believed, were tolerant of delinquent behavior, then their adjustment to the
community was worse.

Do Community Conditions Mediate the Impact of Institutional Effects?

We have found that certain aspects of the focal students' institutional
adjustment, as measured at the time of their release, relate significantly to
their adjustment six months later. Further, we have seen that certain conditions under which they lived during that six months also related to their
adjustment. We turn now to the question of whether those community
conditions mediate the relationship between institutional adjustment and
community adjustment. We are interested in whether their institutional
experiences helped boys to establish the kinds of social relationships after
their release that contributed to their prosocial adjustment.

In order for such a mediating process to have occurred, a certain chain
of events must have taken place, whereby a respondent's social relationships
in the community related on the one side to his institutional adjustment
and on the other side to his adjustment to the community. This would
suggest that institutional adjustment had some effect on the community
variable and that it, in turn, had some effect on boys' adjustment. Furthermore, the two ends of the chain must have been joined in the sense that
there is a highly probable (statistically reliable) relationship between a boy's
institutional adjustment and his adjustment in the community. Thus, we
narrowed this inquiry to those facets of institutional adjustment, post-release
conditions, and post-release adjustment that might plausibly comprise such
a chain of events, as indicated by results presented in the earlier portions
of this chapter.

Five facets of institutional adjustment are reliably related to parallel measures of boys' adjustment six months after their release. These are: (1) boys'

delinquent behavior in the months just prior to their release, (2) their delinquent values, (3) feelings of well-being, (4) interest in school, and (5) besetment. This is the evidence for the durability of the change that occurred during the focal students' institutional stays.

These five facets are also reliably related to satisfaction with the institution six months after departure. We do not consider this an indicator of post-release adjustment, however; it is instead a retrospective view of their previous experience.

In addition to these five facets of adjustment to the community, another critical one is also related to several of the same indicators of adjustment to the institution at boys' release, namely, whether boys were once again in secure placement six months later. Our analysis of this relationship focused only on those boys who were released to the open community, excluding those who spent the entire six months in another institution.

Given these indicators of adjustment at the institution and in the community, what social conditions in the community could have mediated their relationships? We judged that nine community conditions might be mediators because of their relatively strong and consistent relationships to the six indices of boys' post-release adjustment. Though we did not use post-release satisfaction with the institution as a measure of adjustment, we did inquire as to whether their feelings about their experience in retrospect mediated their adjustment to the community. As we will show below, we found that they did not.

We begin our analysis with the first link in the chain. Table 5.11 examines which of the nine social conditions in the community are related to adjustment *at release*. Five of the nine met that criterion for belonging to a causal chain. They are (1) boys' satisfaction with their peer friendships, (2) their assessments of their friends' delinquency, (3) their estimates of their friends' tolerance for delinquent behavior, (4) the degree to which they valued their caregivers' approval, and (5) their retrospective satisfaction with the institution. Note that four of these five community variables indicate something about the nature of boys' reference groups. Together they reflect both the opportunities that the community environment afforded the focal students for associating with prosocial others and the choices the focal students made among these opportunities.

We should point out that these formerly incarcerated delinquents tended to be *less* satisfied with their friends the more they thought that their friends were delinquent ($r = -.06$, $p = .32$) and the more they thought their friends tolerated delinquent behavior ($r = -.17$, $p = .01$). These findings suggest that the respondents who chose or found themselves among more delinquent companions were uneasy about that. They do not seem to have submersed themselves happily into a delinquent subculture after their release. Recall a similar situation during the focal students' residency: the less

Table 5.11
Correlations of Adjustment at Release with Potential Mediators of Adjustment at Six Months,
Controlling for Intake Measures

Potential Mediators

Measures at Release	Satisfaction With Female	School Attendance	Satisfaction With Teachers	Satisfaction With Institution	Desire for Adult Approval
Delinquent Behavior	.03	.01	.06	-.18*	.03
Delinquent Values	.04	.01	-.14	-.11	-.10
Institutional Satisfaction	.13	.06	.11	.45*	.24*
Interest in School	.10	.01	.06	.25*	.11
Besetment	-.09	-.18*	-.07	-.18*	-.11
Well-Being	.08	.04	.03	.13	.08
R^2 Increase	.027	.030	.029	.183*	.064*
R^2 Total	.094	.153*	.128	.314*	.162*

*$p < .05$

Table 5.11 (*continued*)

Potential Mediators

Measures at Release	Delinquent Behavior of Friends	Satisfaction With Friends	Friends' Tolerance for Delinquency	Stigma
Delinquent Behavior	.38*	-.01	.29	.13*
Delinquent Values	.10	-.11	.11	.07
Institutional Satisfaction	-.21*	.06	-.10	-.19*
Interest in School	-.23*	.20*	-.08	-.05
Besetment	.13	.05	.05	.12
Well-Being	-.25*	.16*	-.16*	-.06
R^2 Increase	.175*	.074*	.094*	.045
R^2 Total	.287*	.156*	.152*	.120

*$p < .05$

delinquent they thought their group was, the more attractive it was to them.

Although respondents who rated their satisfaction with the institution higher six months after their release adjusted better to the community than those who were not so satisfied, other evidence indicates that this factor does not qualify as a mediator. (The relevant findings are presented in tables appearing later in this chapter.) The relationship of retrospective satisfaction to post-release adjustment can be explained as simply a continuation of boys' feelings when they were released. In fact, post-release adjustment was more closely associated with satisfaction assessed at release than at the time of the post-release interview. Boys who were happier about their institutionalization when it ended adjusted better later. Whatever changes in these feelings occurred during the next six months did not in themselves affect boys' adjustment.

Many community conditions that plausibly could have mediated the effects of institutional adjustment on successful adjustment after release did not seem to. Among these are how satisfied focal students were with their female caregivers, how well they adjusted to school, and how stigmatized they felt. These conditions did have some effect on boys' adjustment to the community, as we have seen, but they themselves did not seem to be shaped by boys' institutional experiences. Thus, they did not mediate the effect of these experiences on the respondents' integration into their communities. We did not include the number of different placements a youth had in the six months after his release as a community variable in the forementioned analyses because there is good reason to suspect that placements are often changed in response to poor adjustment. Other analyses indicated, however, that the stability of the post-release placement was unrelated to measures of focal students' adjustment at the time of release, so this factor would not have qualified as a mediator in any case.

A comment about our research strategy for mediating community factors before presenting the findings: A condition in the community cannot reasonably be considered as a mediator between institutional and post-release adjustment until another interpretation of the data is ruled out. It is possible that stable features of respondents' personalities were responsible for an only apparently mediating process. For example, the kind of boy who adjusted well to the institution and was responsive to its program might also have responded well to conditions that he found in the community to which he was released. Thus, in the course of this inquiry, we controlled on those aspects of respondents' personalities, such as their delinquent values and their besetment, measured at intake, that were related to adjustment at the institution.

The next stage of the analysis is to determine the degree to which the indicators of social conditions in the community can be said to mediate the relationship between adjustment at release and adjustment six months later.

The more that the community variables mediate, or account for, the relationship, the more the relationship will be reduced by controlling for those variables. The relevant results appear in Table 5.12.

From our examination of the first link in the chain, we know that any mediation we detect will be due largely to boys' reference groups in the community. Table 5.12 indicates that these variables did mediate some of the effects of institutional adjustment on adjustment six months later.

Of all the facets of institutional adjustment, the predictive power of boys' delinquent behavior in the months just prior to their release was most markedly mediated by the boys' reference groups. Boys' delinquent behavior at that time had foreshadowed their delinquent behavior in the community. This relationship was considerably reduced by the mediation of boys' reference groups in the community, as comparisons of the correlations in the first two columns of Table 5.12 show. The correlation of delinquent behavior at the institution with later delinquent behavior declines from .26 to .11 when reference groups are taken into account. A similar pattern involves interest in school at release: its correlation with later delinquent behavior declines from $-.21$ to $-.05$. The entire set of measures of institutional adjustment no longer accounts reliably for the differences in the boys' delinquent behavior in the community when mediation by social conditions in the community is taken into account. (Note the relative increases in R^2 at the foot of the first two columns.)

The findings from Tables 5.11 and 5.12 indicate a pattern in which focal students who engaged in less delinquent behavior and increased their interest in school during their institutionalization were then both more able to gain access to prosocial peer groups after their release and more prone to choose such groups. Furthermore, they tended to be more satisfied with these peer associations, and they were more likely to establish relationships with adults whose opinions, predominantly prosocial, they valued. These relationships then tended to keep the boys from delinquent behavior in the community.

The relationship of respondents' institutional adjustment to their feelings of well-being six months after their release also seems to have depended on the nature of their post-release reference groups. Focal students whose interest in school and sense of well-being had grown and whose besetment had declined tended to find themselves among more satisfying and prosocial reference groups after their release, and this was substantially responsible for the effects of institutional adjustment on their later feelings of well-being.

Boys' community reference groups seem to have played somewhat less of a role in mediating the effects of institutional adjustment on their delinquent values than they did with relation to post-release delinquent behavior and well-being. Of the 12.8 percent of the variance in post-release delinquent values that could be explained by adjustment at release, a little less than half was accounted for by social conditions in the community. Delinquent

Table 5.12
Correlations of Measures at Release with Adjustment Six Months After Release, with and without Controls for Community Mediators

	Measures Six Months After Release									
	Delinquent Behavior		Delinquent Values		Interest in School		Besetment		Well-Being	
	Controls for Community Mediators									
	No	Yes	No	Yes	No	Yes	No	Yes	No	Yes
Measures at Release										
Delinquent Behavior	.26*	.11	.22*	.13	.08	.20*	.25*	.19*	-.04	.00
Delinquent Values	.12	.07	.33*	.28*	-.10	.01	.12	.10	-.06	-.02
Institutional Satisfaction	-.12	.04	-.23*	-.13	.17*	.07	-.17*	-.07	.08	-.11
Interest in School	-.21*	-.05	-.08	.06	.29*	.20*	-.11	-.01	.24*	.14*
Besetment	.08	.03	.08	.03	-.01	.05	.38*	.35*	-.13*	-.04
Well-Being	-.09	.04	-.15*	-.04	.17*	.08	-.10	-.01	.17*	.09
R^2 Increase	.084*	.012	.128*	.076*	.121*	.065*	.125*	.085*	.063*	.037
R^2 Total	.228*	.506*	.275*	.390*	.157*	.356*	.345*	.454*	.206*	.377*

*$p < .05$

NOTE: All correlations also control for selected measures at intake.

values at release continued to predict to delinquent values later. Mediation was more evident for delinquent behavior and well-being at release. Again, if better behavior and more well-being led to more prosocial reference groups, then boys subscribed less to delinquent values after their release. Nevertheless, the mediation of reference groups was constrained by the durability of delinquent values.

The relationship of their institutional adjustment to these youths' interest in school after their release was also mediated by their reference groups in the community. As Table 5.12 shows, the relative levels of boys' interest in school at release tended to remain stable regardless of their later reference groups. In contrast, their feelings of well-being and their delinquent behavior at the time of their release seemed to be related to their subsequent interest in school, largely because of the mediation of reference groups. Greater well-being is associated with more prosocial reference groups, which in turn is associated with more interest in school out in the community.

Focal students' behavior in the months just prior to their release is related to their later interest in school only if their reference groups are taken into account; and then, curiously, the *worse* their behavior the *more* interest in school boys expressed later! This statistically significant finding is known as a "suppressor effect": a relationship between two factors is concealed by their opposing relationships to a third. That the more delinquent respondents at release later actually became more interested in school than their less delinquent peers seems implausible, and we are inclined to believe that this is one of those statistically significant findings that sometimes occur purely by chance.

On the other hand, if we were to take the finding seriously, this would be one interpretation: At their release, the more antisocial boys were more keenly aware than their prosocial peers of their potential for continuing to get into trouble. They might have realized that one way to break out of their delinquent way of life was to succeed at school. Hence, they actually tended to be more interested in school than the focal students who had behaved themselves better in the months prior to their release. Their tendency to associate with more delinquent peers after their release, however, suppressed expression of this interest. When the delinquency of their peer reference group is taken into account, it is revealed that the more antisocial respondents expressed relatively more interest in school than one might have expected, considering whom they had chosen as friends.

The power of the youths' besetment and their delinquent behavior at release to predict their level of besetment six months later were little diminished by controlling for the nature of their reference groups in the community. Reference groups seemed to have played no mediating role here. This finding further corroborates the idea that besetment was, for

Table 5.13
Relationship of Release Variables to Secure Placement Six Months After Release, with and without Controls for Community Mediators

Release Variable	Controlling for Intake Factors Only		Also Controlling for Community Mediators	
	Secure Placement?		Secure Placement?	
	No	Yes	No	Yes
Delinquency at the Institution	13.90	16.70*	13.70	15.80*
Delinquent Values	10.17	10.64	10.19	10.55
Satisfaction with Institution	13.43	12.94	13.36	13.19
Interest in School	10.00	9.40	9.90	9.60
Besetment	33.80	37.00*	34.00	36.30
Well-Being	8.80	7.80*	8.80	8.10

Logistic Regression	Fraction explained	chi sq	df
Unique to Release Variables	.0141	10.031	6
Full Model	.0749	55.650	23

*p < .05

most of the respondents, a fairly stable personality characteristic, relatively unresponsive to the immediate situation.

Finally, we consider the mediating role of reference groups for the relationship between institutional adjustment and whether focal students were reincarcerated six months after their release. We have seen that boys' delinquency at the institution, their besetment, and their sense of well-being predicted reliably to whether they would be in secure placement (note the figures in the two left-hand columns of Table 5.13.) The predictive power of besetment and feelings of well-being declines to insignificance, however, when boys' reference groups are taken into consideration (see the two right-hand columns of Table 5.13). The predictive power of boys' behavior at the institution declines somewhat when reference groups are taken into account, but boys' behavior persists in predicting secure placement reliably better than chance. Thus, boys' emotional state at release seems to have affected their likelihood of reincarceration only insofar as it helped to determine the nature of their community reference groups; the relationship of their behavior to their subsequent institutionalization, on the other hand, seems to have been largely independent of boys' reference groups in the community.

We also examined the relationships of boys'reference groups with the post-release outcomes after controlling for the release variables. Only if those relationships remain strong after taking the release measures into account would it be reasonable to conclude that boys' reference groups mediate in the ways we have described between adjustment at release and adjustment in the community. The relevant relationships, with and without controls for the measures taken at release, appear in Table 5.14 and 5.15. On the whole, controlling for the release measures has little impact on the relationship between the community variables and adjustment six months after release. Almost all significant correlations remain significant after introducing the controls, and typically they are only slightly smaller in magnitude. Accordingly, the explained variance attributable to the community variables is only slightly reduced by taking release measures into account. The exception is retrospective satisfaction with the institution, which is substantially less related to post-release adjustment after controlling for earlier adjustment. This finding led us to discount the importance of the post-release measure of satisfaction with the institution as a mediating variable. The information in Tables 5.14 and 5.15 supports our interpretation of the data as indicating that reference groups had the mediating functions described above.

SUMMARY

Our focal students' responses to institutional treatment were related to their adjustment to the open community after their release. The more their behavior improved during their stay, the more interested in school they had become, and the more satisfied they were with their institutional experience as it was about to end, the more prosocial they were six months later. Compared to those boys who had presented a less positive image, they showed less self-reported delinquency, fewer returns to secure placement, less support for delinquent values, more interest in school, and less anxiety and depression.

Many of these effects of institutional adjustment seem attributable to their enabling or encouraging respondents to adopt more prosocial reference groups in the community. Youths who had adjusted better during their residency tended later to look to adults more than to their peers for approval, especially if peers were perceived as relatively tolerant of delinquent behavior. Unless respondents adopted more prosocial reference groups after their release, prosocial adjustment during the six months after their release was not especially likely to follow from gains they had made in the institution. Positive reference groups proved to be a critical link in the chain of rehabilitation.

Table 5.14

Correlations of Community Mediators with Adjustment Six Months After Release, with and without Controlling for Measures Taken at Release

Community Mediator	Delinquent Behavior		Delinquent Values		Interest in School		Besetment		Well-Being	
	No	Yes	No	Yes	No	Yes	No	Yes	No	Yes
					Control for Measures at Release					
Delinquent Behavior of Friends	.54*	.49*	.32*	.25*	-.23*	-.24*	.20*	.10	-.12	-.05
Satisfaction with Friendships	-.13*	-.10	-.18*	-.19*	.16*	.09	-.19*	-.24*	.20	.17*
Satisfaction with Institution	-.19*	-.13	-.20*	-.11	.15*	.09	-.13*	-.05	.23*	.17*
Desire for Adult Approval	-.23*	-.22*	-.18*	-.16*	.30*	.25*	-.07	-.08	.22*	.21*
Friends' Tolerance for Delinquency	.34*	.32*	.34*	.28*	-.18*	-.20*	.17*	.14*	-.08	-.09
R^2 Increase	.341*	.274*	.169*	.114*	.261*	.194*	.154*	.111*	.198*	.172*
R^2 Total	.479*	.506*	.347*	.390*	.296*	.356*	.385*	.454*	.345*	.377*

*$p < .05$

NOTE: All correlations also control for selected measures at intake.

Table 5.15
Relationship of Community Mediators to Secure Placement Six Months After Release, with and without Controlling for Release Variables

Community Variable	Controlling for Selected Measures at Intake Only		Also Controlling for Release Variables	
	Secure Placement?		Secure Placement?	
	No	Yes	No	Yes
Delinquency of Friends	42.00	60.50*	43.40	52.10*
Satisfaction With Friends	3.27	3.02*	3.26	3.04
Institutional Satisfaction	12.54	11.70*	12.40	12.20
Attachment to Adult Reference Group	10.82	10.45	10.80	10.50
Norms of Peer Reference Group	11.80	12.36*	11.20	11.60
Stigma	2.08	2.29*	2.10	2.19
School Attendance	2.50	2.36	2.47	2.41
Satisfaction With Teachers	3.11	3.26	3.11	3.30

Logistic Regression	Fraction explained	chi sq	df
Unique to Community Variables	.029	20.457*	11
Full Model	.075	55.650*	23

*$p < .05$

Boys' responses to institutional treatment had little effect on some aspects of their adjustment to the community. Although their adjustment at the institution was reliably related to whether they were in secure placement six months after release, it was not related to the number of times they were arrested. Nor was it related to whether they were going to school or holding a job or both. Neither were respondents' reports of their current well-being a function of their earlier institutional adjustment. Apparently the situation in the community shaped boys' adjustment in these respects, exclusive of what they brought to the situation—getting caught and arrested is unlikely, only loosely tied to the impact of the institution on frequency of delinquent behavior; going to school or finding a job depends on the availability of opportunities; and well-being is a reflection of respondents' assessments of the quality of their lives at the moment.

We can construct a probable causal chain of events that begins with those components of the institutional program that contributed to positive change during the focal students' residency, that in turn contributed to prosocial adjustment in the community. This construction involves returning to the data of Chapter 4, in which effective characteristics of staff teams and residents' groups are identified. For this purpose, we focus on those components of the institutional experience that encouraged the focal students to behave better in the months just prior to their release, to become more interested in school, and to be generally satisfied with the program.

The data in Chapter 4 show that focal students who behaved better during their residency belonged to groups that had not developed a delinquent subculture and that, related to the groups' prosocial norms, were more attractive to their members. These youths were most satisfied with their institutional experience if their groups were granted more autonomy by their staff team. Staff teams that put relatively more emphasis on custodial and treatment goals encouraged more interest in school among the boys in their groups. We will postpone further discussion of the implications of these findings for theory and practice until after we have considered the differential effect of the program on different types of delinquent boys.

In one respect, the treatment program had a lasting effect on the focal students regardless of whether they adopted prosocial reference groups. To the degree that they emerged from the institution less beset than they were when they entered, the students were also less beset six months later, even if their reference groups were not necessarily prosocial. Recall that besetment proved to be less responsive to the institutional program than were other facets of the focal students' behavior and psyche. Those who nevertheless became less beset in residency tended to remain more buoyant despite adverse community conditions. One consequence of this was that they related better to their peers than they had before their institutionalization, and this, in turn, may have suppressed the effects of whatever gains they made in the institutional program.

That besetment was fairly stable—that is, a facet of personality—leads us to consider how more and less beset boys may have responded differentially to the treatment program. As we signaled earlier, our research included a test of the usefulness of a typology of delinquents that categorizes them as beset or buoyant. In the next chapter, we explore how these types responded to the program, whether different aspects of the program proved effective for the two types, and whether the two types fared differentially after their release.

NOTES

1. Due to the smaller sample size for the follow-up, the correlation of delinquent behavior with prior interest in school was not reliably different from zero by conventional statistical standards, although it was as strong as it had been at release. That it appeared again indicates that it was probably real.

2. A number of the community variables were undefined for certain subgroups of respondents. There were no data about school factors for respondents who did not attend school, about jobs for respondents who did not have jobs, and about male and female caregivers for respondents who did not have either or both. The correlations reported in Tables 5.9 to 5.13 are based on the subsets who had valid

data for each pair of variables. The R^2 values for the school and job subsets of community variables in Tables 5.9 and 5.10 are also limited to those subsets of respondents. In computing R^2 values for the family variables or for combinations of several types of community variables, limiting the sample to respondents with valid data on all variables would systematically exclude important subgroups of our sample. To avoid this, these regression equations included dummy variables indicating whether or not respondents went to school, had jobs, had male caregivers, and had female caregivers. Once this was done, a constant (the mean of the valid cases) could be substituted for the missing values without biasing the results, and the full sample could be retained in the analysis.

6

THE BUOYANT AND THE BESET

Certain of our findings, together with previous theory and research, suggest that it is illuminating to distinguish among types of delinquents. A two-category typology based on the degree to which heavily delinquent youth manifest anxiety and depression has proven useful for refining our understanding of the causes of delinquency and the effects of treatment programs (Atwood, Gold, & Taylor, 1989; Gold & Mann, 1984; Gold, Mattlin, & Osgood, 1989; Hewitt & Jenkins, 1946).

Chapter 2 reviews the history of this typology, which began with the clinical work of Hewitt and Jenkins. Whereas Hewitt and Jenkins emphasized the quality of delinquents' relationships with their peers, our emphasis is on the delinquents' state of mind. Thus, Hewitt and Jenkins called their two delinquent types "socialized" and "unsocialized," while we refer to the most anxious and depressed as "beset" and their less anxious and depressed counterparts as "buoyant." As we pointed out in Chapter 2, our emphasis integrates typological considerations into a more general theory of delinquent behavior as a defense against a derogated self-image. We believe that the relatively deep anxiety and depression of the beset type indicates that delinquency does not work so well for them as it does for the buoyant. The buoyant and the beset share reasons for adopting a heavily delinquent pattern of behavior, but the beset, we believe, suffer from substantially more psychological problems. These problems develop earlier and include more basic insecurity. It is in this sense that this type of delinquent is more "beset."

Some of the material presented in this chapter has appeared in Gold, Mattlin, and Osgood (1989) in *Criminal Justice and Behavior 16.* Copyright 1989. Reprinted by permission of Sage Publications, Inc.

We hypothesized, therefore, that the beset boys in this study would not respond so well to Positive Peer Culture as the buoyant boys would. The peer group orientation of the treatment would not address the problems of the beset as well for three reasons. First, the beset boys, as Hewitt and Jenkins pointed out, do not get along very well with their peers, and so they would be less influenced by whatever prosocial norms PPC was able to instill in the boys' groups. Second, whatever confidence boys gained in their ability to succeed as students would mean less to the beset than to the buoyant boys because that success would not address a major source of their distress. And third, being in some ways developmentally more immature, beset boys would require more emotional support from adults than PPC ordinarily provided.

We have already presented findings that greater besetment, measured when boys were first admitted to the institution, predicts to poorer adjustment to the institution and to the open community after release. In this chapter we explore the further usefulness of the typology by reviewing data on the differential effects of specific components of the institutional and post-release experiences of the beset and buoyant boys. Specifically, we consider whether positive group norms and scholastic success had less effect on the beset than on the buoyant boys; and whether closer relationships with adults had more effect on the beset than on the buoyant type.

STABILITY

In the analyses of personal characteristics affecting institutional adjustment (presented in Chapter 4) and adjustment to the community (presented in Chapter 5), we treated besetment as a matter of degree rather than type. That is, we placed boys on a continuous scale ranging from most beset to most buoyant and determined what differences that made in their adjustment. A typological investigation required a different strategy. For this purpose, we identified those boys whose besetment was so stable from their admission to their release that it could reasonably be considered a facet of their personalities, and we divided the stable ones into the two distinct types.

An assumption underlying a typological approach is that the typological criterion or criteria are enduring characteristics of the individuals, that is, part of personality. This assumption was not true of all the focal students. For some of them, the level of their anxiety and depression fluctuated widely while they were institutionalized, in general decreasing, almost certainly because the initial measure was elevated by the anxiety-provoking experience of intake.

In order to identify the more stable boys, we took into account their scores on besetment at admission and at release, an average of a year later. The correlation between the two scores is .37, statistically significant at p < .01. The magnitude of this correlation indicates that besetment was unstable among a substantial number of the focal students.

We determined the amount of change in besetment that would constitute instability by taking the reliability of the measure as our guide. The measure's reliability indicates that score a youth would be expected to receive at release, given his score at admission, simply as a consequence of regression to the mean. Change should be gauged relative to this expected score rather than the observed score at intake. The formula we used for our calculations was: predicted score = intake mean + [alpha] (intake score − intake mean). Since the value of Cronbach's alpha for the intake score was .79, then each student's score at release could be expected to deviate from the intake mean by 79 percent of his intake score's deviation from the intake mean. This calculation embodies the assumption of regression to the mean—that more boys with relatively lower intake scores would increase in besetment and more of those with higher intake besetment scores would decline. If release scores deviated by much more or less than this estimate of the true score, then we classified those boys as unstable.

It was necessary to stipulate how much change in score should be tolerated before boys' besetment should be considered unstable. Students whose actual besetment scores at release fell within one standard deviation—nine points—of their estimated true score were classified as stable. This group included 199, or 65 percent, of the 306 boys who had been interviewed at intake and release. An obvious weakness of this classification system is that only about two-thirds of these heavily delinquent boys can be typed. We feel nevertheless that more stringent criteria yielding purer types is desirable at this juncture of research on this typology. We will return to this issue later.

We found that the correlation between besetment and well-being at intake was significantly higher (p < .05) among the unstable (r = −.46) than among the stable (r = −.25). This indicates that the unstable boys' current well-being and their besetment at intake were more closely tied, both being more situationally determined; while the stable boys' besetment was less tied to the situation. At release, the correlation between well-being and besetment was still stronger among the unstable, but not significantly so. The larger difference at intake is to be expected if the intake situation had a more powerful effect on depression and anxiety than release did. Our data indicate that this was the case: Average besetment at intake was 6.2 points higher (p < .01) than the average at release; while the average at release was only 0.1 points higher than the average of scores gathered six months after release.

Perhaps the most telling support for the classification of stability may be found in the autocorrelation of besetment from intake to six months after release. Due to the way in which stability is defined, the correlation between intake and release besetment is automatically higher among the stable than among the unstable (.77 vs. .23). More striking is that besetment at the time of the follow-up, which was not used to identify the stable boys, was significantly more highly correlated with the initial measure of besetment among the stable than among the unstable (.60 vs. .35). The preceding analyses support the validity of our procedure for distinguishing the stable from the unstable beset and buoyant delinquents and allowed us to focus our subsequent analyses on a subset of the sample whose reported anxiety and depression reflected stable typological characteristics.

FINDINGS

Differences in Background Characteristics

There are certain ways in which the backgrounds of the characterologically beset youths were expected to differ from those of the characterologically buoyant. If their levels of anxiety and depression were more than temporary, then beset and buoyant boys hypothetically had different experiences prior to their admission to the institution and the initial assessment of their besetment. We found that the beset boys were significantly younger than the buoyant, suggesting that they got an early start on building a record of delinquency sufficient to be remanded to a secure institution (see Table 6.1). The data also indicate that a smaller percentage of the beset boys had been living with their parents immediately prior to their current institutionalization, and that more of them had experienced out-of-home placements in the past. Most of these out-of-home placements had been occasioned by prior delinquent behavior and involved some sort of detention. The buoyant boys at their initial interview had reported that they had greater success at making friends than the beset boys did. The beset boys, on the other hand, blamed others—parents, peers, authorities—for their incarceration more than the buoyant ones did. They also tended to commit more of their delinquent acts alone. Finally, consistent with their reports of greater anxiety and depression, the beset boys exhibited lower self-esteem than the buoyant boys did. (All of these differences were much more sharply drawn among the stable buoyant and beset than among the unstable.)

These differences in background reinforce our image of the beset boys, relative to the buoyant, as having earlier problems that disturbed their relationships with others and their feelings about themselves. This image led us to expect that they would not adjust as well in the heavily group-oriented PPC program, and that certain components of the program would have more influence upon them. We have already seen that they did not adjust as well to the institution and to the open community after their release. We turn now to the data on how the two types were affected differently by certain facets of the program.

Table 6.1
Key Differences: Buoyant – Beset for Boys with Stable Scores

a.

	n	Buoyant mean	se	n	Beset mean	se	Pdiff
age	101	16.10	.08	98	15.80	.10	.05
% of crimes committed alone[a]	80	32.00	.02	85	43.00	.02	.002
self-esteem	101	66.30	8.90	97	63.74	9.20	.05
success of friendship	101	16.14	2.10	98	15.21	1.90	.001
blaming others	101	8.73	2.70	98	9.52	3.20	.06

b.

	n	%	n	%	Pdiff
% with prior placements	101	34	98	50	.02
% living with parents	100	77	97	58	.004
% living with mother[b]	100	67	97	53	.04
% living with father[c]	100	35	97	26	.16

[a]Limited to the 165 who reported five or more offenses
[b]Natural mother or stepmother
[c]Natural father or stepfather

Effects of the Program on the Buoyant and the Beset

The effects of the program may be of two kinds, mediating or interactive. The mediating kind is due to institutional experiences likely to equally affect all the boys who have them, although one type of delinquent is more prone to have those experiences. The interactive kind is due to experiences that affect the adjustment of one type significantly more than they affect the adjustment of the other, even if the two types are equally likely to have them.

Since we had obtained measures of program features both as each focal student described them and as they appeared to group consensus, we were able to investigate the effects of individual perceptions and group norms on measures of adjustment. These measures included both assessments of the autonomy and closeness to staff felt by the group as a whole and of each student's feelings of relative autonomy and closeness to the staff.

The path diagrams in Figures 6.1 and 6.2 depict adjustment of the stable types at interim and release as a function of their personal autonomy, which was itself a function of besetment at intake and the relative autonomy sensed by the group prior to or early in the boys' stay. (The figures on the paths are standardized coefficients indicating the size of the effect of one variable on the other. The coefficients in parentheses are the effects after the mediating variable, personal autonomy, is controlled. R^2 indicates the amount of variance of the adjustment indicator that is accounted for by the set of predictors.) As we had suspected, the more buoyant boys tended to feel more autonomous. Since personal autonomy itself was a strong positive influence on adjustment at interim and release, the effect of delinquent type on the boys' institutional satisfaction, delinquent values, countercultural attitudes (measured only at interim), and delinquent behavior was mediated by feelings of personal autonomy: the beset boys adjusted less well at the institution partly because they felt more restricted. It should be noted, however, that the group's norm concerning the amount of their autonomy far outweighed boys' delinquent type in determining the amount of autonomy boys experienced personally at interim.

Not all the effects of delinquent type on institutional adjustment were mediated by boys' feelings of personal autonomy. Even after accounting for personal autonomy, whether boys were buoyant or beset was responsible for a significant amount of the variance of adjustment. This is also true of all four facets of adjustment when boys' ties to staff are taken into account.

Boys' feelings of closeness to their staff teams also had a markedly positive impact on their adjustment at interim and release (see Figures 6.3 and 6.4). However, it cannot be confidently asserted that delinquent type worked through staff ties in influencing adjustment, because whether boys were buoyant or beset had no reliable relationship to boys' feelings about staff. However, group ties to staff did work through individual staff ties in influencing adjustment.

We turn now from the mediating effects of autonomy and close ties to staff to their interactive effects. Here we are concerned with whether beset and buoyant boys were differentially affected even if they felt equally autonomous or equally close to staff.

For the most part, autonomy and ties to staff affected the adjustment of

Figure 6.1
Effect of Besetment, Group Autonomy at Intake, and Personal Autonomy on Interim Adjustment****

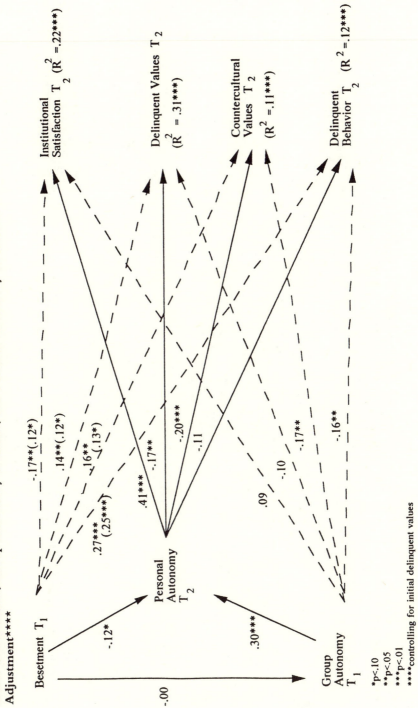

*p<.10
**p<.05
***p<.01
****controlling for initial delinquent values

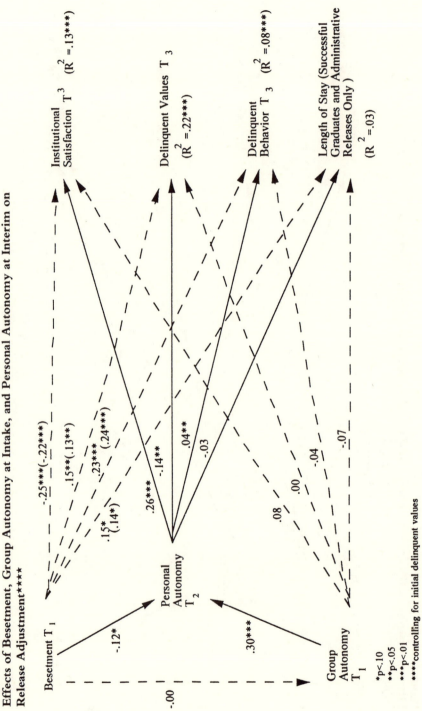

Figure 6.2
Effects of Besetment, Group Autonomy at Intake, and Personal Autonomy at Interim on Release Adjustment****

*p<.10
**p<.05
***p<.01
****controlling for initial delinquent values

Figure 6.3
Effects of Besetment, Group Ties to Staff, and Personal Staff Ties on Interim Adjustment****

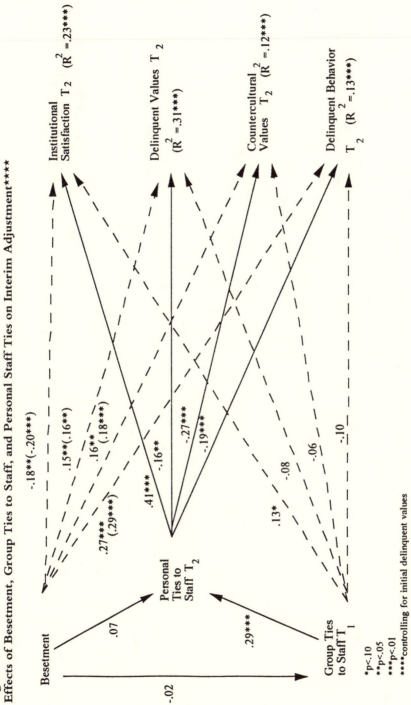

*p<.10
**p<.05
***p<.01
****controlling for initial delinquent values

185

Figure 6.4
Effects of Besetment at Intake, Group Ties to Staff at Interim, and Personal Staff Ties at Release on Adjustment at Release****

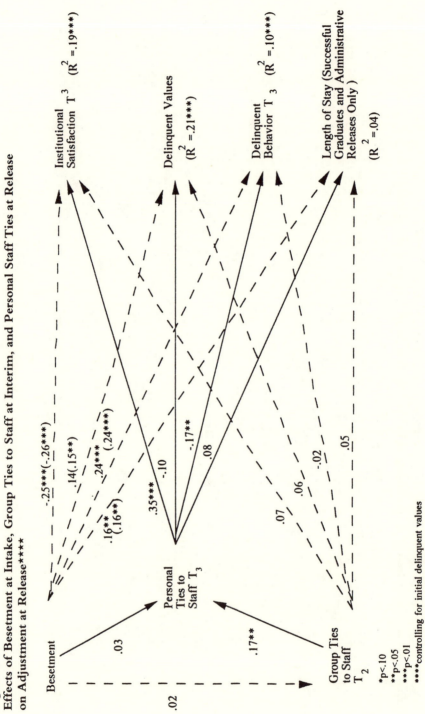

*p<.10
**p<.05
***p<.01
****controlling for initial delinquent values

the two types of delinquents similarly, both after four months' stay and at release. We found only three significant interactions (p < .10); however, all were supportive of our hypotheses. As Figure 6.5 shows, a feeling of greater autonomy at interim was associated with more satisfaction with the institution at the time of release among the buoyant type; autonomy was not related to beset delinquents' satisfaction. Conversely, close ties to staff were significantly associated with less delinquent behavior of beset delinquents at interim and release, but it was not related to the behavior of the buoyant type (see Figure 6.6 for the findings at four months). Of the fourteen possible tests of interactive effects of delinquent type with autonomy or staff ties on adjustment (four indexes at interim, three at release), eleven were in the expected direction, three negligibly in the opposite direction. All of these three involved staff ties.

Finally, we sought to determine whether the kind of group in which a boy was placed affected his adjustment any differently if he was beset rather than buoyant. This is an eminently practical question: Does placing a beset youth in a group with stronger staff ties affect his attitudes and behavior more than it would affect the attitudes and behavior of a buoyant boy? If so, group assignments could be made on the basis of a boy's type (provided that it is known that his categorization is stable).

Searching for interactive effects of buoyant/beset with group characteristics also has some methodological significance. Group characteristics were measured with questionnaires answered by all the boys in a group, so if a group as a whole felt relatively close ties to its staff, it is likely that the staff was encouraging these ties, that they were not solely in the minds of individual beset or buoyant boys. Moreover, groups differed significantly in autonomy and the closeness of their ties to staff. There is reason to believe then that autonomy and ties to staff were group properties, not only perceptions of individuals.

We found little evidence of interaction between delinquent type and group norms about staff ties or autonomy. Only one such interaction is worthy of mention. Group ties to staff at intake helped to reduce delinquent values at interim among the beset, but not among the buoyant. This finding, significant at the .05 level, is similar to the finding in Figure 6.6. This interaction was not significant at release, however.

Significant findings concerning mediating and interaction effects are more prevalent and stronger in our data among the boys we have identified as stable beset or buoyant types. Few of the relationships appear among the unstable youth.

Effects of the Community on the Buoyant and the Beset

We also investigated whether post-release conditions in their communities affected the adjustment of the buoyant and beset boys differently. Just as

Figure 6.5
Relationship Between Personal Autonomy (Interim) and Institutional
Satisfaction (Release) Beset and Buoyant* (Stable Only)

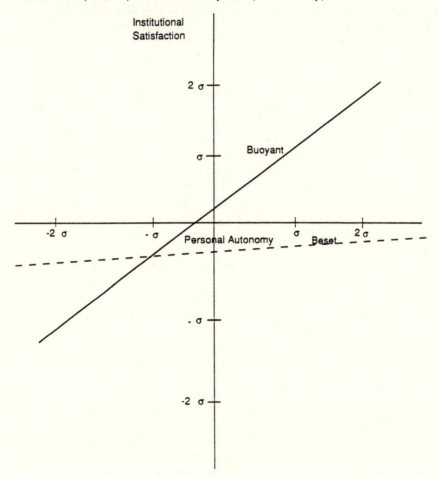

*Holding initial group autonomy and delinquent values constant

Figure 6.6
Relationship Between Staff Ties (Interim) and Delinquency (Interim):
Beset and Buoyant* (Stable Only)

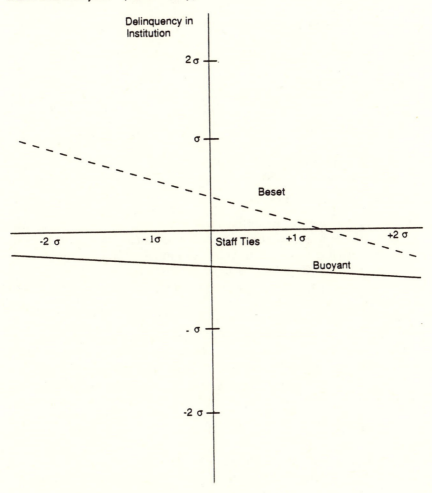

*Holding initial group ties and delinquent values constant

Table 6.2
Comparison of Selected Post-Release Scores Buoyant versus Beset (Stable Only)

Post-Release Variable	n	buoyant mean	se	n	beset mean	se	Pdiff
social support from female caregiver	76	7.16	.19	84	6.80	.18	.19
satisfaction with teachers	54	3.25	.11	68	2.95	.10	.04
relations with teachers	54	22.60	.54	68	20.70	.48	.01
confidence as a student	76	12.69	.31	84	11.38	.29	.002
GPA	55	2.50	.10	68	2.44	.09	.68
satisfaction with job	53	3.04	.13	55	2.73	.13	.10
social support from friends	75	11.41	.28	84	11.18	.26	.55

Note: Mean's adjusted for age and race.

the two types proved to be differentially responsive to elements of their institutional experience, so we expected them to require somewhat different conditions to reintegrate into the open community. Specifically, we hypothesized that the adjustment of beset boys was enhanced more by supportive relationships, and the adjustment of buoyant boys by achievement at school or at work.

These hypotheses were tested with the stable buoyant and beset boys only. These are the boys whose scores on besetment changed little during their institutionalization. We continued to classify boys on the basis of their scores while they were incarcerated, although 27 percent of them changed from buoyant to beset or vice versa over the first six months after their release. That is, their scores crossed over the median at the follow-up. Nevertheless, we wanted to assess how useful the original classification was and maintain the advantages of a longitudinal study of these two types of boys.

Buoyant boys reported finding more social support than the beset boys did when they returned to the open community (see Table 6.2). The former reported better relations with their female caregivers, their teachers, and their friends—that is, with the people who were most prominent in the lives of almost all of them. The difference between the two types was most marked and statistically significant with regard to their teachers. The buoyant boys also reported greater confidence in themselves as students and more satisfaction with their jobs. These data suggest that buoyant boys found conditions in the community more conducive to better adjustment. As we noted in the previous chapter, social support and achievement were related to various indicators of better adjustment.

These data do not speak directly to the question of whether the two types of boys responded differently to conditions they found in the community after their release. To investigate this, it was necessary to examine interaction effects. If the types of boys had experienced the same range of social support and achievement, was the adjustment of the buoyant boys affected more by achievement, and of the beset boys by social support?

We found no evidence that the two types responded differently to achievement at school or to satisfactory employment. Both types tended to adjust better under these conditions. We did find evidence, however, that the post-release adjustment of the beset boys was better enhanced by supportive relationships with their female caregivers. Supportive relationships with their mothers or mother-surrogates were related to greater feelings of well-being for both types of boys, but as shown in Figure 6.7, significantly more so ($p = .03$) for the beset. Similarly, beset boys who remained in the open community reported more support from their female caregivers than beset boys who had to be reincarcerated, while the opposite was true among the buoyant boys. (See Figure 6.8) The differences in the amount of social support reported by those reincarcerated and those not reincarcerated is not statistically significant within either the buoyant or beset types. That the relationships between social support and reincarceration are in opposite directions—the interaction effect—is statistically significant at $p = .05$.

SUMMARY

Distinguishing the buoyant from the beset type of delinquent has proved useful for understanding differences in the boys' adjustment to the institution and to the open community after their release. Characterization as one type or the other appears to have been stable for about half of the focal students from the time they entered the institution until six months after their release, an average of eighteen months later. Thus, about half the boys stayed true to type, displaying relatively high or low levels of anxiety and depression in two quite different environments. They adjusted differently to both environments, and they were differentially affected by certain conditions in both environments. This summary is from the perspective of the beset type.

Beset boys, in comparison to the buoyant, tended to perceive their social relationships through dark lenses. When asked about the people in their lives before, during, or after institutionalization, their reports were less favorable: others were to blame for their incarceration; they didn't make friends easily; they didn't have as much autonomy at the institution; they got little social support from their mothers (or mother-surrogates), teachers,

Figure 6.7
Relationship Between Support from Female Caregivers and Feeling of
Well-Being Six Months After Release for Buoyant and Beset Boys

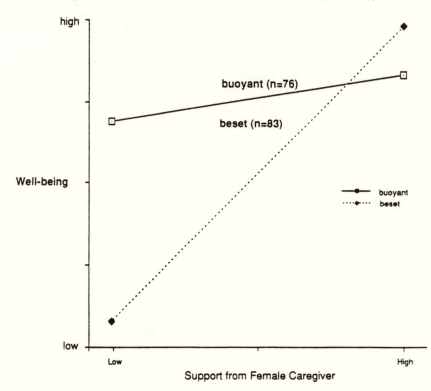

and friends. These findings suggest that the beset boys suffered earlier developmental deficits than the buoyant boys did, resulting in greater mistrust and insecurity. Consistent with this interpretation of the data, beset boys experienced more discontinuity in care, probably came to the attention of authorities at a younger age, and were more likely to be lone delinquents than the buoyant. This more negative outlook affected their adjustment adversely.

Also consistent with the idea that the beset boys suffered from greater deficits in care is their greater responsiveness to relationships with caregivers, compared to the buoyant. Beset boys adjusted better in the institution if they were placed in groups whose members felt closer ties to members of the staff team and especially if they themselves felt closer to staff. They also adjusted better in the community and were more likely to remain in the open community if they felt that their female caregivers provided them with more social support. Warm relationships with caregivers tended to enhance the adjustment to the institution and to the open

Figure 6.8
**Social Support from Female Caregivers for Reincarcerated and Not
Reincarcerated Buoyant and Beset Boys**

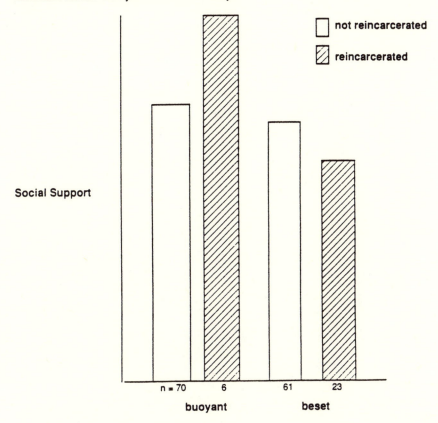

community of all the focal students, the buoyant and the unclassified, as
well as the beset. The beset were markedly more affected by such relationships, however.

These findings have obvious implications for the differential treatment
of the buoyant and beset types of delinquents. We discuss this, along with
other implications of our findings, in the next and final chapter.

7

IMPLICATIONS FOR THEORY
AND PRACTICE

What we have learned in this study is generalizable to a broad range of delinquent adolescents and residential institutions. The youths we observed varied widely in their personal and social characteristics, and as a group resembled delinquent males incarcerated in most other places in the United States in the recent past and for the foreseeable future. While the four participating institutions all practice a heavily group-centered program, some variation of Positive Peer Culture (Vorrath and Brendtro, 1985), this is consistent with other residential treatment programs, which invariably place clients among groups of delinquent peers, for better or worse. The PPC modality simply tries to make use of peer influence. The broad variation in staff teams' delivery of the program among the forty-five groups of boys we studied resembles in many ways programs to be found elsewhere, including the importance attached to group influence.

Furthermore, the implications of our findings can be projected more widely if the findings are raised to a somewhat higher level of abstraction by means of theory. Our study began under the guidance of bodies of theory in social psychology, personality psychology, group dynamics, criminology, and corrections. We can refer the findings back to those theories now and draw implications in terms of principles that should hold wherever the relevant psychological and social conditions prevail.

Our findings have identified certain properties of their staff and group that affected the behavior, attitudes, and emotional states of delinquent boys during their institutionalization and after. No attempt is made here to summarize all of our findings in any detail. Rather, we focus on the more consistent trends that seemed to have the greatest import for the practice of juvenile corrections and for the several bodies of theory from which we drew guidance. We believe that the knowledge gained from documenting and analyzing the experiences of institutionalized delinquent boys can be used to make the more positive experiences more typical.

We begin with social conditions. We attend primarily to the nature of the boys' institutional peer groups, particularly to those group properties that most affected the several facets of residents' adjustment at the institution and after their release. We trace differences in these group properties back to the practices of staff that we believe were at least partly responsible for them. Social conditions also include boys' relationships with their primary caregivers in the community before and after they were institutionalized, and the demographic character of the neighborhoods to which they were released.

We then turn to the consequential personal characteristics these youths brought to their group and staff, especially those characteristics defined as part of the boys' personality by virtue of their stability. We review the findings that reveal how these characteristics shaped adjustment jointly with social conditions.

This chapter concludes with implications for the theories and methods employed in our research. These implications have direct relevance not only to the social sciences but also to the practice of juvenile corrections. We began this study persuaded that theory, research, and practice must be related for the advancement of all three. We close with reflections on what we have learned about their interrelationships.

OVERVIEW OF FINDINGS

Peer Influence

To ignore individual differences among the boys for the moment: although they themselves had all been seriously delinquent, had associated almost exclusively with other heavily delinquent youth on the outside, and seemed motivated to perceive the others in their group as more committed to a delinquent subculture than they actually were, the focal students preferred to be in a group of peers who behaved themselves. They were not in general eager to maintain a delinquent subculture, organizing against the staff and the institution. Expressions of definite support for a delinquent subculture were rare indeed.

It may be that the focal students' greater attraction to more prosocial groups was a direct consequence of the Positive Peer Culture treatment modality, which deliberately aimed for this effect. We believe, however, that it represents a natural tendency for adolescents (and perhaps adults) who are locked figuratively or literally into any delinquency treatment program. PPC perhaps makes better use of this general tendency than other programs do, but the tendency is probably not a consequence of the PPC program alone.

Companions who act out may sometimes provide rewards, such as contraband and the satisfactions of collective defiance of authority. We suspect it is more common that peers' misbehavior entails costs for oneself, in terms such as being victimized, losing privileges for the whole group, and having poorer relationships with both peers and staff. Furthermore, we suppose that boys in treatment realize that getting free of the program depends on their giving evidence of rehabilitation. We suppose, too, that residents understand as well as anyone the importance of peer influence, for better or worse. They realize that it is simply easier to behave if their mates behave and support their good behavior.

Thus, if the group's norms permit them to, boys behave better during their residency, and they feel better that way. To the degree that a group adopts prosocial norms—its members attributing better behavior to their group, less admiration of delinquency, and more cooperation with the staff—group members are happier and more prosocial. Furthermore, when members of more prosocial groups are released, they are more likely to take away with them motives, resources, and attitudes that encourage them to choose more prosocial reference groups and that gain them access to such groups. These reference groups then help them to maintain the prosocial gains they had made during their institutionalization.

Despite incarcerated adolescents' preference for a better behaved, more cooperative group, they cannot create one by themselves. That they all have been seriously delinquent works against them. They bring with them the same, perhaps even more exaggerated, stereotype of delinquents that is abroad in their communities. They fear the potential for violence that they believe their fellows harbor. They cope with this by acting tough themselves and showing a readiness to go along with a delinquent counterculture to which, they believe, their peers subscribed more fiercely than they do themselves. Thus, they unwittingly conspire to altercast one another into the delinquent role.

Furthermore, the intake process obviously does not alter the psychological condition that led them to a delinquent way of life and their consequent incarceration. They arrive still needing their delinquent image even while they had rather be rid of it, if only long enough to get free again. They cannot simply surrender the negative identity that has been keeping them together psychologically or park it at the door. They unpack it with the rest of their belongings. It takes a lot of encouragement before they will give up that identity, and of course, some never do.

The constantly changing membership of the peer group common in residential treatment presents another difficulty to establishing prosocial groups. When a boy's behavior and attitudes improve, he leaves. His bed is taken by a boy as yet unexposed to whatever positive influence prevails, who imports anew the problems that made him prone to delinquency, as well as the expectations about his peers that obscure the group's prosocial norms.

For these personal and social reasons, establishing prosocial norms among groups of institutionalized delinquent boys is hard to do, even while the boys themselves, taken individually, would prefer it that way. The boys must depend on the staff to foster the conditions that make prosocial groups possible.

We have found that certain practices of the staff are more likely to develop prosocial groups. Our findings are strikingly similar to those describing a democratic style of leadership (Lewin, Lippitt, & White, 1939) and effective parenting of adolescents (Baumrind, 1978; Elder, 1962). The staff style that most encourages prosocial groups is called *authoritative* in the literature on parenting. It describes the staff teams that put as much emphasis on boys behaving themselves as on addressing boys' emotional needs.

Guided by the literature on juvenile corrections, we had initially contrasted custodial and treatment orientations in our questions to staff members. Their responses indicated, however, that in their minds these orientations are not inconsistent. Members of those teams whose groups were most prosocial indicated that they both demanded prosocial behavior from their wards and tried to help them overcome their emotional problems. The most effective management style appears to be one that upholds high but reasonable standards of behavior and reacts appropriately to violations. These reactions are infused with concern for the feelings and motives that prompted the misbehavior and address them without minimizing the staff's insistence that the standards prevail.

Our findings also indicate that groups become more prosocial when staff permits them greater autonomy within the limits of standards for good behavior and institutional security. PPC prescribes that the group take responsibility for insuring its members' prosocial behavior. The autonomy of prosocial groups extends beyond the group's responsibility for members' behavior, however, to the widest possible opportunities to arrange its own routines and to plan fun.

An effective staff team usually has to help its group organize to practice autonomy because most youth, especially delinquent youth, are not good at it. We found that it made no difference how many specific matters relating to institutional life were decided by residents rather than staff. In the context of the beneficial effect of group autonomy on group norms, we interpret this finding as a reflection of adolescents' impatience with a lot of inconclusive talk. In our first-hand observations of the groups, we saw signs that institutional life can be tedious indeed if every hour of the day brings a call for a lengthy discussion of "Okay group, how are you going to deal with *that?*" Most groups appear to need active, albeit democratic leadership from staff. Perhaps staff members were aware of this; for when the *staff* reported that the group made a lot of specific decisions, its members adjusted less well during their residency.

Incarcerated adolescents prize their own as well as their group's autonomy. They behave better and feel better when they believe neither staff nor group are overbearing. In the settings in which we conducted this research, physical coercion among the youths or by staff seemed rarely a problem. However, the group-centered program did go overboard sometimes in making individuals subservient to group pressures. Youths adjust better to the institutional experience the less they feel the limitations of incarceration. They are more likely to adhere to the prosocial norms established in their group if staff and the group give them space for self-control.

The positive effects of staffs' management of their groups extends to the adjustment of boys after they are released. A chain of events is set up that eventuates in former residents behaving better and feeling better in the open community. Prosocial peer group norms engendered by staff management lead to better behavior and prosocial change in attitudes and values. These changes carry over most significantly as conditions for acquiring more prosocial reference groups in the community. Focal students emerged from more prosocial peer influence tending to look more to adults than to peers for approval, and to peers who do not admire delinquent behavior very much. The influence of these reference groups in turn encourages more prosocial adjustment after release.

Thus, peer group norms in the institution constitute a consequential piece of social reality. This social reality is not, however, an immediate cause of boys' behavior, attitudes, values, and feelings. What youths perceive their group's norms to be is the immediate determinant of their adjustment. And what the norms actually are, by agreement among all the members in the group, is but one factor in determining what individuals think the norms are.

Apparently, normative consensus was not sufficiently variable among the forty-five groups in this study to make a difference in how accurately individuals perceived the central normative tendency of their group. Consensus in the range that we found had no reliable relationship to how well individual's reports of group norms matched the aggregated report of all the members. Boys' beliefs varied widely within a group about how well the rest of the members behaved, how much they admired delinquent behavior, and how committed they were to a resident counterculture. A focal student could usually find someone in his group who expressed either pro- or antisocial values. It is surprising, and is a testimony to their potential power, that even ragged central group tendencies nevertheless had some influence. We suspect that this is generally true, not only of groups of institutionalized delinquents but also of all natural human groups (as compared to experimental groups in which a strong normative consensus is built for the purposes of research).

Among the other determinants of what boys think their group's norms are, beside the norms themselves, are the personal characteristics that members bring to the group. Residents join their group predisposed to believe that it is more or less antisocial. They confirm their beliefs by projecting their expectations on the group as a whole and on the friends they make within the group. The predictive power of these predispositions means that boys' personalities are another piece of reality that has to be taken into account along with the social reality of the group.

Personality

Two of the personal characteristics of the focal students that we measured when they first arrived proved to be so stable over the time of their residency and proved so predictive of their adjustment then and later that these variables qualify as traits of personality. They are besetment and delinquent values. (See Chapter 4 for the definitions and measures of besetment and delinquent values.)

We had anticipated that the anxiety and depression that constitute besetment would be persistent and consequential personal characteristics. We found besetment, under various labels, prominent in the literature on not only delinquency but on personality in general. We adapted our measure of besetment from those frequently used by others. We brought the theme of besetment to this study as a major topic from our prior research (Gold & Mann, 1984), and we investigated it more systematically than we did delinquent values.

We had not expected that the degree to which boys cleaved to delinquent values would remain so stable and would matter as much as it did. Treatment programs typically aim to change delinquents' values as well as their behavior. Indeed, their pronounced intentions seem to assume that behavioral change depends on changing youngsters' values. We found that incarcerated adolescents do not readily abandon their commitment to delinquent values.

Most of the focal students in this study, seriously delinquent all, fell into the range from devaluing delinquency to only mildly tolerating it. Perhaps this range is displaced toward the positive end somewhat by the respondents wanting to appear prosocial to our interviewers; certainly their past behavior suggested that they had a lot of tolerance for delinquent behavior. In any case, their places in the range of delinquent values, relative to the other focal students, remained fairly constant, even while the focal students as a group subscribed less and less to delinquent values over the time we observed them.

Reducing their besetment and the value they placed on delinquency contributed significantly to boys' rehabilitation. When these remained high, other facets of their adjustment did not improve as much. Whatever pro-social influence their groups tried to exert was blunted.

We found that the effects of peer influence on adolescents' adjustment are qualified by their besetment and delinquent values in two general ways. One is that more beset respondents and respondents who value delinquency more tend to misperceive the positive influences in their social environment. They are apt to minimize the prosocial norms of their group and believe that their friends within the group value delinquency more than they actually do. Beset boys are also less likely to have particular friends in the group and are not as attracted to their group as a whole as buoyant boys are, factors that also inhibit prosocial change.

The other way that boys' personalities qualify the effect of positive social forces is that besetment insulates youths specifically from peer influence while sensitizing them to other prosocial forces. (We did not investigate this function of delinquent values.) One correlate of besetment is distrust of others, and so beset boys do not get along with peers as well. Their group mates, for their part, tend to regard the beset as "sick." Consequently, even when beset adolescents recognize that their group has a fair degree of autonomy, they still tend to feel put upon personally. So the prosocial influence of group autonomy affects them less than it does buoyant youths.

On the other hand, beset boys become more prosocial if they happen to come under the care of a staff team to whom the whole group feels close. Markedly likeable staff touch them more strongly than they touch buoyant residents, for whom peer relationships are the more important.

Thus, the overall effect of this delinquency treatment program was less positive for focal students who were more beset and more committed to delinquent values when they entered it. This was true of youths' adjustment in treatment and after they were released. Indeed, the post-release adjustment of the beset adolescents was worse even than the adjustment of the buoyant ones who had adjusted as badly in the institution as the beset had. Beset boys seem especially resistant to a program that relies heavily on peer influence for its effect. Unless these personal factors are dealt with somehow, they are a drag on rehabilitation.

Effects of School

The effects of going to the institutional school are somewhat independent of both peer influence and of the personality traits that we measured. We found that how much focal students' scholastic test scores improved at the institution and whether they grew more interested in school were not re-liably predicted either by their besetment, their delinquent values at intake, or how prosocial group norms were. Greater interest in school and feelings of well-being were the only prior personal characteristics that predicted these reliably.

If boys' scholastic skills improved and their interest in school grew during their residency, they were more likely to behave better and to feel better as well. Furthermore, increased interest in school tended to persist after residents were released, so that the positive effects of scholastic gains could be seen six months after release. (We do not know how they scored on achievement tests they may taken after their release.) The post-release effects of school-related changes did not depend on the mediation of reference groups in the community. They exerted direct influence over boys' adjustment.

These findings mirror previous ones about the effect of schooling on delinquency (Bowman, 1959; Bowman & Liddle, 1959; Gold & Mann, 1984). Delinquents are notorious for their poor attendance, behavior, and performance at school. It has been suggested that their failure to live up to the demands of the student role is a major provocation for their delinquency (Gold, 1978). When they have some success at school, then their misbehavior subsides. Such success is facilitated by a certain kind of school program.

Two features seem essential to an effective school program for delinquent students. One is that their students are prevented from failing. This is accomplished, without necessarily improving their scholastic skills immediately, by individualizing the curriculum. Each student is presented with learning tasks appropriate to his or her level of skills. The curriculum is not determined by students' age and grade in school, as it typically is in conventional secondary schools. Furthermore, the conventional criteria for assessing performance—norms for grade level and the performance of classmates—are abandoned. Instead, students are encouraged with frequent feedback about the progress that they are making, performing better this week than last week, this month better than last month.

The second essential feature is that teachers give their students uncommonly warm emotional support. The assumption is that the self-respect of school failures is threatened by school. Many turn to delinquency in order to rescue their self-respect, by showing off in this way to an appreciative audience of other youngsters in similar straits. Hostility develops toward adults in authority, especially to teachers, whose evaluations have been denigrating, and defiance of teachers becomes part of the delinquent performance. It takes particularly patient and supportive teachers to ameliorate the perceived threat and overcome the consequent hostility. An effective school is therefore staffed by such people and arranges for its students to spend their school day primarily with but one and secondarily with only a few of them, rather than moving from teacher to teacher frequently.

Rarely do secondary schools incorporate these features. When school systems decide to provide such programs, they locate them in alternative schools. The schools in group-centered residential treatment programs almost by necessity are such alternative schools in at least one of these essential respects. If the residents attend school as a group, as the boys in our study did, then their curriculum must be individualized. The reason is that, unless great pains are taken to compose groups according to scholastic skills, students vary in age, in the last grade they were in before they arrived, and in their scholastic proficiency. They cannot reasonably be put to the same level of schoolwork, and they rarely are. Thus, it is also easier for these institutional schools to provide students with feedback emphasizing individual progress, which they sometimes do.

In the institutions participating in this study, one teacher was primarily responsible for the schooling of each group. In this respect, too, the institutional school programs resembled the model of an effective alternative school quite closely. We did not attempt to measure how supportive each teacher was. Our data seem to confirm previous findings indirectly by showing that the more students liked their teachers, the more their interest in school improved, with the concomitant improvements in their adjustment both at the institution and in the open community that we have described.

IMPLICATIONS FOR THEORY

Corrections

Both the personal characteristics that incarcerated adolescents brought to their institutionalization and the conditions of their detention contributed to the nature of their adjustment to the institution. In other words, we found evidence for both the "importation" and the "pains of imprisonment" hypotheses about the determinants of rehabilitation. Our evidence also suggests that these hypotheses require some revision, at least insofar as they pertain to correctional institutions like the settings of our research.

Our study was of juvenile delinquents incarcerated under apparently benign conditions. From what we could observe, the phrase "pains of imprisonment" seems much too harsh to describe the conditions under which the focal students lived. "Imprisonment" brings to mind rows of barred cells stacked on top of one another; series of heavy, locked doors to be passed through at every forty steps; armed guards; predatory inmates; and so on. The "pains" of such conditions are manifest. The youths in this study, on the other hand, occupied either their own rooms, albeit small and sparsely furnished, or small dormitories, with windows looking out onto broad lawns. They were rarely threatened with violence, either by staff or by peers. Prisons have high walls, but the schools in this study did not even have fences; and the boys often moved without adult supervision among living quarters, school, dining hall, and playing fields. In many important respects, such as housing, meals, facilities for school and play, and medical care, the material quality of their lives was better for most of the residents than it had been at home. And being teenagers rather than adults, the sex life of most of them was not different from what it would have been had they been free.

Still, they were not free. They were often locked into wherever they were at the moment, and they were subject to a twenty-four-hour, year-round schedule that gave them few choices. The pains of their imprisonment consisted primarily of not being able to go where they wanted to go, do what they wanted to do, when they wanted to do it, unlike most U.S. teenagers. Then there was the stigma of being "sent away" and locked up, although we found that they actually felt little stigma in the six months after their release. And almost all of the boys missed their families. As bad as "home" may have been materially, and as erratic, neglectful, and sometimes cruel as their care may have been, they almost invariably wanted to go home. So no doubt, these youths felt some "pains of imprisonment." Their pains were not, however, of the kind or magnitude conceived in the hypotheses of correctional theory.

Nor did the deprivations endured by these adolescents give rise to a fiercely oppositional counterculture supported by a tightly knit and coercively enforced social organization of inmates. What we found, instead, was variation from group to group in the range from negligible to problematic. The most common manifestation of a counterculture was boys' reluctance to "squeal" on their peers, a common norm among American adolescents and adults. This mild level of countercultural development nevertheless had the effect of resisting rehabilitation that it is supposed to have in correctional theory. Deprivation of freedom did shape boys' adjustments. The degree of autonomy—the obverse of deprivation of freedom—that boys felt they and their group enjoyed was related to groups' norms about delinquent values and the attractiveness of groups to their members. Thus, the more freedom residents felt they had, the more prosocial their group and the better their adjustment.

Contemporary correctional theory is not settled on the ultimate effects of "pains of imprisonment" on rehabilitation. There is, on the one hand, the hypothesis that the deprivations of incarceration are detrimental because they generate resistant inmate countercultures. On the other hand is the hypothesis that harsh conditions constitute negative reinforcements and thereby deter delinquency after release. The proliferation of certain punishing treatment programs, like the once-faddish "Boot Camps," demonstrates that some correctional policymakers accept the hypothesis that punishment is rehabilitative.

The findings of this study contradict the idea that the more punishing the institutional experience, the greater is the deterrent effect. The youths who left the institution more unhappy with their experience reported neither more nor less delinquent behavior in the next six months, and they were neither more nor less likely to be reincarcerated. Greater satisfaction with the institution had the more benign effects: boys' delinquent values declined and they were more likely to be attending school and/or holding jobs six months after their release.

Insofar as respondents' personal characteristics determined their adjustment, the importation hypothesis of correctional theory was also supported by our data. Again, this was not attributable to their encouraging a group counterculture. Rather, it was attributable to the way respondents' besetment and commitment to delinquent values governed their perceptions of group norms and of their friends' values, and made focal students differentially responsive to peer influence and relationships with staff members. Professing delinquent values, to the usually small degree that they did, did not lead boys to create or maintain a delinquent counterculture in their group. As for besetment, beset youths tended to be alienated from any peer influence, while buoyant youths preferred that their group be prosocial.

In sum, social norms of groups of incarcerated delinquents that help to determine the effectiveness of rehabilitative programs are shaped both by factors imported in the psyches of the delinquents and by factors generated by the conditions of their incarceration. This is the case even when the conditions of incarceration are not so harsh as to promote a strong resident counterculture. Deprivation of freedom alone is sufficient to encourage delinquent values in a group. The more the deprivation is ameliorated by granting the group some autonomy, the more prosocial the group norms. Residents are differentially predisposed to perceive group norms as pro-or antisocial, however, and differentially predisposed to conform to them.

Our findings also speak to the correctional theory debate over treatment versus custodial orientations. That dichotomy proved false in the institutions we observed. The most effective staff teams attended about equally to making sure residents behaved and to helping them with their social and psychological problems. It did not seem that more effective teams merely struck a balance between the two concerns. Rather, they did both as much as possible and found no contradiction between them.

Theory and research on the effectiveness of rehabilitative programs in corrections have ranged from depressing to ambivalent (Martinson, 1974; Lab & Whitehead, 1988; Andrew et al., 1990). They lean toward the conclusions either that "nothing works" or "not much works very well for any offenders." Our findings will not brighten this situation much because they do not reveal dramatic effects of easily manipulated variables. Our findings do indicate, however, that some variables in correctional theory do make a difference and, therefore, some practices can be expected to work better than others.

Criminology

Our findings shed some light on the causes of delinquency. In the terms of current criminological theory, they reveal that both "strains" and "controls" figure in the delinquent equation. The findings also identify specific strains and specific sources of control.

One source of strain that stands out in our findings is scholastic failure. Consistent with previous findings, the delinquent boys we observed almost invariably were performing below grade and had not been attending school regularly. This in itself does not identify scholastic failure as a cause of delinquency: It is also plausible that their delinquent way of life shaped their attitudes and behavior in school, or that their scholastic failure was an integral part of their delinquency, not a cause of it.

We found evidence for a causal relationship in that those students who had greater gains in achievement scores and increased interest in school came to be better adjusted during residency and after release. While we cannot order the changes that occurred at the institution chronologically, the scholastic gains made at the institution obviously occurred before their release. These scholastic gains predicted to post-release adjustment, regardless of the reference groups the respondents had adopted. They predicted to more prosocial behavior, less commitment to delinquent values, a greater sense of well-being, and a decline in besetment. That they occurred prior to post-release adjustment suggests that they contributed to it.

These findings support the hypothesis that certain strains cause deviant behavior. Thus, delinquency does not vary only with the strength of social controls. Specifically, delinquent behavior is provoked by scholastic failure. One theory is that such failure, with its well-known implications for diminished lifechances, powerfully threatens boys' self-esteem. This threat is particularly conducive to delinquency because delinquency is peculiarly functional for shoring up self-image. We did not find, however, that self-esteem, as we measured it, mediated between scholastic gains and adjustment.

Social control also affects delinquency. There is evidence of its effect both at the institution and in the community. The proximal sources of social control at the institution consist of the staff and the peer group. We found that when the staff insists on good behavior and reacts to misbehavior, boys behave better. Similarly, boys behave better if they perceive that their group maintains more prosocial norms, especially if they like their group. Some might consider peer group norms a provocation to delinquency rather than a form of social control. The pattern of our findings indicates, however, that being more attached to peer groups generally decreases delinquency. When they hold more delinquent norms, peer groups do not so much push their members toward antisocial behavior as show such tolerance that they fail to restrain it.

In the community, reference groups proved critical for the focal students' adjustment. The better their relationships with their primary caregiver, the more they were inclined to follow adults' standards of behavior than peers', and the adults' standards were, on average, considerably more prosocial.

We envision a kind of hydraulic model of provocations and controls and delinquency. Delinquency flows under the pressure of provocations, but its flow can be regulated even to the stopping point by social controls. This model posits that it does not take much provocation to generate some delinquency when controls are quite weak, although delinquency will not flow heavily when the pressure is low. This may be the reason that, as children become adolescents in societies like ours that exert less control at that time, more of them become delinquent, but most do not become not very delinquent.

The hydraulic model also posits that extremely strong controls will hold back delinquency even under the pressure of strong provocations. What happens then to powerfully controlled youngsters who fail at school, or whose self-esteem is otherwise seriously threatened? These youth, according to the model, will be under great pressure. Provoked but denied a delinquent defense, they will therefore be prone to mental illness borne out of psychological conflict.

Personality Psychology

Certain enduring psychological characteristics affected our focal students' adjustment during and after their institutionalization. This constitutes strong testimony to the reality of personality. Behavior and feelings are not altogether malleable, subject only to the environment at the moment. Individuals bring predispositions to situations that affect how they behave, think, and feel.

One of the ways that personality contributes to persons' responses to their contemporary situation is by shaping their perceptions of the situation. The boys we observed perceived important norms of their groups and characteristics of their friends in the group in ways partly predetermined by what they had brought to their encounters months before. Then they acted in the situation as they perceived it.

Moreover, even different youths with the same perceptions of their situation did not necessarily respond the same way to it. Their personalities differentially sensitized them to aspects of the situation. Some were influenced more by the nature of their peer group, others by the nature of their staff team.

Perhaps the most fundamental problem of theory and research on personality is finding the conditions under which certain personal characteristics will endure, that is, become or remain part of personality. We may speculate on that problem on the basis of what we have learned in this study. We found that two of the personal characteristics we measured proved to be enduring and consequential, besetment and delinquent values. We believe that the developmental principle of *critical periods* may account for their enduringness.

By "critical period," we mean a period in the lifecycle when a particular problem of adaptation, rather than others, is especially pressing. The principle is that the solution to that problem at that time will endure as a psychological trait. It will be not altogether unresponsive to later experiences; it will, however, resist change. Modification is possible, but the formative experiences for change must be stronger than they had to be during the critical period when the trait was first developed. The trait will then set the parameters within which persons will find solutions to subsequent problems of adaptation, some of them equally critical.

Solutions are not always found to the pressing problems that arise in critical periods. The situation at the time may not permit solution. The person may remain conflicted about the problem, and according to the developmental principle, that conflicted state will persist. It may manifest itself with neurotic anxiety, or chronic depression, or psychotic estrangement from reality.

To be specific, we suppose that the besetment we found among the boys in our study emerged mostly out of a psychological conflict about personal security. The problem of security, which Erikson (1964) calls the problem of "trust versus basic mistrust," arises in the earliest critical period. It is the main problem of the helpless human infant. The beset boys appear not to have settled on how much to trust others. For example, they tend to blame others for the trouble they get into. Still, they do not become completely alienated from others, for they adjust better under the care of likeable staff members, and peer friends are as important to them as they are to buoyant boys. We imagine that the recurring existential problem of how much to risk oneself at the hands of others is the constant source of the anxiety and depression that besets them.

Put this way, besetment is not born necessarily in a conflict over security, it may emerge out of unresolved conflicts in any critical period. Its enduringness may be greater, however, the earlier the conflict from which it emerges. The reason for this is that unresolved conflicts from one critical period inhibit adaptation to later ones. Thus, besetment over the early crisis of security becomes especially chronic because it means that more kinds of situations present unresolved conflicts.

Nor is besetment, from this perspective, peculiar to delinquents. It may characterize any person far enough along in the lifecycle to exhibit a persistent trait. Its importance to delinquency resides in the way it interacts with other conditions conducive to delinquency to create two distinctive types of delinquents, the beset and the buoyant.

Youth beset with anxiety and depression do not use delinquency in the same way that the more buoyant do. For one thing, they cannot mix comfortably with the so-called "delinquent gang," that mutual admiration society that helps buoyant youth maintain their self-esteem. The beset boys do not trust their peers very much and don't get along well with them.

Also, delinquency does not help them much with their abiding anxiety and depression, for it does nothing to settle their conflict over how much they should trust others. Thus, beset youths' delinquent behavior is more apt, as we have found, to be solo performances; and the best youths' delinquency does not respond in the same way to a treatment program as the buoyant youths' does.

As to the persistence of delinquent values, we note that they are an integral part of the solution to a developmental problem that emerges among some youth with the transition to adolescence. In technologically advanced cultures, poor performance at formal schooling becomes a serious matter when one enters secondary school. It betokens a dismal future. It constitutes an important condition to be taken into account in adapting to the primary developmental problem of adolescence—the formulation of a personal identity.

We mean by "identity" what Erikson alludes to when he writes of "ego identity," that is, a sense of continuity that extends from memories of one's past into anticipations of one's future. An ego identity consists of a conviction that what one was like in the past has helped to determine the kind of person one is at present, and that what one will be like in the future will be partly determined by what one is like in the present.

Erikson rejects the notion that ego identity is the answer to the question, "Who am I?" If it may be said to answer any delineable question, its more precise formulation would be, "What do I want to make of myself, and what do I have to work with?" (Erikson, 1968, p. 314). For youth failing in school in American society today, the painfully obvious answer is, "Not much."

Rather than accept this negative self-image, many school failures formulate a negative identity, an identity that assumes contrary criteria of worth. Delinquent values are well-suited for this solution, for they defy the authorities who mark the failure and glorify acts easily performed if one is motivated enough. It helps enormously if these values are shared with others, so buoyant youth, who get along better with their peers, make a better defense of delinquency than beset youth do.

Delinquent values persist as long as the negative identity formed around them is useful. As long as a youth has little confidence in his or her ability to manage those scholastic tasks that represent the way to get ahead, then he or she will choose another arena in which to gain respect. Thus, Oyserman and Markus (1990) have found that more delinquent youth fear more dismal "possible selves" in their future. Because they offer the possibility of a brighter future, scholastic gains made while they were institutionalized are related to boys' increased interest in schooling and a reduced value for delinquency.

Like besetment, then, delinquent values persist as a personality trait because they precipitate out of dealing with a problem when it is critical.

They are not necessarily accompanied by besetment because they may, at least for the time, provide an unconflicted solution to the critical problem. Buoyant delinquent youth are more troublesome than they are troubled.

We suppose that, in contrast to the besetment that arises out of earlier unresolved conflicts such as conflicts over security, delinquent values are not so ingrained among even seriously delinquent adolescents. Adolescence and young adulthood in our culture constitute the critical period for the formulation of an identity. That is, the critical period has not passed for juvenile delinquents; there is time still for relatively less powerful experiences to make a difference. Some success at school, even after years of failure, can change the nature of their identities and encourage them to abandon delinquent values.

Social Psychology

One contribution to social psychological theory concerns the nature of the effective social environment. If the mission of social psychology is to explain the influence of the social environment on the person, then our findings indicate that the psychological proximity of the social environment should be weighed heavily in social psychological explanations.

By proximity, we mean the degree to which an environment is involved in a process of influence. In the settings of this study, the residential peer group and staff team were the environment in which the influence process of social learning occurred. They were the almost exclusive sources of instruction to residents about how they should act and what their attitudes and values ought to be. The others in a boy's group were his main models for appropriate behavior. Staff and peers dealt out an individual's rewards and punishments. It is in this sense that they were more proximal psychologically than the institution, which exerted its influence, sometimes imperfectly, through them.

We acknowledge that residential institutions for delinquents differ more than the four participating in our study did. All four employed some variation of the PPC modality, and none were deliberately punitive. Perhaps we would have found that differences at the level of the institutions as a whole made more difference had we included other kinds of institutions as well. We suspect, however, that whatever co-variation between institutions and boys' behavior we might have found would have disappeared when we took into account differences among residents' immediate social environments—the staff that had primary responsibility for each boy and the nature of the peer group with which boys lived most closely.

Nor did we find that boys' neighborhoods contributed much, for better or worse, to their post-release adjustment when we factored in what kind of immediate reference groups the boys had. (Except that boys released to neighborhoods with a higher proportion of black residents were likely to be more delinquent and more beset during the subsequent six months.) Neighborhoods do not appear to be as consequential social environments as immediate family, friends, school, and so on. Of course, here too the psychologically more distal social environment may help determine the nature of these more proximal ones; but people in the same neighborhood experience different proximal social environments. These differences are likely to matter more for how people act, think, and feel.

Our findings provide a good example of the importance of psychological proximity for the effects of the social environment. We have proposed that scholastic failure is an important provocation to delinquent behavior. This proposition is valid only in a society in which scholastic failure is possible, that is, in a society where a more or less formal educational institution exists. Such a society is a real, albeit psychological distal, social environment that matters to students, but indirectly. Their school system and their school as a whole, somewhat less distal social environments than their society as a whole, also matter indirectly to students. However, students' immediate educational environment is their class—their teachers and their classmates. These differ within the same distal environments of society and school system, sometimes quite consequentially. We found that the classes attended by the boys during their institutionalization were different in critical respects from the classes they had attended in the open community. Indeed, classes differed within the same residential institution. Because of their proximity, the characteristics of their own class mattered most for boys psychologically.

In one respect at least, even immediate proximity is not close enough for social psychological explanation; for people act in the social environment they perceive. For example, the youths in this study were influenced by the norms of their group, as they understood those norms. The norms as they appeared in the social environment helped to shape individuals' perceptions of them, but not exclusively. Other conditions intervened, conditions in the social environment such as friendships within the group, and conditions internal to the perceivers, such as traits of their personalities.

The mission of social psychology, in other words, is to explain how social conditions become psychological conditions for action, thought, and feeling. This requires tracking the effects of distal social environments to their psychological proximity and understanding their influence from that point.

IMPLICATIONS FOR PRACTICE*

In delinquency services, the practitioner seldom has the chance to stand apart and observe things from a distance. The urgent daily decisions that

*Dale Shears, of the Michigan Department of Social Services, authored this section.

involve young lives in his or her care simply crowd out things like theories and experimental designs.

One of the reasons that practitioners from Michigan's public and private agencies wanted to become involved in the Peer Influence Project in the first place was the opportunity that it provided to look at things that were already going on with the gift of objectivity. Some of the basic premises of institutional treatment for delinquents would be tested.

Testing the Group Treatment Premise

An early theoretical model of how peer processes *might* look in a juvenile institution was hardly flattering: that is, youth might form negative inmate groups in opposition to an essentially coercive environment. These negative peer groups would develop and enforce their own norms. Since only the peer group could guarantee safety against inmate retribution, such negative peer groups could come to represent powerful agents of social control, resisting rehabilitation and strengthening adherence to delinquent values. In such an environment, youth would likely return to the community more deeply confirmed in antisocial ways than when they arrived.

In peer group treatment agencies, staff are constantly alert to the nature of the youth culture and strive to manage that culture in support of the agency's rehabilitative goals. They try to do this through: (1) encouragement of positive group day-to-day decision making (autonomy); (2) use of group sanctions; (3) systematic denial of opportunities for negative group processes to occur "underground" and without visibility; and (4) assignment to groups of a significant role in the release process. The essential question was whether or not treatment programs of this sort were indeed able to establish positive youth cultures.

The research evidence is very encouraging. Youth were uniformly found to view their living environments as safe. Moreover, stronger youth groups, with greater perceived autonomy in their settings, were generally regarded by youth and staff as more positive and prosocial, and focal students had greater attraction to the more prosocial groups. To practitioners, this set of findings was an important validation because it meant that the conditions, at least, for effective group treatment were present.

Differential Youth Responses to Treatment

All of the agencies involved in this study employed youth group treatment programs, but a variety of non-group treatment methods also exist. More needs to be learned about matching the most effective form of treatment to a relevant typology of youth.

This study provides some significant insights in the area of differential diagnosis and treatment with its exploration of the buoyant/beset dimension. A significant number of beset youth display anxiety and depression as a stable personality characteristic, and these youth do not appear to respond as well to peer influence. At the same time, they seem more sensitive to other prosocial forces, such as support and guidance from staff.

These findings suggest that it would be desirable if: (1) a means were found to reliably identify youth with stable besetment from youth who are only situationally beset (due to intake trauma, etc.); (2) non-group treatment programs, which feature the staff/youth relationship as the primary treatment vehicle, were developed; and (3) chronically beset youth were assigned to these programs. It is likely that these special treatment programs would require a higher staff-to-student ratio. A major treatment goal would be to reduce the high levels of anxiety and depression that these youth display.

Delinquent Values as a Personality Feature

Another prominent finding of this study is that a youth's level of delinquent values tends to display the stable characteristic of a personality trait. Adolescents did not readily abandon their commitment to delinquent values during the course of their stay in an institution. Moreover, the value that youth placed on delinquency contributed significantly to their eventual rehabilitation.

To practitioners, the phenomenon of an enduring but underlying pattern of delinquent values is commonly known as surface conformity, or "fronting." The problem is to engage these youth as successfully as possible so as to expose and challenge surface conformity. Group treatment programs attempt to do this in a number of ways: for example, through the provision of opportunities for the youth's problems to surface, and the use of peer group confrontation to challenge fronting. The idea that delinquent values represent an enduring personality feature suggests the need for more intense activities directed at the context in which these values originally emerged as a coping mechanism—the youths' families.

Family Work and Reference Groups

Over the past several years (beginning, for the most part, after this project looked at its focal students), residential treatment programs in Michigan have been moving toward a model in which the youth's family is enlisted as an important contributor in the treatment effort. Family workers have been added to residential treatment staffs, even at the state-operated training schools. This study provides research support that family involvement efforts are worthwhile: in the community after release, the youth's reference groups prove critical to adjustment. Adult standards are, in general, more prosocial, and good relationships to adult caregivers are strongly supportive of rehabilitation. This study's findings also suggest that more work needs to be done in the post-release period, where such efforts are often not well-developed at present. The goal would be to strengthen and support a youth's positive reference groups, both inside and outside the family. Ideally, this work should build upon efforts with the family that were initiated during the youth's stay in residential care.

Successful Schooling and Rehabilitation

Delinquent youth are characterized by their poor attendance, behavior, and performance at school. This study demonstrates that a strong relationship exists between increased interest in school and delinquent rehabilitation. It is exciting to note that when the academic experience is structured so that youth will have the opportunity to experience some successes, even youth with disastrous academic histories can develop an interest in school that tends to persist. To the practitioner, it is especially significant that the post-release effects of school-related changes appear to exert an independent and direct influence over later adjustment in the community.

Successful schooling appears to be an important step down the road to successful rehabilitation. The implications are threefold: (1) residential treatment programs should strive to develop academic programs that successfully whet the interests of youth who have been used only to defeats in school; (2) the significance of academic efforts to the overall rehabilitative effort of the agency should be recognized and highlighted; and (3) efforts should be redoubled in the post-release period to carry the schooling/socializing momentum forward into the community.

Final Thoughts

This study of personality and peer influence in juvenile corrections demonstrates how theory, research, and practice may be coordinated for the betterment of all three. While the study details a complex network of subtle relationships between treatment variables and youth, the underlying picture that emerges is that social influence is going on in the residential treatment setting, that it is not a negative social influence, and that youths' lives may be benefited by these influences.

This study seems to suggest that social bonding may be inherently prosocial. Such bondings and attachments appear to matter—and they matter whether they happen with youth groups, with child care staff, with teachers, with caretakers, or with community reference groups. If we are able to reduce delinquent youths' psychological and social isolation and to assist them in forging these prosocial bonds, we can help them to return to us as members of the community.

IMPLICATIONS FOR RESEARCH DESIGN
AND METHOD

There were some things that we would do differently if we did this study again; and there were some things that we did do differently from previous studies that future studies should also do and improve upon further.

Frequently in this report we have called attention to the fact that our observation of the focal students was mainly by means of interviews. This raises the possibility that what we measured was not the boys' actual delinquent behavior, delinquent values, and so on, but rather the image they presented to our interviewers. These self-presentations may or may not have resembled what these adolescents were like out in the community, in their dormitories, at school, and elsewhere.

We tried to check this possibility by using other methods of measurement as well. We administered questionnaires to staff members and other boys in the focal students' groups, thereby observing the focal students through others' eyes. We also compared focal students' responses to interviews with their records in the community and at the institution.

We found some evidence for the validity of our measures. For example, individuals' reports of their misbehavior at the institution related reliably to their peers' descriptions of their behavior; and focal students' reports of their delinquent values at release distinguished at much better than chance levels which ones would be institutionalized again. However, many official records did not relate reliably to presumably relevant reports by our respondents. Felony arrests on intake records, for example, did not relate reliably to self-reports of their delinquent behavior. Were the respondents' reports invalid or were the records?

The co-variation of several different measures of key variables gives us some confidence in the validity of our findings. We wish now that we had used more multi-method measures, and we urge other researchers to do so as much as possible.

Many studies of delinquency treatment programs have neglected to control properly for conditions aside from the treatment and have thus misattributed outcomes to the program. An important example is that controls need to be imposed on the differential selection of delinquents into different treatment programs. We have refrained throughout this report from comparing the effects of the four participating institutions because it is clear that they treated youths who differed in important ways. One of those ways is that Starr Commonwealth accepts boys younger than the other three centers do. Because younger boys in general do not respond to programs as well as older boys do, it would not be valid to compare Starr's outcomes with the others'. Another way is that residents who run away from the private institutions in this study are sometimes then sent to the public institutions, but not vice versa. This practice assembles different populations of students and so renders uncontrolled interinstitutional comparisons invalid.

Not only have we refrained for these reasons from comparing institutions, we also controlled for differences among groups within institutions with virtual random assignment of boys to groups as well as with statistical methods. Thus, we are in little danger of falsely attributing differences in focal students' adjustment to differences among groups, when these differences were actually caused by the selection of group members.

The most common criterion for sorting delinquents into treatment programs is the seriousness of their delinquency. More serious and committed delinquents are understandably selected for treatment in more restrictive programs. We have seen that previous history of delinquency and degree of commitment to delinquent values affects delinquents' responses to program. So comparison of more with less restrictive treatment programs is likely to be confounded by these consequential differences in their clientele. Little can be learned from such uncontrolled studies. Because the clients in this study were assigned at random to groups, comparisons among groups were free of such confounding differences.

Still, random assignment does not guarantee against important confounding differences among groups. Such differences can occur by chance. Sometimes groups in the institutions we observed are inadvertently loaded with especially difficult boys. To control for such circumstances, it helps to have a large number of groups in a study—the forty-five in this study is a large number by statistical standards—to dilute the effects of a few chance differences. It also helps to have measures of hypothetically important characteristics of group members before they join the group, so that these may be used for statistical control in analyses of later outcomes. Such longitudinal studies are too rare.

There is another advantage to having some assessment of delinquents' characteristics prior to treatment. As we have seen, some of these characteristics interacted with elements of the treatment program to generate outcomes. This would not have been revealed without prior measures. Measures of these personal characteristics taken only at the same time as measures of outcomes could not be distinguished from outcomes.

Longitudinal studies also contribute to determining the direction of causality. We found, for example, that staff characteristics such as granting more autonomy to their groups enhanced the attractiveness of groups to their members and encouraged prosocial group norms. Without some evidence that the staff practice was more stable over time than the group properties were, and generally preceded them in time, we could not attribute causality to the staff practices with as much certainty.

We would have been more certain of causal directions had we been more experimental during the course of this study. Representatives of the participating institutions and we researchers agreed early on that program would not be changed during the course of the study for research purposes. (This did not preclude changes that the institutions wanted to make for other reasons.) There were two reasons for this: First, we realized that a close study of a program always threatens program staff to some degree, and we wanted to minimize that threat by refraining from interfering with the program. Second, we wanted to increase the generalizability of our findings to other programs by observing these in their natural state.

One consequence of this policy is that we did not experiment with changes that our findings suggested might be useful, and then observe their effects. Such experimentation within a longitudinal research design is a powerful method for determining cause–effect relations. Had we, for example, introduced a supplementary treatment program for some of the chronically beset youth, then we could say with much more certainty what led to what.

Another consequence of noninterference with program is that we studied the effects of program within the ranges that program offered. We found, for example, that greater consensus among members about group norms did not improve the accuracy of members' perceptions of the norms. This finding is counter-intuitive. We have speculated that the range of consensus among groups was too narrow to make a difference; few if any groups sent a clear, unified normative message to their members. Had we arranged with staff to increase consensus among some groups, we might have found that consensus at the higher level indeed made a difference.

Many of our findings, while reliable statistically, indicate that the differences we found among groups account for only a very small proportion of the differences in focal students' adjustment. While this may reflect the most that group properties can do, it may also be attributable to the lack of variation in some group properties, such as normative consensus in the example above. The probability levels indicate that certain variables are almost undoubtedly interrelated, that if one changes, others also will change. The figures on "amount of variance accounted for" indicate how closely related variables are; that is, how much change one could expect in one if the other changes. Our measures do not account for much variance in boys' adjustment. This may be due, however, to the narrow range of differences among hypothetically causal conditions. Were these differences widened, they might make a greater difference in outcomes.

One could experiment in the future with programs that aim to maximize positive effects by increasing the level of certain staff practices and group properties. The most promising variables to work with are those that make some difference according to the findings of this study. These include such variables as the authoritativeness of staff supervision, the amount of autonomy staff grants to its group, boys' recognition of the prosocial norms of their group, and boys' scholastic gains. Or one could attempt to enhance boys' adjustment after their release with a follow-up program that aims particularly to help boys adopt prosocial reference groups. This experimentation should be done systematically.

Field experiments are an especially powerful scientific tool, and they also have great practical potential. It is not so much because, in contrast to laboratory studies, they take place in the "real world." In most senses of the term, the laboratory situation is as real as any other. Rather, it is that the conditions under which field experiments are conducted are more prevalent than the conditions of an academic laboratory. Thus, their findings are more widely generalizable.

Perhaps social psychology has been led to exaggerate the influence of people's social environment and underestimate the influence of the personal qualities that people bring to their situation. Laboratory conditions are advantageous for the thorough control over conditions and the close observation of variables that define an experiment. However, laboratory studies fail to engage many of their subjects' motives, attitudes, and resources. Laboratory conditions do not usually include the personal characteristics that are active under most other circumstances. That is one reason why their findings have limited generalizability. Clearly the effects of the social environment of the adolescents in this study were affected by the personal characteristics that made them more responsive to some elements of their social environment than to others.

Nor do laboratory experiments ordinarily invoke important social conditions that are prevalent in other environments. There are advantages to experimental simplification. Social psychological processes can be observed more clearly when only one or a few are allowed to operate at the time. If the effects of these processes were simply additive, then studying only one or a few at a time would not limit the generalizability of the findings. These processes often interact, however, and their simultaneous operation generates something different from an additive effect.

The design of the study reported here was only quasi-experimental. We researchers did not exercise experimental controls, but, rather, we took advantage of those that occurred naturally. Nor did we systematically vary hypothetically important components of the treatment program; instead, we measured the variation that we found. Further research will contribute more knowledge to the advance of theory and practice the more experimental it is. This will require even closer collaboration between researchers and practitioners than we have enjoyed, as close and as gratifying as ours has been.

REFERENCES

Akers, R. L. (1977). *Deviant behavior: A social learning perspective*. Belmont, CA: Wadsworth.

Akers, R. L., Hayner, N. S., & Gruniger, W. (1974). Homosexual and drug behavior in prison: A test of the functional and importation models of the inmate system. *Social Problems, 21,* 410–422.

Akers, R. L., Krohn, M. D., Lanza-Kaduce, L., & Radosevich, M. (1979). Social learning and deviant behavior: A specific test of a general theory. *American Sociological Review, 44,* 636–655.

Allen, J. P., Aber, J. L., & Leadbeater, B. J. (1990). Adolescent problem behaviors: The influence of attachment and autonomy. *Psychiatric Clinics of North America, 13,* 45–467.

Andrews, D. A., Bonta, J. G., & Hoge, R. D. (1990). Classification for effective rehabilitation: Rediscovering psychology. *Criminal Justice and Behavior, 17,* 19–52.

Atwood, R., Gold, M., & Taylor, R. (1989). Two types of delinquents and their institutional adjustment. *Journal of Consulting and Clinical Psychology, 57,* 68–75.

Atwood, R. O., & Osgood, W. (1987). Cooperation in group treatment programs for incarcerated adolescents. *Journal of Applied Social Psychology, 17,* (11), 969–989.

Baumgartel, H., (1957). Leadership style as a variable in research administration. *Administrative Science Quarterly, 2,* 344–360.

Baumrind, D. (1978). Parental disciplinary patterns and social competence in children. *Youth and Society, 9,* 239–276.

Berelson, B., Lazarsfeld, P. F., and McPhee, W. (1954). *Voting*. Chicago: University of Chicago Press.

Berk, B. (1976). Organizational goals and inmate organization. *American Journal of Sociology, 71,* 522–534.

Bowman, P. H. (1959). Effects of a revised school program on potential delinquents. *Annals of the American Academy of Political and Social Science, 322,* 53–62.

Bowman, P. H., & Liddle, G. P. (1959). Slow learners in the secondary schools. Chicago: University of Chicago Quincy Youth Development Project.

Brehm, J. W. (1966). *A theory of psychological reactance*. New York: Academic Press.

Buehler, R. E., Patterson, G. R., & Furniss, J. M. (1966). The reinforcement of behavior in institutional settings. *Behaviour Research and Therapy, 4,* 457–467.

Clemmer, D. (1958). *The prison community*. New York: Holt, Rinehart, & Winston.

Cloward, R. A., & Ohlin, L. E. (1960). *Delinquency and opportunity: A theory of delinquent gangs*. New York: Free Press.

Coates, R. B., Miller, A. D., & Ohlin, L. E. (1978). *Diversity in a youth correctional system*. Cambridge, MA: Ballinger.

Cohen, A. K. (1955). *Delinquent boys*. New York: Free Press.

Cronbach, L. J. (1951). Coefficient alpha and the internal structure of tests. *Psychometrika, 16,* 297–334.

D'Angelo, R. V., (1973). *The influence of three styles of leadership on the process of an organizational development effort*. Unpublished doctoral dissertation. Berkeley, CA: University of California.

Elder, G. H., Jr. (1962). Structural variations in the child-rearing relationship. *Sociometry, 25,* 241–262.

Elliot, D. S., & Ageton, S. S. (1980). Reconciling race and class differences in self-reported and official estimates of delinquency. *American Sociological Review, 45,* 95–110.

Elliot, D. S., Huizinga, D., & Ageton, S. S. (1985). *Explaining delinquency and drug use*. Beverly Hills, CA: Sage.

Empey, L. T. (1982). *American delinquency: Its meaning and construction* (rev. ed.). Homewood, IL: Dorsey Press.

Empey, L. J., & Erickson, M. L. (1972). *The Provo experiment: Evaluating community control of delinquency*. Lexington, MA: Lexington Books.

Empey, L. T., & Lubeck, S. G. (1968). Conformity and deviance in the "situation of company." *American Sociological Review, 33,* 760–774.

Empey, L. T., & Rabow, J. (1961). The Provo experiment in delinquency rehabilitation. *American Sociological Review, 26,* 679–695.

Erikson, E. H. (1963). *Childhood and society* (rev. ed.). New York: Norton.

Erikson, E. H. (1968). *Identity, youth, and crisis*. New York: Norton.

Eynon, T. G., & Simpson, J. E. (1965). The boy's perception of himself in a state training school for delinquents. *Social Service Review, March,* 31–37.

Eysenck, H. (1970). *Crime and personality*. London: Granada Press.

Festinger, L. (1957). *A theory of cognitive dissonance*. Stanford, CA: Stanford University Press.

Festinger, L., Schachter, S., & Back, K. (1950). *Social pressures in informal groups: A study of human factors in housing*. New York: Harper & Bros.

Field, E. (1967). *A validation study of Hewitt and Jenkin's Hypothesis*. London: HMSO.

French, J. R. P., Jr., & Raven, B. (1959). The basis of social power, In D. Cartwright, *Studies in social power* (pp. 150–167). Ann Arbor, MI: Institute for Social Research.

French, J. R. P., Jr., Morrison, H. W., & Levinger, G. (1960). Coercive power and forces affecting conformity. *Journal of Abnormal and Social Psychology, 61,* 91–101.

Gold, M. (1966). Undetected delinquent behavior. *Journal of Research on Crime and Delinquency, 3,* 27–46.

Gold, M. (1978). Scholastic experiences, self-esteem, and delinquent behavior: A theory for alternative schools. *Crime and Delinquency, 24,* 290–308.

Gold, M., & Douvan, E. (eds.). (1969). *Adolescent development: Readings in research and theory.* Boston: Allyn & Bacon.

Gold, M., & Mann, D. W. (1984). *Expelled to a friendlier place: A study of effective alternative schools.* Ann Arbor: University of Michigan Press.

Gold, M., & Mann, D. W. (1972). Delinquency as defense. *American Journal of Orthopsychiatry, 42* (3), 463–479.

Gold, M., & Petronio, R. J. (1980). Delinquent behavior in adolescence. In J. Adelson (ed.), *Handbook of adolescent psychology.* New York: Wiley.

Gold, M., Mattlin, J., & Osgood, D. W. (1989). Background characteristics and responses to treatment of two types of institutionalized delinquent boys. *Criminal Justice and Behavior, 16,* 5–33.

Heider, F. (1958). *The psychology of interpersonal relations.* New York: Wiley.

Hewitt, L. E., & Jenkins, R. L. (1946). *Fundamental patterns of maladjustment.* Springfield, IL: State of Illinois.

Hindelang, M. J., & Weis, J. G. (1972). Personality and self-reported delinquency. *Criminology, 10,* 268–294.

Hindelang, M. J., Hirschi, T., & Weis, J. G. (1981). *Measuring delinquency.* Beverly Hills, CA: Sage Publications.

Hirschi, T. (1969). *Causes of delinquency.* Berkeley, CA: University of California Press.

Hirschi, T., & Hindelang, M. J. (1977). Intelligence and delinquency: A revisionist review. *American Sociological Review, 42,* 571–587.

Jensen, G. F., & Jones, D. (1976). Perspectives on inmate culture: A study of women in prison. *Social Forces, 54,* 590–603.

Jessor, R., & Jessor, S. L. (1977). *Problem behavior and psychosocial development: A longitudinal study of youth.* New York: Academic Press.

Jones, J. A. (1964). The nature of compliance in correctional institutions for juvenile offenders. *Journal of Research in Crime and Delinquency, 1,* 82–95.

Joreskog, K. G., & Sorbom, D. (1983). *LISREL VI user's guide.* Chicago, IL: International Educational Services.

Jussim, L., & Osgood, D. W. (1989). Influence and similarity among friends: An integrative model applied to incarcerated adolescents. *Social Psychology Quarterly, 52,* 98–112.

Kandel, D. B. (1978). Homophily, selection and socialization in adolescent friendships. *American Journal of Sociology, 84,* 427–436.

Kaplan, H. B. (1980). *Deviant behavior in defense of self.* New York: Academic Press.

Kelley, H. H., & Woodruff, C. L. (1956). Members' reactions to apparent group approval of a counternorm communication. *Journal of Abnormal and Social Psychology, 52,* 67–74.

Kelley, H. H., & Volkart, E. H. (1952). The resistance to change of group-anchored attitudes. *American Sociological Review, 17,* 679–695.

Kenny, D. (1979). *Correlation and causality.* New York: Wiley.

Lab, S. P., & Whitehead, J. T. (1988). An analysis of juvenile correctional treatment. *Crime & Delinquency, 34,* 60–83.

Lab, S. P., & Whitehead, J. T. (1990). From "nothing works" to the "appropriate works": The latest stop on the search for the secular jail. *Criminology, 28,* 405–417.

Lerman, P. (1968). Evaluative studies of institutions for delinquents: Implications for research and social policy. *Social Work, 13* (July), 55–64.

Lerman, P. (1989). *Counting youth in trouble living away from home: Recent trends and counting problems.* Ann Arbor: University of Michigan Center for the Study of Youth Policy.

Lewin, K. (1943/1951). Defining the "field at a given time." In K. Lewin, *Field theory in social science.* New York: Harper.

Lewin, K., Lippitt, R., & White, R. K. (1939). Patterns of aggressive behavior in experimentally created "social climates." *Journal of Social Psychology, 10,* 271–299.

Lippitt, R., & White, R. K. (1943). The "social climate" of children's groups. In R. G. Barker, J. Kounin, & H. Wright (eds.), *Child behavior and development* (pp. 485–508). New York: McGraw-Hill.

Martin, F. P., & Osgood, D. W. (1987). Autonomy: A source of pro-social influence among incarcerated adolescents. *Journal of Applied Social Psychology, 17,* 97–107.

Martinson, R. (1974). What works? Questions and answers about prison reform. *Public Interest, 35,* 22–24.

Mathiesen, T. (1968). A functional equivalent to inmate cohesion. *Human Organization, 27,* 117–124.

McCord, W., McCord, J., & Zola, I. K. (1959). *Origins of crime.* New York: Columbia University Press.

Mead, G. H. (1934). *Mind, self and society.* Chicago: University of Chicago Press.

Megargee, E. I. (1984). A new classification system for criminal offenders: VI. Differences among the types on the adjective checklist. *Criminal Justice and Behavior, 11,* 349–376.

Megargee, E. I., & Bohn, M. J., Jr. (1979). *Classifying criminal offenders: A new system based on the MMPI.* Beverly Hills, CA: Sage.

Miller, W. B. (1958). Lower class culture as a generating milieu of gang delinquency. *Journal of Social Issues, 14,* 5–19.

Misumi, J., & Nakano, S. Y. (1960). A cross-cultural study of the effect of democratic, authoritarian and laissez-faire atmospheres in children's groups. *The Japanese Journal of Educational and Social Psychology, 1,* 10–22.

Mosley, D. C. (1987). System four revisited: Some new insights. *Organization Development Journal, 5,* 19–24.

Murray, C. A., & Cox, L. A., Jr. (1979). *Beyond probation.* Beverly Hills, CA: Sage Publications.

Newcomb, T. M. (1943). *Personality and social change.* New York: Dryden.

Newcomb, T. M. (1950). *Social Psychology.* New York: Dryden.

Newcomb, T. M. (1953). An approach to the study of communicative acts. *Psychological Review, 60,* 393–404.

Newcomb, T. M., Koenig, K., Flacks, R., & Warwick, D. P. (1967). *Persistence and change: Bennington College and its students after twenty-five years.* New York: Wiley.

Nunnally, J. C. (1967). *Psychometric theory.* New York: McGraw-Hill.

Orwell, G. (1953). *Such, such were the joys.* New York: Harcourt, Brace, pp. 32–34.

Osgood, D. W., Gold, M., & Miller, C. (1986, October). *For better or worse?: Peer attachments and peer influence among incarcerated adolescents.* Paper presented at the annual meeting of the American Society of Criminology, Atlanta, GA.

Osgood, D. W., Gruber, E., Archer, M. A., & Newcomb, T. M. (1985). Autonomy for inmates: Counterculture or cooptation? *Criminal Justice and Behavior, 12,* 71–89.

Oyserman, D., & Markus, H. R. (1990). Possible selves and delinquency. *Journal of Personality and Social Psychology, 59,* 112–125.

Pearson, K. (1896). Mathematical contributions to the theory of evolution III. Regression, heredity, and panmixia. *Philosophical transactions of the Royal Society of London. Series H., 187,* 253–318.

Persons, T. M. (1958). The relationship between psychotherapy with institutionalized boys and subsequent community adjustment. *Journal of Consulting Psychology, 31,* 137–141.

Platt, A. J. (1977). *The child savers, The invention of delinquency* (2nd ed.). Chicago, IL: University of Chicago Press.

Pollock, M., & Colwill, N. L. (1987). Participatory decision-making in review. *Leadership and Organization Development Journal, 8,* 7–10.

Prescott, P. S. (1981). *The child savers: Juvenile justice observed.* New York: Knopf.

Propper, A. (1976). *Importation and deprivation perspectives on homosexuality in correctional institutions: An empirical test on their relative efficacy.* Unpublished doctoral dissertation, University of Michigan, Ann Arbor.

Quay, H. C. (1964). Dimensions of personality in delinquent boys as inferred from the factor analysis of case history data. *Child Development, 35,* 479–484.

Quay, H. C. (1964). Personality dimensions in delinquent males as inferred from the factor analysis of behavior ratings. *Journal of Research in Crime and Delinquency, 1,* 33–37.

Quay, H. C. (1987). Patterns of delinquent behavior. In H. C. Quay (ed.), *Handbook of juvenile delinquency.* New York: Wiley.

Raven, B. H., & French, J. R. P., Jr. (1958). Legitimate power, coercive power, and observability of social influence. *Sociometry, 21,* 83–97.

Rubin, Z. (1973). *Liking and loving.* New York: Holt, Rinehart, & Winston.

Sanson-Fisher, R., Seymour, F., & Baer, D. (1976). Training paraprofessional staff to increase appropriate conversation by delinquents within a correctional institution. *Journal of Behavior Therapy and Experimental Psychiatry, 7,* 243–247.

Sakurai, M. M. (1975). Small group cohesiveness and detrimental conformity. *Sociometry, 38,* 340–357.

Schaeffer, E. S. (1959). A circumplex model of maternal behavior. *Journal of Abnormal and Social Psychology, 59,* 226–235.

Selo, E. (1979). *Inmate misconduct in juvenile correctional institutions: A comparative study.* Unpublished doctoral dissertation, University of Michigan, Ann Arbor.

Sewell, W. H., Haller, A. O., & Portes, A. (1969). The educational and early occupational attainment process. *American Sociological Review, 34,* 82–92.

Sherif, M. (1948). *An outline of social psychology.* New York: Harper and Row.

Shore, M. F., & Massimo, J. L. (1966). Comprehensive vocationally oriented psychotherapy for adolescent delinquent boys: A follow-up study. *American Journal of Orthopsychiatry, 36,* 609–615.

Street, D., Vinter, R., & Perrow, C. (1966). *Organization for treatment.* New York: The Free Press.

Sutherland, E. H., & Cressey, D. R. (1955). *Principles of criminology* (5th ed.). Philadelphia: J. B. Lippincott.

Sykes, G. (1958). *The society of captives.* Princeton, NJ: Princeton University Press.

Sykes, G. M., & Messinger, S. (1960). The inmate social system. *Theoretical Studies on Social Organization of the Prison, 15,* 5–19.

Thomas, C. W. (1970). Toward a more inclusive model of the contraculture. *Criminology, 8,* 251–262.

Thomas, C. W. (1977). Theoretical perspectives on prisonization: A comparison of the importation and deprivation models. *Journal of Criminal Law and Criminology, 68,* 135–145.

Tittle, C. R. (1969). Inmate organization: Sex differentiation and the influence of criminal subcultures. *American Sociological Review, 34,* 492–504.

Tittle, C. R. (1972). *Society of subordinates: Inmate organization in a narcotic hospital.* Bloomington: Indiana University Press.

Vinter, R. D., Newcomb, T. M., & Kish, R. (eds.). (1976). *Time out: A national study of juvenile corrections programs.* Ann Arbor: National Assessment of Juvenile Corrections, University of Michigan.

Vorrath, H., & Brendtro, L. K. (1985). *Positive peer culture.* Chicago: Aldine.

Wellford, C. (1967). Factors associated with adoption of the inmate code: A study of normative socialization. *Journal of Criminal Law, Criminology, and Police Science, 58,* 197–203.

Ziller, R., Hagey, J., Smith, M., & Long, B. (1969). Self-esteem: A self-social construct. *Journal of Consulting and Clinical Psychology, 33,* 84–95.

AUTHOR INDEX

SUBJECT INDEX

Acceptance of treatment, 54–55. *See also* Institutional adjustment, measure of

Adjustment, general. *See* Institutional adjustment

Adrian Training School, 20, 21

Anxiety. *See* Besetment

Areal measures, 153–57. *See also* Community influences

Arrests, 57, 130. *See also* Community adjustment; Prior characteristics of youth, measure of

Attraction to group or peers, 80–85. *See also* Perception of groups, accuracy and group influence

Autonomy, 14–15, 66; and besetment, 11, 182–87; measure of, 69, 71, 86. *See also* Group properties; Perceptions of groups; Staff team properties

Balance theory, 15

Besetment, 9–12, 177–93, 207–10; and autonomy, 11; and community influences, 187–91; definition of, 9; and institutional adjustment, 63, 181–87; and institutional influences, 181–87; measure of, 63, 130; and

prior characteristics, 180; stability, 178–80; and staff ties, 11; theoretical background, 9–12. *See also* Community adjustment; Institutional adjustment

Boysville, 20, 23

Buoyant. *See* Besetment

Caregiver, rating of community adjustment, 138. *See also* Community adjustment, measure of

Census data, 44, 153–57. *See also* Community influences

Coercive power, 14–15

Cognitive dissonance, 15

Cohesiveness of group: and group influence, 80; measure of, 69, 71. *See also* Group properties

Community adjustment, 125–76; and community influences, 153–72; and institutional adjustment, 139–53, 163–72; measure of, 127–31; and prior characteristics of youth, 132–39

Community influences, 18, 44, 153–72; and besetment, 187–91; and community adjustment, 153–72; and institutional adjustment, 163–72

Conditions of institutional life, 7. *See*

About the Authors

MARTIN GOLD is a Research Scientist at the Institute for Social Research and Professor of Psychology at the University of Michigan. He has written at length in the field of social psychology and delinquency, and his books include *Delinquent Behavior in an American City* (1970) and *Expelled to a Friendlier Place: Study of Effective Alternative Schools* (1984).

D. WAYNE OSGOOD is Associate Professor of Sociology and Director of the Bureau of Social Research at the University of Nebraska, Lincoln. He is the author of *Cognitive Structure: Theory and Measurement of Individual Differences* (1979). He has also written at some length on juvenile delinquency and adolescent behavior problems.